# The Applied Economics of Transport

This book provides an introduction and overview to nine applied financial studies on the theme of transport. The book addresses a wide range of topics, from value based trading of real assets in shipping, to the determinants of efficiency and productivity in European railways, to the market for used cars. The studies employ a variety of applied techniques across a range of countries, analysing a range of different modes of transport.

This book was originally published as a special issue of *Applied Economics.*

**Mark P. Taylor** is Dean of Warwick Business School, UK, and is a leading international authority in open economy macroeconomics and international finance. Although interested in broad research subjects, he focuses particularly on empirical work on exchange rates. Amongst his many published works are studies on the presence of nonlinearity in real and nominal exchange rate movements, on the long-run behaviour of real exchange rates, on the nature and effectiveness of official foreign exchange market intervention and on the micro-structural effects of European Central Bank interest rate announcements.

# The Applied Economics of Transport

*Edited by*
**Mark P. Taylor**

Routledge
Taylor & Francis Group
LONDON AND NEW YORK

First published 2012
by Routledge
2 Park Square, Milton Park, Abingdon, Oxon, OX14 4RN

Simultaneously published in the USA and Canada
by Routledge
711 Third Avenue, New York, NY 10017

*Routledge is an imprint of the Taylor & Francis Group, an informa business*



This book is a reproduction of *Applied Economics*, volume 41, issue 22. The Publisher requests to those authors who may be citing this book to state, also, the bibliographical details of the special issue on which the book was based.



*British Library Cataloguing in Publication Data*
A catalogue record for this book is available from the British Library

ISBN13: 978-0-415-69307-3

Typeset in Times New Roman
by Taylor & Francis Books

**Disclaimer**
The publisher would like to make readers aware that the chapters in this book are referred to as articles as they had been in the special issue. The publisher accepts responsibility for any inconsistencies that may have arisen in the course of preparing this volume for print.

# Contents

# The applied economics of transport: introduction and overview

Mark P. Taylor
*Editor, Applied Economics Series*

We provide an introduction and overview to the nine applied studies making up this special theme on transport. The studies cover a wide range of national and regional experience and employ a variety of applied techniques.

This special theme on the economics of transport brings together nine applied studies covering a range of national and regional experience in the area of transport economics, using a variety of applied techniques.

In the first article, Sigbjorn Sodal, Steen Koekebakker and Roar Adland use a real options valuation model with stochastic freight rates to investigate market efficiency and the economics of switching between the dry bulk and the tanker markets in international shipping. A dry bulk carrier is replaced with a tanker when the expected net present value of such a switch is optimal from a real options-based decision rule. Depending on the development of the markets, a reversal may take place later. The cost and demand parameters upon which the decisions to switch are made, including the stochastic characteristics of freight rates, are estimated from an empirical analysis that is updated every week throughout a 12-year time period from 1993 to 2005. The authors conclude that the second-hand market for bulk ships seems to have been efficient most of these years in the sense that market switching usually did not pay off, with one major exception: it seemed profitable in expectation to leave the dry bulk market and enter the tanker market over a significant period of time, shortly after the millennium shift, and to return to dry bulk market about 3 years later.

Peter Schulze and Alexander Prinz, examine container trans-shipment at German ports using the Seasonal Autoregressive Integrated Moving Average (SARIMA) model and the Holt–Winters exponential smoothing approach. The models are designed especially to take account of the seasonal behaviour of the quarterly data used. The authors consider the dynamic development in this sector for the whole container throughput and also for the destinations Asia, Europe and North America, which are the world's three main economic regions. The data runs from the first quarter of 1989 to the fourth quarter of 2006 and the authors provide detailed quarterly forecasts for the years 2007 and 2008.

According to forecasting error, measures such as Mean Square Error and Theil's U, the SARIMA-approach yields slightly better values of modelling the container throughput than the exponential smoothing approach. The forecast results indicate further strong growth for German container handling in total, and especially for the destinations Asia and Europe.

Only the container transshipment between Germany and North America shows rather small increases up to the end of 2008.

Next, Chen-Hsiu Laih and Kuan-Yu Chen develop the optimal step toll scheme which is levied to bulk ships for a queuing port. Bulk ships' arrival times at the port are rationally dispersed after pricing this toll scheme. Consequently, the queuing time at the anchorage to all bulk ships is rationally decreased. Laih and Chen derive the bulk ships' equilibrium arrival rate distributions during the queuing period before and after establishing the optimal step toll scheme. Their article also shows bulk ship owners' decisions of arrival time adjustment under the optimal step toll scheme. Based on these results, the authors find some bulk ships that paid no toll under the optimal step toll scheme maintain the same arrival times at the anchorage as they did in the original nontoll equilibrium situation. New arrival times at the anchorage for other bulk ships that paid the optimal step toll are postponed when compared with their original arrival times in the nontoll equilibrium situation.

In their contribution, Antonio Couto and Daniel Graham evaluate the economic performance of European railways over the period 1972 to 1999. The cost structure of the railway industry is analysed using a stochastic frontier approach estimated within the framework of a translog cost system. The results confirm that European railways experience significant cost increases due to an inefficient behaviour. In contrast to the previous studies, however, the estimates indicate a much greater role for allocative rather than technical inefficiency. Overall, inefficiencies can essentially be explained by the supply of excess capacity and by the over-employment of labour inputs. Regarding productivity, it appears to be technological progress, and not levels of efficiency or scale economies, that provide the most convincing explanation for variance in growth rates within the sample.

Germà Bel and Xavier Fageda argue that, from a public interest perspective, there could be a justification for constraining market mechanisms with the aim of progressive redistribution. However, some policies might be based on selfish motivations of government agents. In their article, Bel and Fageda examine empirically whether the infrastructure policy is based only on public interest motivations or if it is also based on the private motivations of policy makers. In this way, Spanish infrastructure policy provides a useful policymaking field to test hypotheses concerning the behaviour of policy makers. The authors find some evidence regarding the strength of political motivations in explaining such behaviour. In fact, results from their analysis show that political motivations can eventually play a more relevant role than social welfare maximization.

Winand Emons and George Sheldon start by noting that the celebrated lemons model assumes that owners of used cars have an information advantage over potential buyers with respect to the quality of their vehicles. Owners of bad cars try to sell them to ill-informed buyers while owners of good cars hold on to theirs. Consequently, the quality of traded automobiles tends to be sub-average. In contrast to previous empirical work, the authors investigate both the behaviour of buyers and sellers, testing for adverse selection by sellers and for quality uncertainty among buyers with a sample consisting of all 1985 cars registered in the Swiss canton of Basle-City over the period 1985 to 1991. The results support both adverse selection and buyer uncertainty, suggesting that a lemons problem exists.

In their article, Anna Matas and Jose-Luis Raymond provide a comparison of different formulations for hedonic regression analysis in order to construct a quality-adjusted price index for the Spanish car market over the period 1981 to 2005. Specifically, the authors address the issue of instability of coefficients over time, and propose two alternative estimation procedures based, firstly, on a moving sample of observations and, secondly, on a moving average of estimated coefficients in single-period equations. The statistical tests applied support the proposed methodologies. Two conclusions can be emphasised ON empirical grounds. Firstly, the study concludes that, taking quality changes into account, car prices in Spain deflated by CPI declined by 40% between 1981 and 2005. This result is robust to the alternative estimation procedures employed in the study. Secondly, an analysis of sigma-convergence shows that for quality-adjusted prices a clear trend in $\sigma$-convergence emerges between 1986 and 1992, whereas such a trend does not exists for observed prices. The authors link this result to Spain's integration into the European Community.

Peter Loeb, William Clarke and Richard Anderson develop a set of models for the determinants of automobile fatalities with particular attention devoted to the effects of increased cell phone usage. Cell phones have been associated with both life-taking and life-saving properties. However, prior statistical evaluations of the effects of cell phones have led to fragile results. The authors develop, in this article, econometric models using time series data, allowing for polynomial structures of the regressors. The models are evaluated with a set of specification error tests providing reliable estimates of the effects of the various policy and driving related variables evaluated. The statistical results indicate the effect of cell phones is nonmonotonic depending on the volume of phones in use, first having a net life-taking effect, then a net life-saving effect, finally followed with a net life-taking effect as the volume of phone use increases.

Finally, Juyi Shen applies two recent stated choice survey datasets of Japan to investigate the difference between the Latent Class Model (LCM) and the Mixed Logit Model (MLM) for transport mode choice. A detailed comparison is carried out, focusing on comparing the values of time savings, direct choice elasticities, predicted choice probabilities and prediction success indices. Furthermore, a test on nonnested model is also utilized to help determine which model is superior to another one. The results suggest that the LCM performs better than the MLM in both datasets.

# Value based trading of real assets in shipping under stochastic freight rates

Sigbjørn Sødal, Steen Koekebakker and Roar Adland

The article uses a real options valuation model with stochastic freight rates to investigate market efficiency and the economics of switching between the dry bulk and the tanker markets in international shipping. A dry bulk carrier is replaced with a tanker when the expected net present value of such a switch is optimal from a real options based decision rule. Depending on the development of the markets a reversal may take place later. The cost and demand parameters upon which the decisions to switch are made, including the stochastic characteristics of freight rates, are estimated from an empirical analysis that is updated every week throughout a 12-year time period from 1993 to 2005. The second-hand market for bulk ships seems to have been efficient most of these years in the sense that market switching usually did not pay off, with one major exception: it seemed profitable in expectation to leave the dry bulk market and enter the tanker market over a significant period of time shortly after the millennium shift, and to return to the dry bulk market about three years later. These points in time corresponded with an unprecedented boom period in the tanker and dry bulk freight markets, respectively, and the result suggest that agents in the second-hand market were slow to adjust their expectations. In retrospect, such an investment policy also happened to be profitable compared to staying put in the tanker market, even after accounting for transaction costs.

## I. Introduction

Timing of investment is a key to success in international shipping. This is because freight rates are sometimes very high for long enough periods of time to make a ship look more like a money machine than a normal production unit. In other periods they are close to or even below average long-run costs including normal returns to capital. In this article we apply a real options based model to study the optimal timing of investment in the sense of switching between the two main freight market segments in bulk shipping, namely that for tankers (the sea transport of crude oil and oil products) and dry bulk carriers (the sea transport of dry commodities such as iron ore, coal and grain). The model is calibrated to real world data on freight rates and second-hand ship values, and it seems to do a fairly good job in estimating when a switch from one market segment to the other could be profitable. The model and the empirical results are also used to discuss market efficiency.

The theoretical real options model used here is in the tradition of McDonald and Siegel (1986). The modelling of combined entry–exit decisions was introduced by Mossin (1968) and generalized in a modern real options framework in Brennan and Schwartz (1985) and Dixit (1989). Leahy (1993) showed how to interpret such models in a perfectly competitive market, which is our framework of analysis.[1]

According to Koopmans (1939), the short-term supply curve in bulk shipping can be characterized by two distinct regimes, depending on whether or not the fleet is fully employed. When the fleet sails at close to the maximum capacity, the aggregate supply function becomes almost perfectly inelastic resulting in very high freight rates. Conversely, when the available supply exceeds demand, leading to lower freight rates and vessel unemployment, the least cost-efficient vessels withdraw from the market, resulting in a series of perfectly elastic steps in the short-term supply function. Boom periods have historically been followed by periods of depressed freight rates, due to a strong supply side response through newbuilding activity. This cyclical nature of the freight rates in turn leads to cyclical and very volatile ship prices. Obviously a ship has greater value if freight rates and operating income are high, but if changes in ship values are predictable then there is money to be made from market timing. In shipping this is referred to as *asset play*. An asset play investor has typically a fairly short investment horizon compared to the typical lifetime of a ship of 25 years or more. Another timing strategy is to switch between freight market segments based on the freight rate differential and relative ship values. If asset play or market segment switching provides easy profits, then the (second-hand) market for ships is not informationally efficient. In this article we focus on the latter investment strategy, but before describing our own model we give a brief review of the maritime economic literature concerning ship valuation, investment strategies and market efficiency.

What is the value of a ship? The maritime literature has borrowed heavily from financial economics over the past decades. Beenstock (1985) and Strandenes (1984) introduce the present value model of ships in maritime economics. The price of a ship today is the discounted value of the ship the next period plus the freight revenue during the period. This present value relationship says that the market is efficient if market participants discount future cash flows properly. If market participants are rational (or semi-rational as suggested by Strandenes (1984)), then markets are efficient. Such a framework suggests that ship prices are largely unpredictable. This conclusion spurred a series of empirical investigations of market efficiency by Vergottis (1988), Hale and Vanags (1992), Beenstock and Vergottis (1993b), Glen (1997), Kavussanos and Alizadeh (2002), Tsolakis *et al.* (2003) and Adland and Koekebakker (2004).

Kavussanos and Alizadeh (2002) test the efficient market hypothesis within the rational expectation framework in the market for new and second-hand dry bulk ships. They follow the VAR methodology of Campbell and Schiller (1988), which enables a direct test of the joint hypothesis of rational expectation and market efficiency. The conclusion from the empirical part of their study is that the efficient market hypothesis must be rejected for the dry bulk sector. Birkeland and Tvedt (1997) discuss asset play in tanker trades under the assumption of mean-reverting freight earnings. In their model a company owns at all times a minimum of one and a maximum of five ships. The model is only in part based on economic valuation in the sense that an asset transaction occurs when an *ad hoc* markup of expected revenues over costs is observed. Adland and Koekebakker (2004) investigate asset play strategies in the second market for bulk ships. They use an entry–exit model where the buy and sell signals are generated by technical trading rules. They find that profits from trading rules exceed a simple buy and hold strategy in both the dry bulk and tanker sectors. However, these trading rules are governed by short term trends in the asset values, leading to frequent trading. Moreover, when the strategies are adjusted for transaction costs and illiquidity in the second-hand market, the excess profits evaporates, leading to the conclusion that the sale and purchase markets (S&P) for ships are fairly efficient.

Asset pricing can be viewed in absolute or relative terms. The present value model of ship value is an absolute valuation relationship, relating freight revenues to the price level of an asset. Absolute asset pricing is a difficult exercise with wide error margins, which also explains the mixed results reported above. But what about the relative price of ships in different market segments? The law of one price says that two assets that produce the same future payoff should sell at the same price and is an example of perfect relative pricing. If it does not hold, arbitrage opportunities exist. Chen and Knez (1995) argue that in the more general case where markets are integrated, assets with similar payoffs across future states should have

[1] See Speight and Thomson (2006) and Hőlzl (2005) for recent applications of such real options theory.

similar prices. In a measure-theoretic framework they develop relative price bounds that allow for examination of near integrated markets.

The concept of relative valuation has been used for generating trading strategies in the general financial literature. For instance, Gatev *et al.* (2006) conduct an empirical study of relative pricing in the stock market using a trading strategy called pairs trading, explained as follows: Pick two common stocks that have moved together in the past. If they deviate in value, buy the cheap one and sell the expensive one. If history repeats itself, prices will converge once more and the speculator will profit. Turning to bulk shipping, there are two main sectors, the dry bulk and tanker markets. Since ships are typically designed to operate in one of these markets only, high freight rates in one market segment does not automatically produce high freight rates in the other segment. However, Beenstock and Vergottis (1993a) argue that freight rates in these two markets cannot drift too far apart due to shipbuilding and scrapping activity, as well as the existence of a special ship type (the *combination carrier*) that can operate in both segments. Their arguments are as follows: increased contracting of tankers reduces the potential future supply of new dry bulk carriers as shipbuilding capacity is scarce. This will ultimately lower tanker freight rates relative to dry bulk freight rates. Furthermore, in times of strong transportation demand for oil relative to dry bulk commodities, the fleet of combination carriers will switch to the tanker market from the dry bulk market and increase supply in the short run until increased newbuilding activity and subsequent deliveries restore the market balance. Such a switch reduces the tanker rates relative to dry cargo rates. Following this line of reasoning, the two freight markets are more integrated the older the fleet of dry or tanker vessels (making scrapping a viable option) and the larger the fleet of combination carriers. When two markets are integrated, then so should ship prices be according to Chen and Knez (1995). Very few combination carriers have been built over the last 30 years. The share of such ships in the total bulk fleet has declined from more than 10% to less than 2% today over this period. Thereby the two bulk market segments have become less integrated. See Sødal *et al.* (2008) for a discussion.

In this article we propose to use a real options based entry–exit model for switching between these two market segments in shipping. We assume that a ship operator will always own and operate one ship, but he can switch back and forth between the two segments. If he initially operates in oil transportation, then, in order to make a switch, he must sell his oil tanker and buy a dry bulk carrier. The discussion above suggests that these market segments are integrated, indicating that the freight rate in one segment cannot drift too far away from the freight rate in the other segment. The key variable in the model is therefore the freight rate differential, which is modelled by an Ornstein-Uhlenbeck (mean-reverting) process.

Imagine a perfectly competitive market with two truly comparable valued ships – one dry bulk carrier and one tanker – and where switching could occur at no cost. In such a market switching would take place immediately if the observed freight rate differential deviated from the theoretical value that reflects the long-term cost differential. When transaction costs are introduced, an upper and lower barrier to switching will exist due to the combination of uncertainty and irreversibility. These barriers for investment are identified by the entry–exit model of this article. If ships in the two segments are priced efficiently, the freight rate differential can be expected to lie between the two barriers (inside the hysteresis band). If the freight rate differential moves outside this band of inaction, there is an indication of inefficient relative pricing as switching is expectedly profitable.

The rest of the article is organized as follows: Section II provides some basic insights in the decision problem of the article by a general discussion of market switching and market efficiency. Section III contains the theoretical model. In Section IV the estimation and calibration routine is explained. Empirical results are presented and discussed in Section V, while Section VI concludes.

## II. Market Switching and Market Efficiency

Suppose that a ship owner with restricted access to capital and other resources is bound to operate exactly one ship in either of two markets. One market is considered the default market that yields a default cash flow. A fixed entry cost is required to initiate operations in the other market. Operations in the latter market may then be suspended by incurring a fixed exit cost. Then a second entry may take place, and so it goes. When is it optimal to switch from one market to the other? The answer is well known from the real options theory on entry and exit under uncertainty. As long as the freight rate processes satisfy certain characteristics, it is optimal to enter when the net freight rate differential (in terms of earnings) exceeds a fixed, upper trigger level.

A similar rule applies in the reverse case; i.e. a return to the base case market occurs when a certain lower differential is reached. Irreversible transaction costs and uncertainty explain the inertia. When the freight rate (differential) is between the two trigger levels it is optimal to remain in the current state of operation. The cost parameters and the characteristics of the price process will determine the exact location of the triggers.

What if the firm is not alone with this option to invest or disinvest, but one firm among a large number of (potential) entrants? Then one should expect massive entry as soon as entry is optimal for a single firm. Such an increase of supply will prevent the freight rate from rising far above the trigger rate for investment. In the theoretical ideal situation with a large number of identical entrants, the freight rate will not increase a dollar above the trigger level, but the trigger level will act like a reflecting upper barrier for the freight rate. Similarly, the exit trigger will act like a lower reflecting barrier. This theoretically ideal evolution of prices is illustrated in Fig. 1, which plots a simulated random walk with and without two specific barriers.

The grey line in Fig. 1 shows how freight rates would have been in the case of a single monopolistic firm, i.e. without aggregate supply adjustments. The black line shows the constrained process with two specific barriers. The lower barrier is touched first. This leads to a positive differential between the constrained and the unconstrained process. The differential stays constant as long as the constrained random variable wanders between the two barriers, but it will drift off in some direction in the very long run as one of the processes is unconstrained. The unconstrained process in Fig. 1 can be interpreted as a more fundamental demand process than the solid line price process, as the unconstrained process does not depend on the supply side in an industry context.

When the firm is to determine the trigger price at which to invest or divest, it does not matter which one of the two processes is used. This striking result is due to Leahy (1993). In other words, the firm's decisions can be based on myopic preferences. Profits are affected as the true price process is bounded in both ends, but the optimal decision rules are not.

No real market where prices are unregulated will produce price ceilings and price floors as exact as those shown in Fig. 1. One reason is that firms are never identical in terms of costs. There will also be slight differences in terms of quality, branding etc, making any real market different from a market with perfect competition. Other distortions also come into effect. The prices will often stay relatively close to some mean value in the very long run, but with no absolute price ceiling or floor. With a sufficiently large variation of competing technologies a mean-reverting price process could therefore result. The long-term mean price should be closely related to long-term costs as long as the markets are efficient, with free entry and free exit.

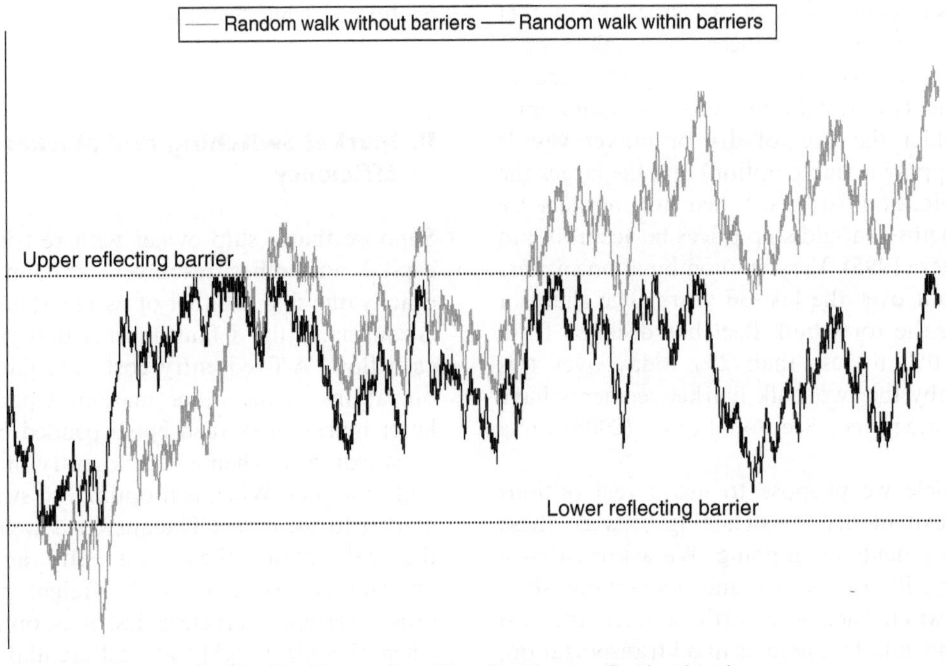


**Fig. 1. Random walk with and without reflecting barriers**

At least three candidates for a stochastic process exist that may be used when searching for the optimal decision rules in markets as discussed above: (1) the underlying demand process, (2) a price process without mean-reversion but with barriers or (3) a mean-reverting price process without barriers. The last candidate is the most promising one for our purposes, considering not only the available information on the world's bulk markets, but also the technical challenges that arise with the two other alternatives.

The analysis in the subsequent sections applies a mean-reverting price process without price ceilings and price floors, and with parameters that are estimated from historical data. Referring to the theoretical discussion above, one should keep in mind that a random walk between an upper and a lower price barrier that fluctuate over time, might well be a more realistic representation of the exact price process.

## III. Theoretical Model

In this section we describe an optimal asset play strategy in terms of a policy for switching between the two market segments, *dry bulk* and *tankers*, based on the general discussion above. The technical tool is a real options model that is spelled out in detail in the Appendix. Sødal *et al.* (2008) use a similar model to value the flexibility embedded in combination carriers that can operate in both market segments. This requires another empirical setup and a different interpretation of variables.

The decision maker is a shipping firm with some kind of capacity constraint that prevents it from operating many different assets at the same time. However, the firm is able to switch between the two ship types depending on what ship is expectedly more profitable from available information on freight rates, ship prices and costs. More precisely, we make the following assumptions:

(1) An investor must at all time own exactly one ship that can operate in exactly one of the two market segments. He is allowed to switch back and forth between the two market segments an infinite number of times by selling and buying ships of comparable size.
(2) The buying and selling of ships is done in the second-hand market. The price of a second-hand ship in each of the two segments is denoted by $I_{\text{wet}}$ and $I_{\text{dry}}$.
(3) All ships are assumed to have infinite lifetime.
(4) The discount rate is constant ($\rho$).
(5) The transaction cost of a switch – i.e. brokerage fees etc. – is also constant ($F$).

The appropriateness of these assumptions is discussed in the empirical section below. The most important variable in the theoretical model is the differential (the spread) between freight rates in the dry bulk and tanker freight market segment. The dynamics of the freight rate spread is described by an Ornstein-Uhlenbeck (O-U) process

$$\mathrm{d}p = \mu(m - p)\mathrm{d}t + \sigma \mathrm{d}z \tag{1}$$

where $p(= p_{\text{wet}} - p_{\text{dry}})$ is the freight rate differential between the two market segments, $m$ is the long run mean for this spread, $\mu$ is a mean-reverting speed parameter, $\sigma$ is a volatility parameter and $\mathrm{d}z$ is the increment of a Wiener process.

What is the value of a switch compared to staying put in the initial market segment? A switch incurs investment costs plus either a short or a long position in the freight rate differential. Look first at the investment costs. The total investment cost when switching from the dry bulk segment to the tanker segment is

$$A = F + I \tag{2}$$

where $I = I_{\text{wet}} - I_{\text{dry}}$. The similar total cost for a switch the other way, denoted $B$, equals

$$B = F - I \tag{3}$$

since the component $I$ of the total investment now has been reversed. When the price of the second-hand oil tanker exceeds that of the dry bulk carrier by more than the brokerage fee, $B$ will be negative. Still we have $A + B > 0$, which is required for irreversibility (i.e. one cannot get rich by switching back and forth all the time).

Next, look at the freight rate differential. Denote the expected, discounted value of future freight differentials at time $t$ by $V_t$, assuming no further switches. This revenue would be obtained by switching to the other sector and remaining there forever. For the given O-U process it becomes

$$V_t = E\left[\int_t^{\infty} p_s e^{-\rho s}\mathrm{d}s\right] = \left[\int_t^{\infty} (m + (p_s - m)e^{-\mu s})e^{-\rho s}\mathrm{d}s\right] = \frac{p_t}{\rho + \mu} + \frac{\mu m}{\rho(\rho + \mu)} \tag{4}$$

where $E[\cdot]$ is the expectations operator and $p_t$ is the current freight rate differential; see Dixit and Pindyck (1994, p. 74). Equation 4 shows that $V_t$ is a linear function of the current differential, $p_t$. By Ito's lemma, $V_t$ follows the O-U process

$$dV = \mu(\tilde{m} - V)dt + \tilde{\sigma}dz \tag{5}$$

where $\tilde{m} = m/\rho$ and $\tilde{\sigma} = \sigma/(\rho + \mu)$, and where the time subscript has been omitted.

Suppose that the shipping firm is initially in the tanker segment but has decided to switch to the dry bulk segment when the freight rate hits a certain $p_H$, and to return when another freight rate $p_L$ ($< p_H$) is hit next. The Appendix shows that the value of the switching opportunities equals

$$W_0 = \frac{Q(p_0, p_H)(V_H - A - Q(p_H, p_L)(B + V_L))}{1 - Q(p_L, p_H)Q(p_H, p_L)} \tag{6}$$

where $p_0$ ($<p_H$) is the current freight rate differential and $V_H$ and $V_L$ are expected net present values of future earnings evaluated at the trigger points $p_H$ and $p_L$, assuming no further switches. $Q(x, y)$ is a discount factor function that applies to the motion from a current freight rate $x$ to another freight rate $y$. Thus $Q(x, y) = 1$ for $x = y$ and $0 \leq Q(x, y) < 1$ for $x \neq y$. The discount factor function is specific to the stochastic process. It could also matter whether the motion is upward or downward, so generally $Q(x, y) \neq Q(y, x)$. For the O-U process the Appendix shows that the discount factor is

$$Q(p_L, p_H) = \frac{M(p_L) + U(p_L)}{M(p_H) + U(p_H)} \tag{7a}$$

$$Q(p_H, p_L) = \frac{M(p_H) - U(p_H)}{M(p_L) - U(p_L)} \tag{7b}$$

where $p_H > p_L$, and where $M(\cdot)$ and $U(\cdot)$ are defined as follows:

$$M(p) = H\left(\frac{\rho}{2\mu}, \frac{1}{2}, \frac{\mu}{\sigma^2}(p - m)^2\right) \tag{8a}$$

$$U(p) = \frac{2(p-m)\sqrt{\mu}}{\sigma} \frac{\Gamma((1/2)+(\rho/2\mu))}{\Gamma(\rho/2\mu)} \times H\left(\frac{1}{2} + \frac{\rho}{2\mu}, \frac{3}{2}, \frac{\mu}{\sigma^2}(p-m)^2\right) \tag{8b}$$

Here $\Gamma(\cdot)$ is the Gamma function while $H(\cdot)$ is the confluent hypergeometric (Kummer) function. The latter function has a series representation as follows (Slater, 1960):

$$H(\theta, b, z) = 1 + \frac{\theta}{b}z + \frac{\theta(\theta+1)z^2}{b(b+1)2!} + \frac{\theta(\theta+1)(\theta+2)z^3}{b(b+1)(b+2)3!} + \cdots \tag{9}$$

In order to determine whether it is optimal to switch market, the value function (6) with underlying definitions is maximized with respect to $p_L$ and $p_H$. If the firm is currently operating in the tanker market, a switch to dry bulk is induced if the current freight rate differential exceeds $p_H$. Likewise, a switch in the other direction is induced by a freight rate differential below $p_L$. Based on the main result in Leahy (1993), it can be argued that the two market segments are efficient in a relative sense (i.e. relative to each other) if the observed freight rate differential stays within the hysteresis band $[p_L, p_H]$. In the next section we present the data along with a discussion of the modelling assumptions above.

## IV. Modelling Assumptions and Parameter Estimation

Under the stated assumptions, optimal investment boils down to the question on when to sell a dry bulk carrier and replace it with an oil tanker and vice versa. The decision will depend on the current second-hand price differential for ships, $I_0$, the discount rate, $\rho$, the current freight rate differential, $p$ and the stochastic properties of the freight rate differential as given by (1) under appropriate estimates for $m$, $\mu$ and $\sigma$.

### *Newbuilding and second-hand ship values*

The ship types we consider are Suezmax oil tankers and Capesize dry bulk carriers, which are of comparable size (around 150 000 dwt). The switching model could be of interest to several ship types and market segments, but to reduce the significance of errors in variables not modelled explicitly it is natural to choose ships that are comparable in size and costs. If one ship were much more expensive or is characterized by economies of scale or scope (such as a combination carrier) one would have to put more effort into modelling other operations within the firm, other investment options and the opportunity costs of capital. Such issues can be more or less ignored when restricting to markets that are fairly similar and easy to characterize as they mainly differ in freight rates and second-hand prices in the short-run.

Figure 2 plots the newbuilding prices for Suezmax and Capesize bulk carriers between 1986 and 2005. The clear upward shift in oil tanker newbuilding prices early in the 1990s is probably related to the

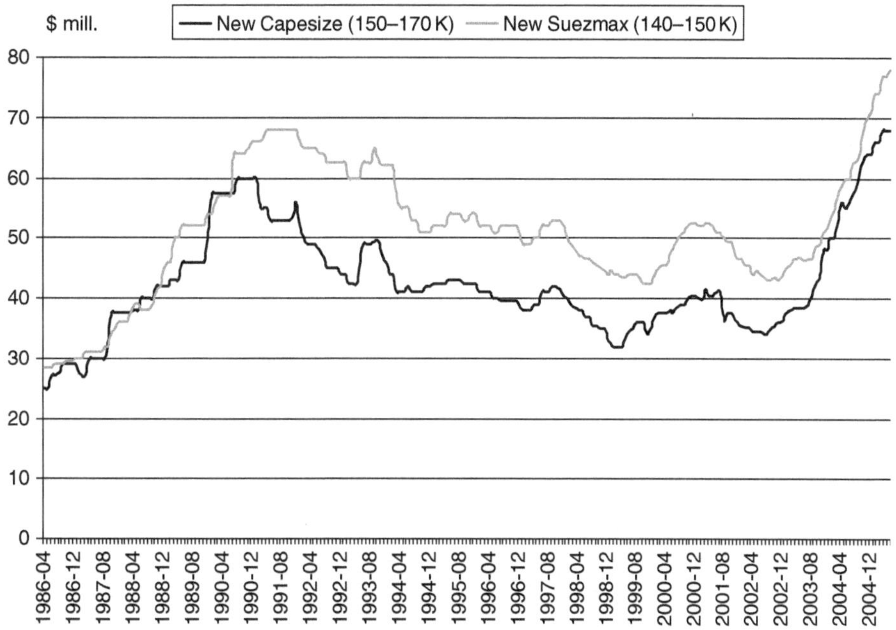


**Fig. 2. Newbuilding prices in the bulk ship market (Clarksons, 2005)**

double-hull requirement that was introduced around that time.[2]

In our model we focus on second-hand values, or more specifically on the price difference between an oil tanker and a dry bulk carrier that are both five-year old. Figure 3 shows the price development for such ships.

The lowest (thin) line in Fig. 3 represents the variable $I$ in the theoretical model and shows that the price differential is positive during most of the data period. This means that tankers are usually more expensive than dry bulk carriers. In practice this results from greater steel consumption due to the double hull requirement and the fact that tankers are more complex in terms of construction and onboard equipment. The assumption that all ships are five years of age is trivial as long as second-hand markets are balanced in the sense that second-hand ships of different age are priced correctly relative to each other. That is reasonable as all such ships are available immediately. The economics of investment in new ships is more complicated due to delivery lags which also fluctuate. In general, delivery lags can have spurious effects on investment; see Bar-Ilan and Strange (1996) and Sødal (2006).

Since all ships are assumed to have infinite life-times, the discount rate must be raised accordingly to account for depreciation. The volatility of freight rates dominates discounting in the short run, so infinite life-times is probably not a crucial assumption in the model. The empirical analysis will show that success with the market switching strategy does not depend highly on interest rates but mostly on how decisions are made conditional on the evolution of freight rates and second-hand prices.

It should also be emphasized that the model considers all costs to be fixed. Selling one ship and buying another one is regarded as a net investment based on the current price differential. This means that the investment strategy does not consider explicitly the uncertainty of second-hand prices. Since the uncertainty of freight rates, which is indeed modelled, tends to be positively correlated with price uncertainty for ships, this simplifying assumption could have systematic erroneous impact on investment valuation. Since uncertainty of freight rates is modelled explicitly, however, the magnitude of the error is intuitively small albeit in principle unknown.[3]

### *Freight rate differential*

Figures 2 and 3 indicate that second-hand prices are more volatile than newbuilding prices. The recent experience in the second-hand market is exceptional,

[2] Note the graphical illusion after 2003, which indicates a smaller price differential than the actual one due to rising absolute prices. Still the differential is somewhat lower than in the previous years.
[3] See Dixit and Pindyck (1994, ch. 6) for a model with combined price and cost uncertainty.

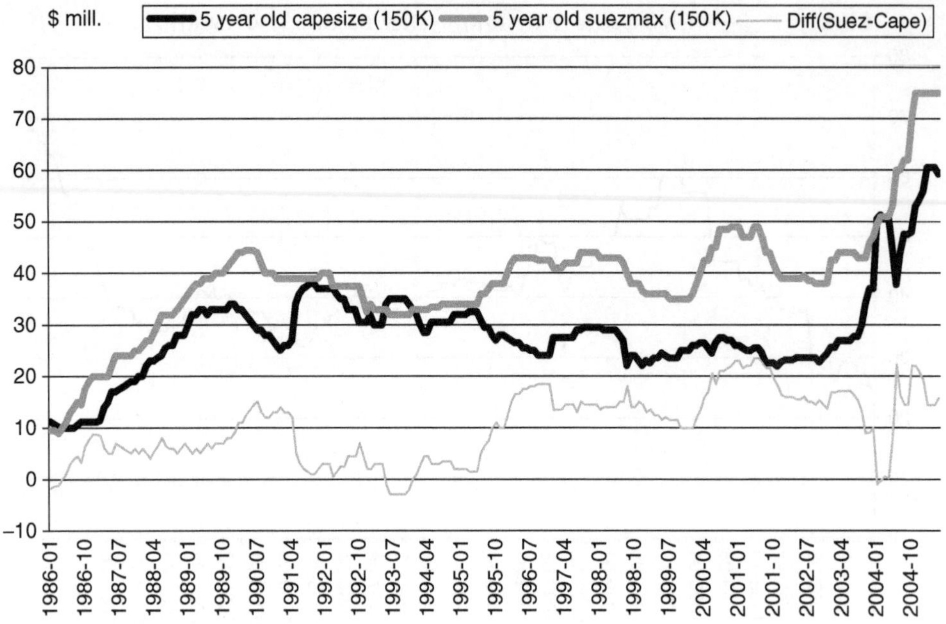


**Fig. 3. Second-hand prices in the bulk ship market (Clarksons, 2005)**

with the price for five years old ships at some occasions even exceeding the newbuilding price. Record-high freight rates is the main explanatory factor, as the opportunity cost of waiting many years for the delivery is correspondingly high. This is seen from Fig. 4, which plots monthly spot freight rates in the dry bulk and the tanker market after 1990.

Figure 4 demonstrates increasing uncertainty and increasing freight rate spread over time as the overhang of tonnage created in the 1970s and 1980s slowly disappeared and gave way to a tight balance of supply and demand. The thin line in Fig. 4 is the freight rate spread which is the driving process in the model. The volatility increases dramatically in the end of the sample period, so the empirical estimates will vary depending on the choice of data period. Some changes could be predicted by the market, partly due to increased newbuilding costs for oil tankers following from political decisions and technological change, and partly due to a shrinking combination carrier fleet, all of which could be observed. This suggests that the parameters of the O-U process are not constant over time. One might have picked a more sophisticated stochastic process for the freight rate differential, but then the analytical tractability of the model would be lost.[4] Another possibility, the one we pursue, is to re-estimate the parameters when new observations enter the sample window.

### *Parameter estimation*

The discrete time counterpart to the O-U process in (1) is the AR(1) process given as

$$p_t = \alpha + \beta p_{t-1} + \varepsilon_t \qquad (10)$$

where $\alpha$ and $\beta$ are constants and $\varepsilon \sim N(0, S^2)$. Here $X \sim N(a, b)$ means that a random variable $X$ is normally distributed with mean $a$ and variance $b$. In this model, unbiased estimates of $\alpha$ and $\beta$ can be found from an ordinary least squares regression. The relationships between the parameters in the discrete time model in (10) and the continuous time version in (1) are given by

$$\mu = \frac{-\ln \beta}{\Delta} \qquad (11a)$$

$$m = \frac{\alpha}{1 - e^{-\mu\Delta}} \qquad (11b)$$

$$\sigma = \sqrt{S^2 \frac{2\mu}{1 - e^{-2\mu\Delta}}} \qquad (11c)$$

where $S$ is the SD of the residuals of the regression and $\Delta$ is the time between observations measured in years. We will use weekly data on the freight rate differential, resulting in $\Delta = 1/52$. In the next section the model is calibrated to real world data. As discussed above, the model must be re-estimated frequently to adjust for changing market conditions.

[4] Time-varying volatility for second-hand dry cargo ship prices of different sizes is studied in Kavussanos (1997).

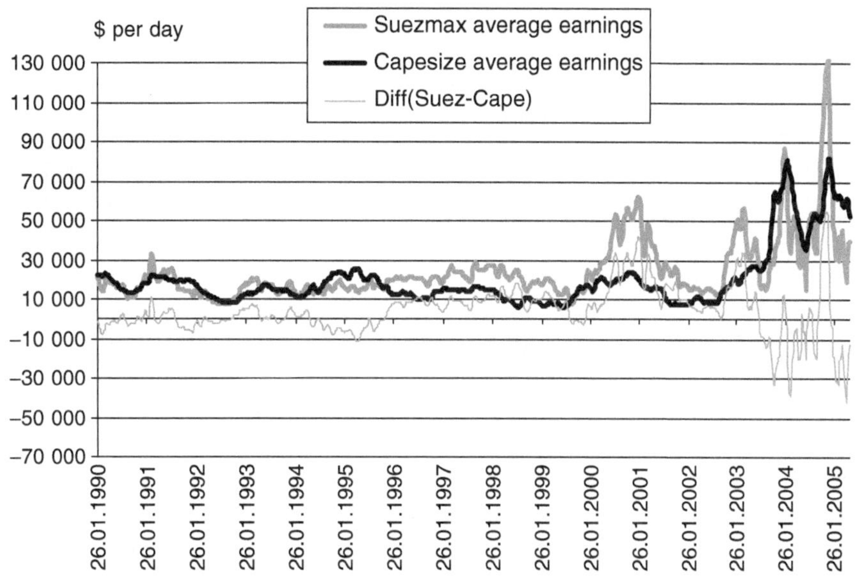


**Fig. 4. Freight rates in the bulk market (Clarksons, 2005)**

We will use a sample window of three years for the model estimation. For a slowly mean-reverting process, although unbiased, one would need a long time series to get precise estimates of the parameter $\alpha$ in (10) and consequently the long run mean, $m$ in (1). Therefore the long run mean is instead derived from an equilibrium argument. Differences in newbuilding prices between tankers and dry bulk carriers are likely to translate into equivalent freight rate differences in the long run for a competitive market. As long as the discount rate and the newbuilding cost differential are stable over time, and since the O-U process is symmetric around its mean, it can be argued that $m$ will correspond to the annualized capital cost difference between tankers and bulk ships. This is used in the empirical analysis, which assumes

$$m = \rho I_0 \tag{12}$$

where $\rho$ is a constant discount rate and $I_0$ equals 75% of the newbuilding price differential between new ships and five-year old ships.[5] Newbuilding prices fluctuate but the price differential between tankers and bulk ships of comparable size can be expected to fluctuate less due to integrated shipbuilding markets. This follows from the fact that many shipyards can produce both types of ships and that, at the aggregate level, the capacity (per time unit) to produce ships is constrained.

## V. Empirical Analysis

When uncertainty is limited to freight rates and the process for the freight rate differential is autonomous as it is here (i.e. not depending on calendar time), the optimal policy follows from the discussion in Section II. The firm should switch market segment, selling the tanker and buying a dry bulk carrier, when the freight rate differential exceeds the second-hand price differential by a certain upper margin. The decision to return is based on a similar rule.

### *Parameter estimation and model calibration*

In practical market switching situations historical data will be combined with other knowledge to form plausible predictions for freight rates and other variables. In our context, backward-looking empirical behaviour would tend to underestimate the importance of change. We use a sample window of three years for parameter estimation. Three years is a normal delivery lag for new ships and can be seen as a typical long-term response time on the supply side when the market is exposed to demand changes. Data and estimation details are given below:[6]

(1) We have collected weekly spot freight rate in the dry and tanker sector and computed the freight rate differential for the period 12 January 2001 to 20 May 2005, a total of 802

[5] Twenty-five percent value reduction is close to the average long-term price differential between new ships and five-year old ships in this market, bulk carriers as well as tankers.
[6] All our data was kindly provided by Clarkson Research (2005).

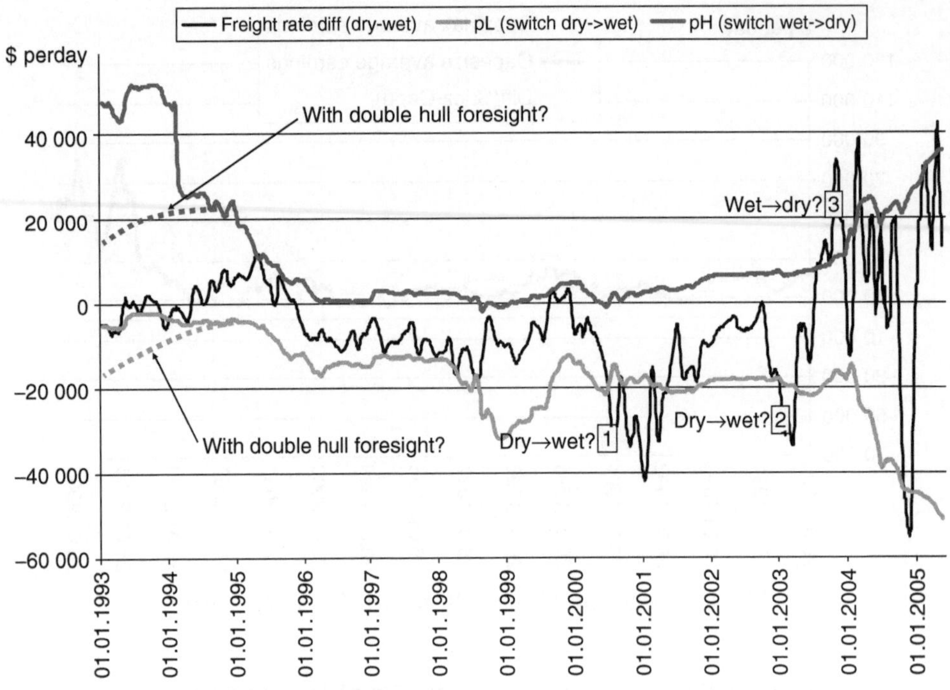


**Fig. 5. Freight rate differentials and optimal switching barriers in the bulk market**

observations. On 18 December 1992, we use the previous three years of data (154 observations) and run an OLS regression for the AR(1) model described in (10). The estimates for $\sigma$ and $\mu$ are computed from (11a) and (11c).

(2) Monthly prices for Suezmax tankers and Capesize bulk carriers for the period January 1990 to May 2005 are used to compute differences in newbuilding prices. For December 1992 we use the previous three years of data (36 observations) as an estimate for $I_0$. The base case discount rate is set to $\rho = 0.1$ (10% year) embodying 5–6% interest and 4–5% depreciation. The parameter $m$ is computed from (12).

(3) Monthly observations of second-hand prices for Suezmax tankers and Capesize bulk carriers over the period January 1990 to May 2005 are used to compute differences in second-hand prices. In December 1992 we use the prevailing price difference as an estimate of $I$.

(4) The market switching strategy consists of determining the optimal triggers $p_L$ and $p_H$ from (6) using the parameter values found in step 1–3, and to switch market whenever it is optimal from the given decision policy. (The optimal triggers are found by maximizing the value function, $W_0$, numerically over a grid.)

(5) The sample window is then moved one week ahead, and steps 1–4 are repeated until the end of the sample (20 May 2005). The estimated trigger points, $p_L$ and $p_H$, are recorded at each recalibration.

Note that since we only have monthly prices on ship values, and the model is calibrated weekly, the parameter values of $I$ and $m$ can only change every fourth week.

## VI. Results

Figure 5 shows the development of the freight rate differential and the optimal barriers for investment between December 1992 and May 2005. All three types of data are computed weekly, but the figure plots the average values over the last four weeks, reflecting that even an asset play strategy requires a reasonable response time and the fact that some empirical data are based on monthly observations. The main conclusion is that the market seems to have been efficient in a relative sense during most of the sample. The freight rate is located in between the barriers up until July 2000. The strategy under such conditions is to sustain operations. The freight rate approaches and is apparently reflected by one of the investment thresholds at several occasions. The theory discussed in Section II makes it reasonable to believe that the true stochastic process could be a random walk within two barriers as opposed to a process with an always active mean-reversion force. Alternatively, it could be a combination of these alternatives. For practical purposes the difference may not be crucial: what matters are the estimates for the investment triggers.

We note that the double-hull requirement increased the long-term investment costs for tankers relative to dry bulk carriers. A well-functioning market will anticipate such a change by expecting relatively higher future freight rates in oil trades than present and historical rates. Accordingly, both thresholds in Fig. 5 would be lowered in the first part of the data period by accounting for this external effect.

The resulting decision policy implies that a switch to the tanker market would be profitable for several months in the second half of the year 2000. The size and duration of the shock in terms of freight rates outside the hysteresis band of in-action can be interpreted as a clear advice. A slightly less clear advice to switch appears early in 2003, before an advice to invest in dry bulk later the same year. The trigger points in mid-2000 and late 2003 corresponds very well with the start of the recent boom markets in the tanker and dry bulk freight markets, respectively, with freight rates in the latter case rapidly reaching levels never before seen in the recent history of the global shipping markets. This suggests that either the agents in the second-hand markets were slow to change their expectations or that the rolling window estimation procedure of our empirical implementation is incapable of incorporating this structural change in freight rate levels and volatility sufficiently quickly. The markets have been extremely volatile from then on. This is reflected in the decision policy with a time lag since the policy is based on a three-year sliding average. Still the hysteresis band widens up fast, so the recommendation is to stay constantly in dry bulk trades. (There is a very short exceptional period early in 2005, in a market situation wilder than hardly ever before in peace-time. Most investors would probably hesitate to follow the advice of a model like this one literally under such circumstances.)

The real history is but one possible among an infinite number of paths for the evolution of the market prices. Therefore the economic implications of following the recommendation of the decision policy do not say much about the quality of the policy. More extensive testing is needed for that. Puzzling enough, however, a ship owner who initially operated in the dry bulk market, switching to the tanker market in July 2000 as recommended by the market switching strategy, and returning in October 2003, would have made excess profit compared to nonswitching strategy. He would have paid 10 million dollars more for the tanker he bought in July 2000 than for the one he sold in October 2003, in addition to one million dollars in transaction costs. However, the net present value of the freight income would have been more than 14 million dollars higher, implying a net gain of 3.7 million dollars when ignoring some minor interest payments. A firm that missed the opportunity in 2000 but switched to the tanker trades in January 2003 and returned in October 2003 would also have made a small gain. Freight earnings but also the price for the tanker purchased in January 2003 would have been lower, and the net gain around one million dollars.

Except for interpretation, the theoretical model used here is like one derived by Sødal *et al.* (2008). The latter reference studies the profitability of combination carriers, a ship type capable of operating in both of the bulk market segments in question. It does not investigate relative market efficiency, but only the value of flexibility based on a pure valuation approach. A combination carrier increases in value as the hysteresis band between the tanker and dry bulk sector increases. The main variable of interest, the freight rate differential, need not be outside the bands in order for such an investment to be profitable. Few such dual-purpose ships have been built during the last decade due to high price tags. Sødal *et al.* (2008) conclude that the profitability of combination carriers has increased, so this situation may well change in the near future. If it does, the dry bulk and tanker freight markets will become more integrated once again. The empirical set-up behind the investment rules of this article adjusts automatically to such changing circumstances as they evolve.

### *Sensitivity analysis*

As shown in Fig. 6, the conclusions above appear not to be very sensitive to changes in the discount rate, which has been varied from 7 to 15%. This result is comforting as the discount rate was treated simplistically to make the model tractable.

Figure 7 shows that the model is also quite insensitive to changes in transaction costs. The brokerage fee is usually not a fixed amount but a certain percentage of the price (the seller usually pays around 1% commission), but it is treated as a fixed parameter in the model for technical reasons. Varying this parameter between $300 000

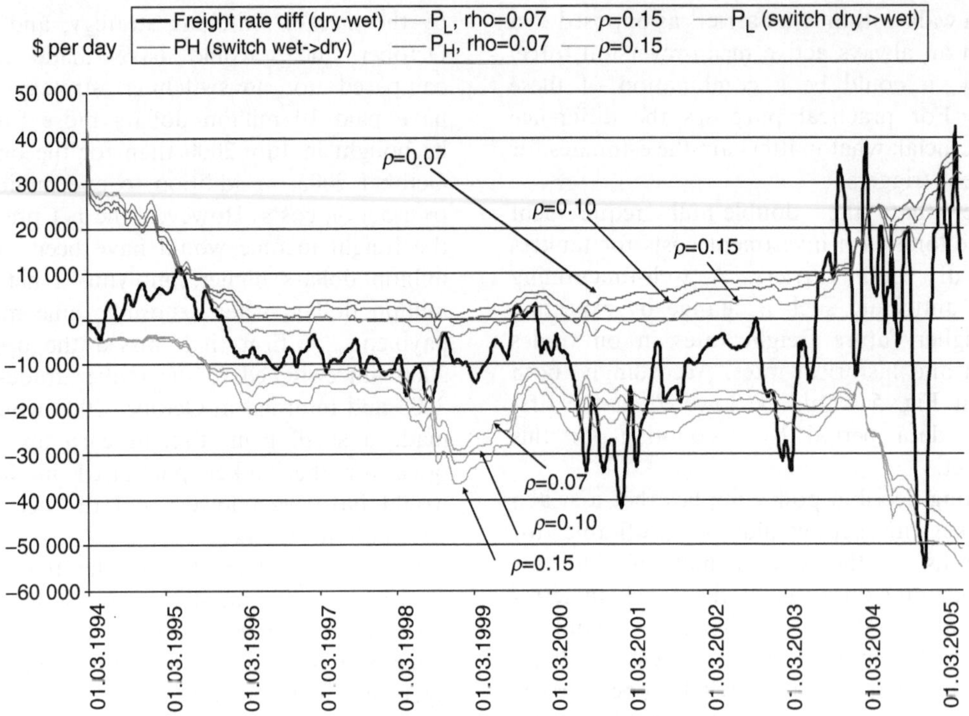


**Fig. 6. Optimal switching barriers under various discount rates**

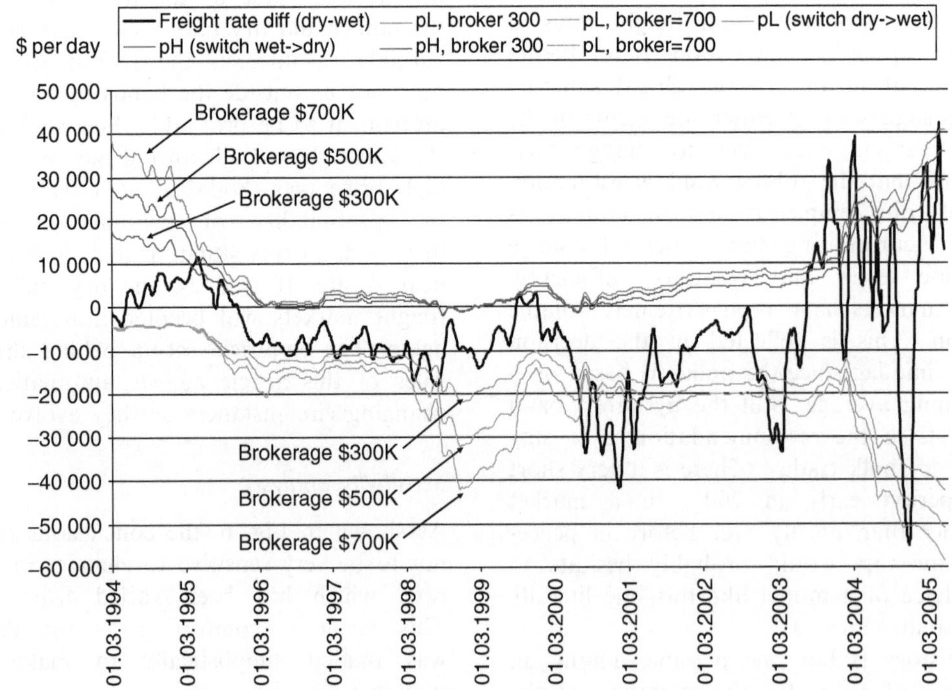


**Fig. 7. Optimal switching barriers under various switching costs**

and $700 000 does sometimes make a difference with respect to the location of the barriers, but one that apparently does not very often matter for the decision on whether to switch market or not.

We conclude that the base case discount rate and switching cost – i.e. 10% and $500 000, respectively – are representative for the model even if the exact choice of these numbers can always be questioned in such a simplified model.

## VII. Concluding Remarks

In this article we have provided a model for switching between integrated markets, based on economic valuation using real options techniques. An investor should switch market if two markets are integrated and prices of real assets in the other market drop sufficiently in a relative sense. The opposite applies for the investor to switch back. This provides a framework for analysing the relative efficiency of two integrated markets. If money can be made from timing the markets, the two markets are inefficient in a relative sense.

In the empirical analysis we applied the model to two main market segments in international shipping: the tanker market and the dry bulk market. The model was calibrated to real world data using a three-year estimation window. It turned out that the freight rate differential remained inside the estimated hysteresis band most of the time. This indicates that no excess profits can usually be made from the switching strategy – the markets are informationally efficient in a relative sense. At the end of our sample, however, the model indicates market timing abilities. In fact, all the switches suggested by the model would have paid off. Still it is much too early to pass the judgement that these market segments are informationally inefficient. First, the model identifies only a few excess profit opportunities and it is not evident how to judge the statistical significance of these results. Second, testing for market efficiency, in an absolute or relative sense, often encounters the 'joint-hypothesis' problem. Our model is based on the assumption that the freight rate differential process adequately picks up the uncertainty in the investment situation and that it can be described by an O-U process. Misspecification of the underlying uncertainty may mistakenly be taken as evidence of relative inefficiency.

For the stochastic and highly volatile shipping markets one should not pay much attention to the results from a single example. Future work should include more extensive testing of the market switching strategy with more market segments, a variety of time periods and adjustments for changes in technologies and economic policies of significance to shipping markets. Revisions that could make the strategy more realistic should also be considered. This includes explicitly modelling the second-hand markets for ships, more rigorous lifetime considerations and improved modelling of frequent market segment switching.

One possible application of the model would be to link it with the pairs trading strategy considered in Gatev *et al.* (2006). They use an *ad hoc* trading rule (sum of squared deviations between two normalized price series) to determine the thresholds. Here we have presented an economic valuation model for determining such thresholds.

## Acknowledgements

This research has been supported by Agder Maritime Research Foundation, Norway.

## References

Adland, R. O. and Koekebakker, S. (2004) Market efficiency in the second-hand market for bulk ships, *Maritime Economics and Logistics*, **6**, 1–15.

Bar-Ilan, A. and Strange, W. C. (1996) Investment lags, *American Economic Review*, **86**, 610–22.

Beenstock, M. (1985) A theory of ship prices, *Maritime Policy and Management*, **12**, 215–25.

Beenstock, M. and Vergottis, A. (1993a) The interdependence between the dry cargo and tanker markets, *Logistics and Transportation Review*, **29**, 3–38.

Beenstock, M. and Vergottis, A. (1993b) *Econometric Modelling of World Shipping*, Chapman & Hall, London, UK.

Birkeland, S. and Tvedt, J. (1997) Freight rates and tanker values – empirical findings and implications for asset play, Working Paper 25, SNF/Norwegian School of Economics, Bergen, Norway.

Brennan, M. J. and Schwartz, E. S. (1985) Evaluating natural resource investments, *Journal of Business*, **58**, 135–57.

Campbell, J. Y. and Schiller, R. F. (1988) Stock prices, earnings and expected dividends, *Journal of Finance*, **43**, 661–76.

Chang, H.-B., Choi, J. Y. and Chang, Y.-T. (1996) Price behavior in the Baltic freight futures market, IAME, Annual Conference Proceedings 1996 (International Association of Maritime Economists).

Chen, Z. and Knez, P. J. (1995) Measurement of market integration and arbitrage, *Review of Financial Studies*, **8**,, 287–325.

Clarkson Research (2005) Shipping Intelligence Network, www.clarksons.net

Dixit, A. K. (1989) Entry and exit decisions under uncertainty, *Journal of Political Economy*, **97**, 620–38.

Dixit, A. K. and Pindyck, R. S. (1994) *Investment Under Uncertainty*, Princeton University Press, Princeton, New Jersy, USA.

Dixit, A., Pindyck, R. S. and Sødal, S. (1999) A markup interpretation of optimal investment rules, *Economic Journal*, **109**, 179–89.

Gatev, E. G., Goetzman, W. N. and Rouwenhorst, K. G. (2006) Pairs trading: Performance of a relative value arbitrage rule, *Review of Financial Studies*, **19**, 797–827.

Glen, D. (1997) The market for second-hand ships: further results on efficiency using cointegration analysis, *Maritime Policy and Management*, **24**, 245–60.
Hale, C. and Vanags, A. (1992) The market for second-hand ships: some results on efficiency using cointegration, *Maritime Policy and Management*, **19**, 131–40.
Hőlzl, W. (2005) Tangible and intangible sunk costs and the entry and exit of firms in a small open economy: the case of Austria, *Applied Economics*, **37**, 2429–43.
Kavussanos, M. G. (1997) The dynamics of time-varying volatilities in different size second-hand ship prices of the dry-cargo sector, *Applied Economics*, **29**, 433–43.
Kavussanos, M. G. and Alizadeh, A (2002) Efficient pricing of ships in the dry bulk sector of the shipping industry, *Maritime Policy and Management*, **29**, 303–30.
Kavussanos, M. G. and Alizadeh, A. (2003) The price-volume relationship in the sale and purchase market for dry bulk vessels, *Maritime Policy and Management*, **30**, 321–37.
Koopmans, T. (1939) *Tanker Freight Rates and Tankship Building*, Economic Institute Report 27, Haarlem, The Netherlands.
Leahy, J. (1993) Investment in competitive equilibrium: the optimality of myopic behaviour, *Quarterly Journal of Economics*, **108**, 1105–33.
Mossin, J. (1968) An optimal policy for lay-up decisions, *Swedish Journal of Economics*, **70**, 170–7.
McDonald, R. and Siegel, R. (1986) The value of waiting to invest, *Quarterly Journal of Economics*, **101**, 707–28.
Slater, L. J. (1960) *Confluent Hypergeometric Functions*, Cambridge University Press, Cambridge, UK.
Speight, A. E. H. and Thompson, P. (2006) Is investment time irreversible? Some empirical evidence for disaggregated UK manufacturing data, *Applied Economics*, **38**, 2265–75.
Strandenes, S. P. (1984) Price determination in the time-charter and second-hand markets, Working Paper 6, Centre for Applied Research, Norwegian School of Economics and Business Administration, Bergen, Norway.
Sødal, S. (2006) Entry and exit decisions based on a discount factor approach, *Journal of Economic Dynamics and Control*, **30**, 1963–86.
Sødal, S., Koekebakker, S. and Adland, R. (2008) Market switching in shipping – a real option model applied to the valuation of combination carriers, *Review of Financial Economics* (Forthcoming).
Tsolakis, S. D., Cridland, C. and Haralambides, H. E. (2003) Econometric modelling of second-hand ship prices, *Maritime Economics and Logistics*, **5**, 347–77.
Vergottis, A. (1988) An econometric model of world shipping, PhD-thesis, City University Business School, London.

## Appendix 1: the value function $W_0$

This appendix derives the value function $W_0$ given by Equation 6, using the discount factor approach to investment as in Dixit *et al.* (1999) and Sødal (2006). Consider the optimal timing problem of when to enter or exit a market for which the expected net present value of remaining in the market forever equals a stochastic variable $V$ as described in the text. The evolution of the net present value is given by the Ito process

$$dV = \mu_V dt + \sigma_V dz \tag{A1}$$

where the O-U case in Equation 5, for which $\mu_V = \mu(\tilde{m} - V)$ and $\sigma_V = \sigma$, is one example. The entry cost is a constant, $A$, and the exit cost a similar constant, $B$. We require $A + B > 0$ to establish some irreversibility in the model, but either $A$ or $B$ could be negative. The initial value of the stochastic variable is a fixed $V_0$, the firm is not operating initially, and $V_0$ is so low that immediate entry is not optimal. (The optimal decision policy does not depend on $V_0$, so this initial value is just a technical necessity.)

As argued by Dixit (1989) and others, the optimal decision is to enter as soon as a certain $V_H$ is reached and to exit as soon as a certain $V_L$ ($<V_H$) is reached after the first entry. Then re-entry will take place the next time $V_H$ is hit, and so on. The firm finds the optimal policy by a two-step procedure. First, the current expected net present value of a decision policy that uses two *arbitrary* values $V_L$ and $V_H$ is found. Then the *optimal* policy is found by maximizing this expected net present value with respect to $V_H$ and $V_L$.

The (net present) value of the firm at the initial point, $W_0 = W(V_0)$, can be written

$$W_0 = Q(V_0, V_H)(V_H - A + F(V_H)) \tag{A2}$$

where $Q(V_1, V_2) \equiv E[e^{-\rho T}]$ is a decreasing function in $V_2$ for a fixed $V_1$, equivalent to the expected discount factor when moving from $V_1$ to $V_2$ for the first time $T$ is the first-hitting time from $V_1$ to $V_2$; see Dixit *et al.* (1999). The formula (A2) can be explained as follows: starting outside the market at $V_0$, all future revenues and costs are discounted by $Q(V_0, V_H)$ to account for the time until the first entry. Then the entry cost $A$ is incurred, after which the value of the firm is $V_H$ plus the value of further investment options, $F(V_H)$.

Exit will take place as soon as the stochastic variable hits $V_L$. This implies that the value of the remaining investment options at time of entry can be written as

$$F(V_H) = Q(V_H, V_L)(-V_L - B + W_L) \qquad \text{(A3)}$$

This formula reflects that the net present value of further operations at time of exit, $V_L$, is lost at time of exit when the exit cost $B$ is incurred. The firm still has value $W_L$ as it keeps the option to enter and exit later on. As long as $V_0 < V_L$ it must also hold that

$$W_0 = Q(V_0, V_L)W_L \qquad \text{(A4)}$$

because the value of the firm when $V = V_L$ is the discounted value of its initial value. The discount factor when moving from $V_0$ to $V_H$ can be decomposed into two legs – from $V_0$ to $V_L$ and from $V_L$ to $V_H$– as follows; see Dixit *et al.* (1999):

$$Q(V_0, V_H) = Q(V_0, V_L)Q(V_L, V_H) \qquad \text{(A5)}$$

By definition we also have $Q(V_i, V_j) = Q(p_i, p_j)$ for $i,j$ = 0, $L$ or $H$. Then Equation 6 in the text is obtained by combining (A2) through (A5).

As in Dixit *et al.* (1999), the discount factor $Q(p_1,p_2)$ for the O-U process (A1) is found by solving the differential equation

$$\frac{1}{2}\sigma^2 Q''(p_1, p_2) + \mu(m - p_1)Q'(p_1, p_2) - \rho Q(p_1, p_2) = 0 \qquad \text{(A6)}$$

The primes denote first and second derivatives of $Q$ with respect to the first argument. Sødal *et al.* (2008) show that the solution to Equation A6 can be written as

$$Q(p_1, p_2) = K_1 M(p_1) + K_2 U(p_1) \qquad \text{(A7)}$$

where $K_1$ and $K_2$ are constants and the definitions of $M(p_1)$ and $U(p_1)$ follow from Equations 8a and b. The discount factor for upward moves, given by Equation 7a is found by imposing appropriate boundary conditions that fix $K_1$ and $K_2$. A two-step procedure is needed. First, a conditional discount factor function $Q(p_L, p_H | p < p_L)$ will be derived, describing the discount factor when moving from $p_L$ to $p_H$ ($> p_L$) without hitting a certain $p < p_L$ first. Then we let $p \to -\infty$. The process is continuous, so $Q(p_L, p_H)$ will be reached in the limit as any finite value $p_H$ will be hit before $p$ (with probability one).

The boundary conditions are $Q(p_H, p_H | p < p_L) = 1$ and $Q(p, p_H, | p < p_L) = 0$. The first condition reflects no discounting if the intial value equals the destination value, $p_H$. The second condition reflects that the destination, $p_H$, is never hit before $p$ if starting at $p$. Hence,

$$K_1 M(p_H) + K_2 U(p_H) = 1; \quad K_1 M(p) + K_2 U(p) = 0 \qquad \text{(A8)}$$

Solving (A8) for $K_1$ and $K_2$, inserting into (A7) and letting $p \to -\infty$ gives the desired result. To arrive at Equation 7a, the following asymptotic property of the Kummer function is applied (see Slater 1960):

$$\lim_{z \to \infty} H(\theta, b, z) = \frac{\Gamma(b)}{\Gamma(\theta)} e^z z^{\theta - b} \qquad \text{(A9)}$$

This condition implies that $M(p)/U(p) \to \pm 1$ as $p \to \pm\infty$, which combined with the Gamma function property $\Gamma(1/2) = 2\ \Gamma(3/2)$ establishes Equation 7a. Equation 7b is derived similarly.

# Forecasting container transshipment in Germany

Peter M. Schulze and Alexander Prinz

In this article, we examine container transshipment at German ports using the Seasonal Auto-Regressive Integrated Moving Average (SARIMA) model and the Holt–Winters exponential smoothing approach. Our models are designed especially to take account of the seasonal behaviour of the quarterly data used. We consider the dynamic development in this sector for the whole container throughput and also the destinations Asia, Europe and North America, which are the world's three main economic regions. Our data runs from the first quarter of 1989 to the fourth quarter of 2006. We provide detailed quarterly forecasts for the years 2007 and 2008. According to forecasting error measures such as mean square error and Theil's U, the SARIMA-approach yields slightly better values of modelling the container throughput than the exponential smoothing approach. Our forecast results indicate further strong growth for German container handling in total and especially for the destinations Asia and Europe. Only the container transshipment between Germany and North America shows rather small increases up to the end of 2008.

## I. Introduction

Seaborne trade laid the foundations for the rapid and mostly steady growth of world trade during the past decades. Especially the rapidly increasing container transport, measured in TEU (20 ft Equivalent Unit), is an important indicator to represent the dynamics of world trade. Despite the fact that, in 2005, container ships accounted only for 14% (as share of the world gross tonnage) of world seaborne trade (Heymann, 2006, p. 4) the value of goods transported in containers is much higher – oil and gas tankers as well as bulkers are more significant according to weight.

Worldwide container transshipment grew with an annual rate of about 11% between 1995 and 2005. Forecasts predict annual growth rates of about 10% until 2010 (Heymann, 2006, p. 6).

In 2005, Germany held about 9% of the world's real exports (in prices and exchange rates of the year 2000) (Deutsche Bundesbank, 2006, p. 33) and more than 3% of the rapidly growing market of container transshipment. Furthermore, Germany controls one-third of the world's container fleet. Put into figures, German shipping companies controlled 1157 of the 3499 container ships in 2006 (ISL, 2006a, p. 23).

Quantitatively analytical literature on international container throughput, as well as on container transport, is rather scant: on the one hand, there is no freely accessible broad supranational database for international maritime shipping. On the other hand, the theoretical side of this theme is mostly integrated into general logistics, at least in scientific publications. Some institutions like Drewry Shipping Consultants Ltd., London (Drewry), Institut für

Seeverkehrswirtschaft und Logistik, Bremen (ISL) and Ocean Shipping Consultants Ltd., Surrey (OSC) regularly publish analyses for certain market segments on a descriptive-empirical base, and sometimes medium-term forecasts without giving the methodology.

We present quantitative short-run forecasts by using quarterly data for the German container throughput, separated by the world's main economic areas Asia, Europe and North America, the so-called triad of globalization. These three regions cumulate around 80% of global container shipment. As well, we provide forecasts for the German container throughput in total. These forecasts are important for logistics companies, e.g. shipping companies, port authorities and shipyards. Using quarterly data and therefore catching seasonal effects, it is possible to give a detailed outlook for a manageable time period. Given attention to the seasonal structure of the data, forecasts can account for this level of detail. This can be a great advantage for companies when allocating capacities. The methodologies we use are two univariate time-series approaches: the traditional exponential smoothing analysis of Holt–Winters and the Auto-Regressive Integrated Moving Average (ARIMA) framework adapted to Seasonal data (SARIMA). Certain model specifications of these two approaches are formal equivalents, so another question here is to see whether, when applied, they lead to similar results.

Next, we outline the main estimation and forecast equations. This theoretical part is followed by some remarks on the database. The principle part contains estimation, diagnosis and interpretation of the main results. Finally using forecast error measures, we compare the results of the two approaches and present our forecast results.

## II. Estimation and Forecast Techniques

High frequency data often exhibit seasonal behaviour, that is, there are returning characteristics within certain periods of a year. For data with higher than annual frequency it is therefore often appropriate to make seasonal adjustments. Traditionally, seasonality is seen as some kind of pollution of the data. In modern time-series analysis, trend and seasonality is seen as a chance to lead to more exact forecasts. Especially in business matters, knowledge of seasonal changes can help to improve outcomes or reduce costs. From the theoretical point of view, taking account of seasonality may reduce forecasting errors.

In the SARIMA methodology (Newbold and Bos, 1994, pp. 319–25), the original data series are differenced by linear transformation until the data seems to be stationary and the estimated autocorrelation function (ACF) and partial autocorrelation function (PACF) show only a few significant, easily interpretable autocorrelations. The linear transformation is done by differencing the data. Nonseasonal and seasonal differencing filters are applied. Seasonal differencing consists of subtracting the values of two observations that are $L$ periods apart. For quarterly data, the double differencing filter, which is a combination of a nonseasonal and a seasonal differencing filter, amounts to

$$\Delta_1\Delta_4 = (y_t - y_{t-1}) - (y_{t-4} - y_{t-4-1}) \quad (1)$$

The forecasting equation for the one-step-ahead out-of-sample forecast of the often used so-called airline model (Box and Jenkins, 1970, pp. 300–22) SARIMA(0,1,1)(0,1,1) applied to quarterly data, is

$$\begin{aligned}\hat{y}_{T+1} &= y_T + y_{T-3} - y_{T-4} + \beta_1 \cdot e_T \\ &\quad + \beta_4 \cdot e_{T-3} + \beta_1\beta_4 \cdot e_{T-4}\end{aligned} \quad (2)$$

with the $\beta$s being the estimated coefficients of the MA-terms $e$.

For $h = 6, 7, \ldots$ we get

$$\hat{y}_{T+h} = \hat{y}_{T+h-1} + \hat{y}_{T+h-4} + \hat{y}_{T+h-5} \quad (3)$$

which indicates that after $h = 5$, the estimated MA-parts have disappeared.

We then use the Holt–Winters algorithm for seasonal time series based on the exponential smoothing approach (Newbold and Bos, 1994, pp. 199–210). This technique is capable of producing short-term forecasts for a large collection of time series with a trend and additive or multiplicative seasonal variation. The model of the time series $y_t$ $(t = 1, 2, \ldots, T)$ with linear trend and multiplicative seasonality consists of the following three equations:

$$a_t = \alpha_1 \frac{y_t}{s_{t-L}} + (1 - \alpha_1)(a_{t-1} + b_{t-1}) \quad (4)$$

$$b_t = \alpha_2(a_t - a_{t-1}) + (1 - \alpha_2)b_{t-1} \quad (5)$$

$$s_t = \alpha_3 \frac{y_t}{a_t} + (1 - \alpha_3)s_{t-L} \quad (6)$$

In these equations, $\alpha_1$, $\alpha_2$ and $\alpha_3$ $(0 \leq \alpha \leq 1)$ are smoothing coefficients, $a_t$ in (4) yields the current level estimate, $b_t$ in (5) shows the estimate of current slope and $s_t$ in (6) determines the current seasonal factor. $L$ here denotes the number of periods per year in the data, e.g. for quarterly data $L = 4$.

Forecasts in the case of a linear trend and multiplicative seasonal factor can be made by

$$\hat{y}_{t+h} = (a_t + b_t \cdot h)s_{t-L+h} \quad (7)$$

with $h = 1, 2, \ldots$. The additive and multiplicative algorithm may yield quite different forecasting values. So, the concrete dataset leads to considerations about the combination of the model parts as well as the choice of values for the smoothing terms. This decision has been taken by using the model with the smallest forecasting error.

It can be shown that under certain conditions the additive Holt–Winters model is theoretically equivalent to the seasonal ARIMA model (SARIMA) (Mills, 1990, pp. 180–3) and the interesting question to answer is whether the two approaches lead to equivalent forecasting results in applications. The estimations are compared by using the forecast error measures (Greene, 2003, p. 113) root mean square error (RMSE) and Theil's U which is defined as

$$U = \frac{\text{RMSE}_{\text{(forecast)}}}{\text{RMSE}_{\text{(naive)}}} \quad (8)$$

In our model, for Theil's U we use the value of the prevailing last period $y_{t-4}$ as forecasting value of the naive model.

## III. Database

The worldwide container transshipment has increased with impressing two digit growth rates during the past few years. Figure 1 visualizes this dynamic, obviously, exponential growth for the years 1985–2005.

This development is driven by the high-growth rates of world trade, further globalization with the division of labour, the decentralization of production, the liberalization of trade and also the increasing economic importance of China. Especially, the Asian market is the driving force for global container shipments. Many Asian countries depend on seaborne trade because of their insular location or missing landside infrastructure. Figure 2 gives the distribution of the container handling in 2005, itemized by continent. Asia handles nearly 57% of the world's container transshipment. Also, the world's six biggest container ports (Singapore, Hongkong, Shanghai, Shenzhen, Pusan and Kaohsiung) are located in Asia. In 2005, these ports cumulated a volume of 101 220 million TEU which was 25.5% of the world's container throughput, and these ports are still experiencing dynamic growth. Thirteen of the 20 biggest container ports of the world (by means of container handling) are located in Asia. Europe handles a proportion of about 20%. The biggest ports here are Rotterdam, Hamburg and Antwerp (the world's seventh, eighth and twelfth largest container ports), which cumulate a volume of 23 862 million TEU. American container harbours, of which Los Angeles and Long Beach are the biggest, handle 18% of the world's container throughput.

The following analysis is based on quarterly time-series data of German container transshipment in million TEU, provided by the Federal Statistical Office of Germany (Statistisches Bundesamt). The analysed time period is 1989:01 to 2006:02. We focus on possible seasonal variations of container transshipment.

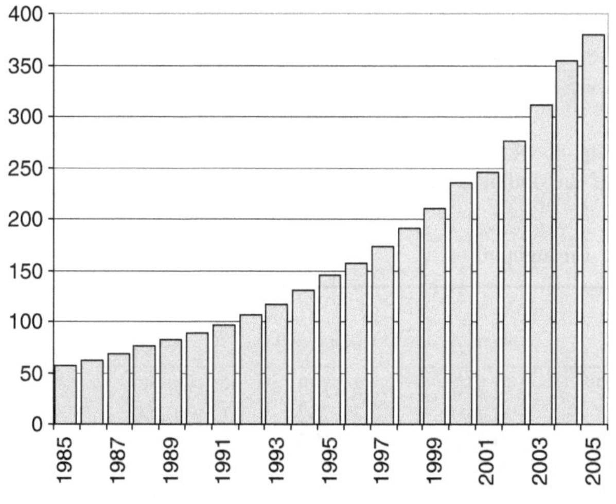


**Fig. 1. Container transshipment 1985–2005 (in million TEU) worldwide**
*Source*: ISL (2006b).

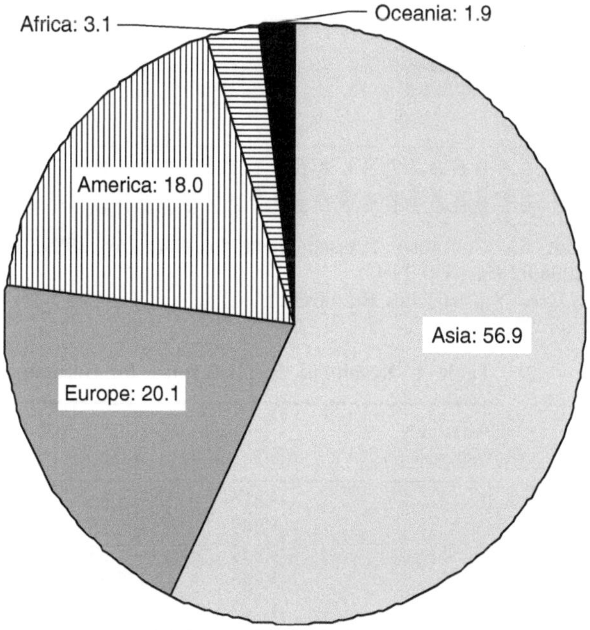


**Fig. 2. Container handling 2005 divided to continents in %**
*Source*: ISL (2006c).

## IV. Model Analysis

The analysis will concentrate on the container transshipment at German ports with destination to one of the three main regions of container shipping Asia, Europe and North America. We will give forecasts for each of these destinations separately and for the container throughput at German ports in total. The development of the latter for the time period 1989:01 to 2006:02 (in 1000 TEU) is shown in Fig. 3.

The graph in Fig. 3 exhibits a nonlinear trend with seasonal variations. The seasonal variations show a strong downward movement at the beginning of each year. Graphs for the three regions look similar and are not presented here.

Using the double differencing filter according to Equation 1 on German container handling leads to estimated ACF and PACF values visualized in Fig. 4.

The PACF shows two significant values at lags 4 and 8. The significant ACF value at lag 4 ($\hat{\rho} = -0.454$) is a typical feature of many doubly differenced seasonal time series. It takes values nearly $-0.5$ which may suggest overdifferenced seasonal data. Therefore, we additionally apply a unit root test for quarterly series to identify the most appropriate differencing filter for $y_t$.

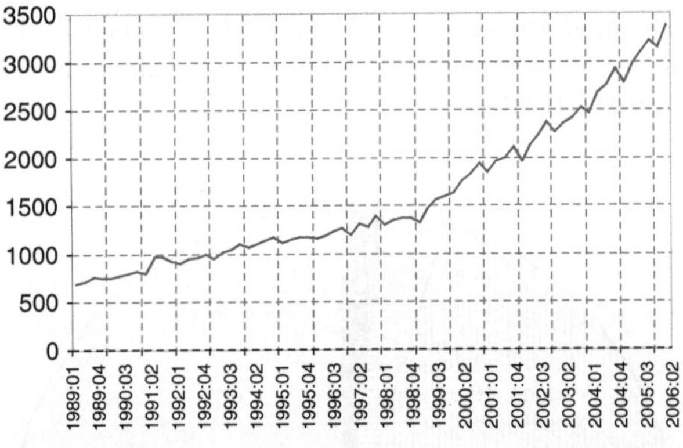


**Fig. 3. Container transshipment in Germany 1989:01–2006:02 (in 1000 TEU)**
*Source*: Statistisches Bundesamt.

To confirm the use of the correct differencing filter, we carry out the HEGY unit root test for quarterly data with different auxiliary regressions (Hylleberg *et al.*, 1990). Table 1 gives the results for the double differenced container handling in Germany (SDTEU).

The series are tested with different specifications: without a deterministic term (0), with a constant (C), constant and seasonal dummies (C, SD), constant and linear trend (C, Tr) and constant, seasonal dummies and linear trend (C, SD, Tr). If $\pi_1 = 0$, the null hypothesis 'presence of a nonseasonal unit root' cannot be rejected; if $\pi_2 = 0$, a half-yearly unit root is present, and the corresponding tests are designed as $t(\pi_1)$ and $t(\pi_2)$. To test for seasonal (quarterly) unit roots, one has to test the complex unit root $\pi_3 \cap \pi_4 = 0$ by an $F$-statistic $F(\pi_3, \pi_4)$. If both $\pi_3$ and $\pi_4$ are zero, the joint null hypothesis cannot be rejected, and a seasonal unit root is present.

Nearly all values at $T = 48$ and the conventional significance level of 5% are smaller than the corresponding critical values (Hylleberg *et al.*, 1990, pp. 226–7). The values for $\pi_4$ are greater than the respective critical values, but that does not restrict the results in general. So, the nulls are rejected and stationarity by double differencing is achieved. The last column of Table 1 indicates the $p$-values of the LM-test on autocorrelation in the error term which indicates no autocorrelation.

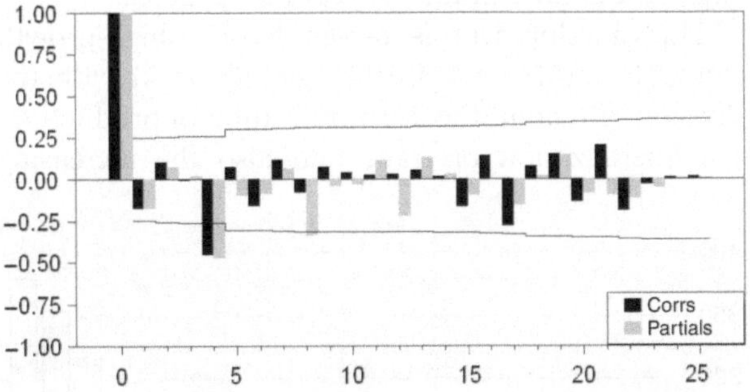


**Fig. 4. Estimated ACF (Corrs) and PACF (Partials) values of the double differenced German container throughput**

**Table 1. Results of the HEGY test for German container throughput**

| Auxiliary regressions | $t(\pi_1)$ | $t(\pi_2)$ | $t(\pi_3)$ | $t(\pi_4)$ | $F(\pi_3, \pi_4)$ | LM-sign |
|---|---|---|---|---|---|---|
| 0 | −5.816 | −5.565 | −8.543 | 0.752 | 37.733 | 0.259 |
| C | −5.949 | −5.562 | −8.537 | 0.780 | 37.732 | 0.160 |
| C, SD | −5.839 | −5.535 | −8.482 | 0.722 | 37.193 | 0.118 |
| C, Tr | −5.946 | −5.527 | −8.519 | 0.741 | 37.540 | 0.101 |
| C, SD, Tr | −4.375 | −3.495 | −4.789 | 1.185 | 12.931 | 0.108 |

*Notes*: HEGY unit root test: testing for seasonal integration in the series SDTEU. Effective sample: 1992:03 to 2006:02.

These considerations lead to the identification of a SARIMA(0,1,0)(2,1,0) model. Furthermore, we identified several other possible SARIMA models, but the model mentioned above proved to be best.

Analogously, for the three destinations Asia, Europe and North America we identified similar models. Table 2 shows the details of the estimation results of the respectively best model for each destination and total German container handling (World), concerning significance and autocorrelations of the error term. Estimations were done with WinRATS 6.3 using the Gauss–Newton algorithm.

The first row gives information about the chosen model. The values in parenthesis in the coefficient rows give the $p$-values of the $t$-tests for the coefficient estimators. 'Q-sign' indicates the $p$-values of the Box–Pierce statistic on no autocorrelation in the error term. Constants have been generally omitted, because of nonsignificance.

As an alternative to the SARIMA analysis, the Holt–Winters method provides an easy way to analyse and predict seasonal time-series. For the smoothing coefficients in Equations 4–6 we apply, as commonly made in applications, $\alpha_1 = 0.20$, $\alpha_2 = 0.25$ and $\alpha_3 = 0.30$. Other $\alpha$-values were tested, though they did not change the results substantially, but rather led to unstable outcomes.

After inspection of the original series for the different regions, we chose the following specifications: an exponential trend with a multiplicative seasonal factor for the destination Asia and the whole German container throughput, while for the destinations Europe and North America we assume a linear trend combined with a multiplicative season.

To compare the two methods – SARIMA and Holt–Winters exponential smoothing – concerning their predictability we computed two measures for *ex post* forecast errors, the RMSE and Theil's U. Table 3 gives details on the results.

The RMSE shows a mean deviation between 22 000 and 30 000 TEU for the three destinations, but 57 000 TEU for the total German container transshipment. These differences arise from the overall strongly different and heterogeneous development of the world's economic regions. Due to RMSE there are remarkable differences between the two types of models: the RMSE values of the SARIMA approach are about 10% smaller for the destinations Asia and Europe, and more than 30% for the whole container handling. For the destination North America, the exponential smoothing approach obviously led to better results.

For Theil's U we use the observed value with a lag of four quarters as 'naive forecasts'. Experience shows that values smaller than 0.5 for Theil's U lead to useful forecasting results (in the past). Again, only the value for North America leads to a value greater than 0.5, which means that the two approaches produce better results than the 'naive model', but it should not be used for *ex ante* forecasts. For all datasets except North America, the SARIMA $U$-values are smaller than those of the Holt–Winters model. Therefore, the SARIMA approach should be used for *ex ante* forecasting rather than the Holt–Winters approach.

**Table 2. Estimation results for the different SARIMA models**

| | Asia | Europe | North America | World | |
|---|---|---|---|---|---|
| SARIMA | (0,1,0)(1,1,0) | (0,1,0)(0,1,1) | (1,1,0)(1,1,0) | (0,1,0)(2,1,0) | |
| Iteration steps | 2 | 2 | 7 | 2 | |
| AR | | | −0.4916 (0.0001) | | |
| SAR | −0.5724 (0.0000) | | −0.4465 (0.0003) | −0.5909 (0.0000) | −0.3313 (−0.0092) |
| SMA | | −0.7192 (0.0000) | | | |
| Q-sign | 0.4397 | 0.6419 | 0.6122 | 0.5969 | |

**Table 3. Model types and forecast errors**

| | Holt–Winters exponential smoothing | | | | SARIMA | | |
|---|---|---|---|---|---|---|---|
| Region | Trend | Season | RMSE | U | Type | RMSE | U |
| Asia | Exponential | Multiplicative | 26.37 | 0.3118 | (0,1,0)(1,1,0) | 24.72 | 0.2923 |
| Europe | Linear | Multiplicative | 29.99 | 0.4132 | (0,1,0)(1,1,0) | 27.39 | 0.3666 |
| North America | Linear | Multiplicative | 22.57 | 0.7885 | (1,1,0)(1,1,0) | 24.12 | 0.8070 |
| World | Exponential | Multiplicative | 57.08 | 0.3116 | (0,1,0)(2,1,0) | 43.16 | 0.2356 |

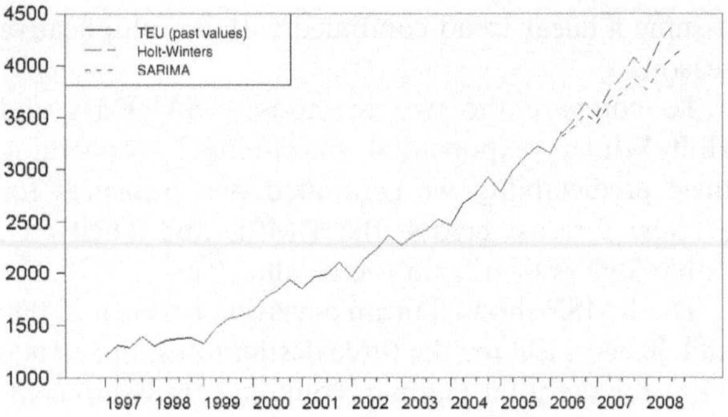


**Fig. 5. SARIMA and Holt–Winters forecasts for the whole container throughput in Germany (in 1000 TEU)**

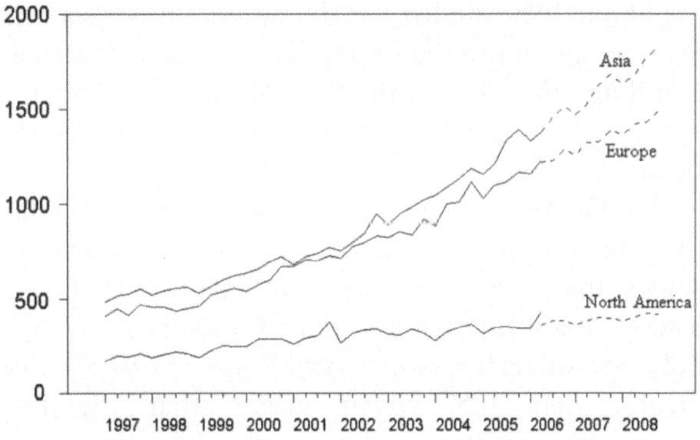


**Fig. 6. SARIMA forecasts for destinations Asia, Europe and North America (in 1000 TEU)**

The identified SARIMA models will lead to better and more stable forecasts, given stationarity. Visualizing these findings, Fig. 5 compares the forecasting results of the SARIMA and the Holt–Winters model for the whole German transshipment from 2006:03 until the end of 2008. It can be seen that the Holt–Winters approach overestimates the development of the container throughput in the future.

In Fig. 6, the forecasts of the SARIMA-models are shown for the three regions Asia, Europe and North America. Table 4 contains the numerical forecasting values. Taking a look at the graphical illustration, the seasonal variation which is inherent in the quarterly data can be found in the forecast values as well.

Our forecasts give a continuingly positive outlook for the container industry in Germany. Especially, the destinations Asia and Europe are the driving forces for development. We forecast that within the forecasting period the German container throughput will rise by 22.8% in total, for the destination Asia we predict a gain of 25.3% and for Europe 21.5%. A moderate increase of 9.5% is given for the destination North America.

**Table 4. Forecasting values for container throughput (in 1000 TEU)**

| | World | Asia | Europe | North America |
|---|---|---|---|---|
| 2006:03 | 3416.163 | 1457.342 | 1225.300 | 382.019 |
| 2006:04 | 3536.961 | 1512.480 | 1285.345 | 381.409 |
| 2007:01 | 3450.250 | 1466.651 | 1257.379 | 360.268 |
| 2007:02 | 3645.487 | 1520.959 | 1319.417 | 384.123 |
| 2007:03 | 3744.720 | 1626.133 | 1326.679 | 397.893 |
| 2007:04 | 3876.864 | 1682.909 | 1386.725 | 394.591 |
| 2008:01 | 3774.378 | 1627.252 | 1358.758 | 381.691 |
| 2008:02 | 3967.375 | 1679.497 | 1420.796 | 403.133 |
| 2008:03 | 4075.730 | 1769.483 | 1428.058 | 420.350 |
| 2008:04 | 4195.274 | 1825.322 | 1488.104 | 418.233 |

Given such detailed forecast information as in Table 4, port authorities can do their planning more efficiently. Furthermore, capacity planning of shipping companies can be positively influenced.

## V. Conclusions

This analysis discusses SARIMA and exponential smoothing models for estimating and forecasting quarterly data of the German container transshipment (measured in TEU). Different models are identified and tested for the whole German container throughput and for the throughput with the destinations Asia, Europe and North America. The SARIMA models are examined by the ACF and PACF, the HEGY test on stationarity for quarterly data, the Box–Pierce statistic and *t*-tests.

Although there is, theoretically, equivalence between the two types of models, the SARIMA models perform slightly better than the Holt–Winters approach – expressed by the forecasting measures MSE and Theil's U.

The quarterly forecasts up to the end of the year 2008 show a permanent dynamic growth of German container throughput, especially with the destinations Asia and Europe. A moderate increase can be anticipated for the container handling concerning North America.

The methodologies we use can be easily applied to many kinds of time-series data. Given more detailed data, for example on smaller aggregates such as a small group of countries, valuable information on the further development in a special sector can be produced. For Germany, container handling with the destination of Baltic Sea abutters could be of particular interest.

## References


Box, G. E. P. and Jenkins, G. M. (1970) *Time Series Analysis, Forecasting and Control*, Holden Day, San Francisco.

Deutsche Bundesbank (2006) *Monatsbericht*, **12**, Frankfurt/Main.

Greene, W. H. (2003) *Econometric Analysis*, 5th edn, Prentice Hall, Upper Saddle River, NJ.

Heymann, E. (2006) Containerschifffahrt, Deutsche Bank Research, Nr. 347.

Hylleberg, S., Engle, R. F., Granger, C. W. J. and Yoo, B. S. (1990) Seasonal integration and cointegration, *Journal of Econometrics*, **44**, 215–38.

Institut für Seeverkehrswirtschaft und Logistik (ISL) (2006a) Shipping Statistics and Market Review (SSMR), World Merchant Fleet by Ownership Patterns, Vol. 51, Issue 4.

Institut für Seeverkehrswirtschaft und Logistik (ISL) (2006b) Shipping Statistics and Market Review (SSMR), General Cargo and Container Shipping, Vol. 51, Issue 6.

Institut für Seeverkehrswirtschaft und Logistik (ISL) (2006c) Shipping Statistics and Market Review (SSMR), World Port Development, Vol. 51, Issue 11/12.

Mills, T. C. (1990) *Time Series Techniques for Economists*, Cambridge University Press, Cambridge.

Newbold, P. and Bos, Th. (1994) *Introductory Business and Economic Forecasting*, 2nd edn, South-Western Publishers, Cincinnati (Ohio).

Statistisches Bundesamt, Seeschifffahrt, Fachserie 8 Reihe 5, 1990–2007, Wiesbaden.

# Economics on the optimal port queuing pricing to bulk ships

Chen-Hsiu Laih and Kuan-Yu Chen

This article develops the optimal single step toll scheme which is levied to bulk ships for a queuing port. Bulk ships' arrival times at the port will be rationally dispersed after pricing this toll scheme. Consequently, the queuing time at the anchorage to all bulk ships will be rationally decreased. This article shows bulk ships' equilibrium arrival rate distributions during the queuing period before and after establishing the optimal single step toll scheme. This article also shows bulk ship owners' decisions of arrival time adjustments under the optimal single step toll scheme. Based on these results, we find some bulk ships that paid no toll under the optimal single step toll scheme to maintain the same arrival times at the anchorage as they did in the original nontoll equilibrium situation. New arrival times at the anchorage for other bulk ships that paid the toll are postponed when compared with their original arrival times in the nontoll equilibrium situation.

## I. Introduction

When a bulk ship arrives at a queuing port, the port officers will guide her to wait at general anchorage. When a bulk ship berth becomes vacant and available, a pilot will shepherd her to the berth where it unloads and loads. Generally speaking, this situation is similar to auto-vehicles queuing at a road bottleneck especially in the morning rush hour. In order to make the efficient use of the bulk ship berth, this article develops a series of pricing schemes to bulk ships at a queuing port.

Laih (2008) has developed the optimal single- and multi-step toll schemes to container ships at a queuing port. Unfortunately, these toll schemes are not suitable for bulk ships. For this purpose, this article derives the optimal single step pricing to bulk ships at a queuing port. This article also derives the consequent changes of bulk ships' arrival schedules at the queuing port after collecting the optimal single step toll scheme. Consequently, bulk ship owners' arrival time adjusting decisions from the nontoll to the tolled cases can be predicted before the toll scheme is established at a queuing port. All of these are important issues for bulk ship owners and the port bureau if the port queuing pricing to bulk ships is considered to put into practice by the authorities.

The related literatures concerning to pricing a queuing bottleneck are raised as follows. A model of pricing a queuing bottleneck was first developed by Vickrey (1969). In his model, nontoll equilibrium is illustrated and the optimal variable toll, which eliminates queuing completely, is determined to stagger commuters' departure times. Small (1982) derived and estimated a disaggregate econometric model for the choice of trip schedule by automobile commuters. He found that, on average, urban commuters will shift their schedules by 1 o 2 minutes towards the early side, or by 1/3 to 1 minutes towards the late side, in order to save a minute of travel time. Laih (1994) developed a flexible pricing mechanism including the optimal single- and multi-step tolls to relieve commuting queuing in the morning at a road bottleneck. He showed that $n/(n+1)$ of the total queuing time that exists under the nontoll equilibrium can be eliminated with the optimal *n-step* toll. Laih (2004) provided a methodological framework to forecast commuter behaviour changes from the no toll case to both the optimal single- and multi-step toll cases. When the charging steps increased one by one, the framework of the single optimal step toll, the related equilibrium costs, the equilibrium departure rates and moving tracks of departure time of auto-commuters vary regularly. These complete and regular information not only facilitate policy makers for the application of the optimal single step toll scheme, but it can also be used to predict the entire auto-commuters' behaviour in the system of toll collection. Moreover, Laih *et al.* (2006) and Laih and Chen (2007) designed an optimal single- and multi-step toll schemes, respectively, to container ships by cost equilibrium approach for a queuing port. All values of equilibrium queuing cost, operating cost and in patterns of equilibrium arrival time shifted under the optimal single- and multi-step toll schemes are obtained. With these toll schemes, arrival times of container ships at the queuing port will be rationally dispersed. Consequently, the queuing time for port entry can be decreased. These papers also derived the consequent changes of container ships' arrival schedules at the queuing port after collecting the optimal single- and multi-step tolls. Decisions of adjusting the arrival time from the nontoll to the tolled cases can be predicted before these toll schemes are established. Unfortunately, however, the above results are not suitable for bulk ships at a queuing port. This problem will be dealt within the following sections.

The rest of the article is structured as follows. The basic model including the equilibrium total cost and the optimal time-varying toll scheme to bulk ships at a queuing port are derived in Section II. Based on the basic model, Section III develops the optimal single step toll scheme, inscribed within the optimal time-varying toll scheme, to bulk ships for practical purposes. Equilibrium queuing costs to bulk ships and bulk ships' equilibrium arrival rates at the anchorage under the optimal single step toll scheme are derived in Section IV. A framework used to predict bulk ship owners' decisions of arrival time adjustments from the nontoll to the tolled cases are established in Section V. Finally, the main results provided in this article are addressed in Section VI.

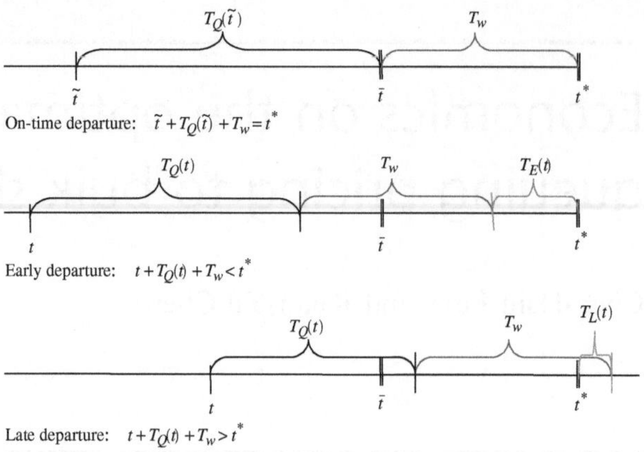


**Fig. 1. Bulk ships' departure patterns at a queuing port**

## II. The Basic Model

Basic assumptions for a queuing port model are as follows. First, the assumed background in this article is that arrived bulk ships have to queue at the anchorage until a vacant berth for cargo loading/ unloading becomes available. This may be a result of increase in demand or supply of bulk cargos attracting more ships calling the port. Secondly, the sequence of entering the berth at a queuing port follows the principle of first come first serviced. Thirdly, except this queuing port, there are no other alternative ports existed. Fourth, apart from the queuing cost at the anchorage, other costs to a bulk ship owner in our model include the wharfage for a bulk ship alongside the berth, the dispatch fee or revenue loss due to early or late departure from the queuing port, respectively, and the toll (if any).

In Fig. 1, There are three kinds of departure patterns to all bulk ships: on-time departure $(\tilde{t}+T_Q(\tilde{t})+T_w=t^*)$, early departure $(t+T_Q(t)+T_w<t^*)$ and late departure $(t+T_Q(t)+T_w>t^*)$. Among these three situations, $\bar{t}$ and $t^*$ are Estimate Time of Arrival (ETA) and Estimate Time of Departure (ETD), respectively, to all bulk ships. $\tilde{t}$ is defined as a bulk ship's arrival time at the anchorage which allows the berthing time just the same as ETA after queuing. $t$ is the time point when a bulk ship arrives at the anchorage of the port. $T_Q(t)$ is the length of queuing time period at the anchorage and varies in accordance with $t$. For simplicity, $T_Q(t)$ is assumed to be a linear function. $T_w=t^*-\bar{t}$ is the average (fixed) operation time length that each bulk ship staying at a berth for all cases in Fig. 1. $T_E(t)=t^*-(t+T_Q(t)+T_w)$ and $T_L(t)=(t+T_Q(t)+T_w)-t^*$ in Fig. 1 are defined as the time lengths of early departure period and late departure period, respectively.

According to Fig. 1, we obtain the total costs to all bulk ships from the time arriving and queuing at the anchorage until the time leaving the port:
on-time departure:

$$\begin{aligned} TC(\tilde{t}) &= \alpha \cdot T_Q(\tilde{t}) + w \cdot T_w \\ &= \alpha \cdot T_Q(\tilde{t}) + w \cdot (t^* - \tilde{t}) \\ &\tilde{t} + T_Q(\tilde{t}) + T_w = t^* \end{aligned} \tag{1}$$

early departure:

$$\begin{aligned} TC(t) &= \alpha \cdot T_Q(t) + w \cdot T_w + \beta \cdot T_E(t) \\ &= \alpha \cdot T_Q(t) + w \cdot T_w \\ &\quad + \beta \cdot \left[t^* - \left(t + T_Q(t) + T_w\right)\right] \\ &t_q \leq t + T_Q(t) + T_w < t^* \end{aligned} \tag{2}$$

late departure:

$$\begin{aligned} TC(t) &= \alpha \cdot T_Q(t) + w \cdot T_w + \gamma \cdot T_L(t) \\ &= \alpha \cdot T_Q(t) + w \cdot T_w \\ &\quad + \gamma \cdot \left[\left(t + T_Q(t) + T_w\right) - t^*\right] \\ &t^* < t + T_Q(t) + T_w \leq t_{q'} \end{aligned} \tag{3}$$

In (1)–(3), $\alpha$ represents the time cost per hour to $T_Q(t)$, then $\alpha T_Q(t)$ means the queuing time cost, which consists of personnel expense, depreciation cost of the ship, expense for repairing, insurance fee, interests, petrol fee for maintenance and desalination fee. These expenses are indispensable while ships queue at the anchorage during the queuing period $[t_q, t_{q'}]$, where $t_q$ and $t_{q'}$ represent the start and the end times of queuing at the anchorage, respectively. $w$ represents the wharfage per hour for $T_w$ to a bulk ship, the total wharfage $w{\cdot}T_w$ should be paid by bulk ship owners in most cases of tramp shipping. In (2) and (3), $\beta$ and $\gamma$ represent the time cost per hour for $T_E$ and $T_L$, respectively. In tramp shipping, the ship owner should pay the dispatch fee to the consignor if the ship's departure time becomes earlier than ETD due to the consignor's prompt arrangements for cargos being loaded/unloaded. For the early departure case in Fig. 1, the dispatch fee is $\beta \cdot [t^* - (t + T_Q(t) + T_w)]$. On the other hand, the ship owner has to suffer revenue losses on delaying the next voyage if the ship's departure time becomes later than ETD. For the late departure case in Fig. 1, the revenue loss is $\gamma \cdot [(t + T_Q(t) + T_w) - t^*]$.

Equilibrium obtains when no individual bulk ship has an incentive to change the arrival time, $t$. This implies that the total cost $TC(t)$ to each bulk ship must be the same at all times during the queuing period $[t_q, t_{q'}]$. In other words, the equilibrium condition is $\mathrm{d}TC/\mathrm{d}t = 0$. For this purpose, differentiating (2) and (3) with respect to $t$, then we obtain (4) and (5), respectively, as follows:

$$\frac{\mathrm{d}TC(t)}{\mathrm{d}t} = \alpha \cdot \frac{\mathrm{d}T_Q(t)}{\mathrm{d}t} + \beta \cdot \left[-1 - \frac{\mathrm{d}T_Q(t)}{\mathrm{d}t}\right] = 0$$

$$\frac{\mathrm{d}T_Q(t)}{\mathrm{d}t} = \frac{\beta}{\alpha - \beta} \quad \text{for } t_q \leq t + T_Q(t) + T_w < t^* \tag{4}$$

$$\frac{\mathrm{d}TC(t)}{\mathrm{d}t} = \alpha \cdot \frac{\mathrm{d}T_Q(t)}{\mathrm{d}t} + \gamma \cdot \left[1 + \frac{\mathrm{d}T_Q(t)}{\mathrm{d}t}\right] = 0$$

$$\frac{\mathrm{d}T_Q(t)}{\mathrm{d}t} = \frac{-\gamma}{\alpha + \gamma} \quad \text{for } t^* < t + T_Q(t) + T_w \leq t_{q'} \tag{5}$$

Because $(\alpha - \beta)$ in (4) is positive in practice, (4) and (5) represent the positive and negative slopes of the linear relationship between $T_Q(t)$ and $t$ in early and late departure situations, respectively. Using (4) and (5), the equilibrium queuing time length can be easily calculated. Take $\bar{t}$ for example, $T_Q(\bar{t})$ can be obtained as $(\bar{t} - t_{q'}) \cdot -\gamma/\alpha + \gamma$. Following the definition of $\tilde{t}$, we have $\tilde{t} + T_Q(\tilde{t}) = \bar{t}$, then

$$\tilde{t} + \frac{\beta}{\alpha - \beta} \cdot \left(\tilde{t} - t_q\right) = \bar{t} \tag{6}$$

$$\tilde{t} + \frac{-\gamma}{\alpha + \gamma} \cdot \left(\tilde{t} - t_{q'}\right) = \bar{t} \tag{7}$$

Next, since $T_w$ is defined as the average (fixed) time length that each of $N$ bulk ships staying at a berth, the queuing time length for $[t_q, t_{q'}]$ can be obtained as

$$t_{q'} - t_q = T_w \cdot (N - 1) \tag{8}$$

Solving (6)–(8), we then obtain three arrival time values $\tilde{t}$, $t_q$ and $t_{q'}$ as follows:

$$\tilde{t} = \bar{t} - \frac{\beta \cdot \gamma}{\alpha(\beta + \gamma)} \cdot T_w \cdot (N - 1) \tag{9}$$

$$t_q = \bar{t} - \frac{\gamma}{\beta + \gamma} \cdot T_w \cdot (N - 1) \tag{10}$$

$$t_{q'} = \bar{t} + \frac{\beta}{\beta + \gamma} \cdot T_w \cdot (N - 1) \tag{11}$$

Because all bulk ships have the same cost in equilibrium, by substituting $T_Q(\tilde{t}) = \bar{t} - \tilde{t}$ and (9) into (1), or substituting $T_Q(t_q) = 0$ and (10) into (2), or substituting $T_Q(t_{q'}) = 0$ and (11) into (3), the equilibrium total cost per bulk ship during $[t_q, t_{q'}]$ can be obtained as

$$ETC = \frac{\beta \cdot \gamma}{\beta + \gamma} \cdot T_w \cdot (N - 1) + w \cdot \left(t^* - \bar{t}\right) \tag{12}$$

$\Delta t_q a t_{q'}$ in Fig. 2 represents the queuing cost, $\alpha{\cdot}T_Q(t)$, in the nontoll equilibrium. Based on (4) and (5), slopes of $\overline{t_q a}$ and $\overline{a t_{q'}}$, can be easily obtained as $\alpha\beta/(\alpha - \beta)$ and $-\alpha\gamma/(\alpha + \gamma)$, respectively.

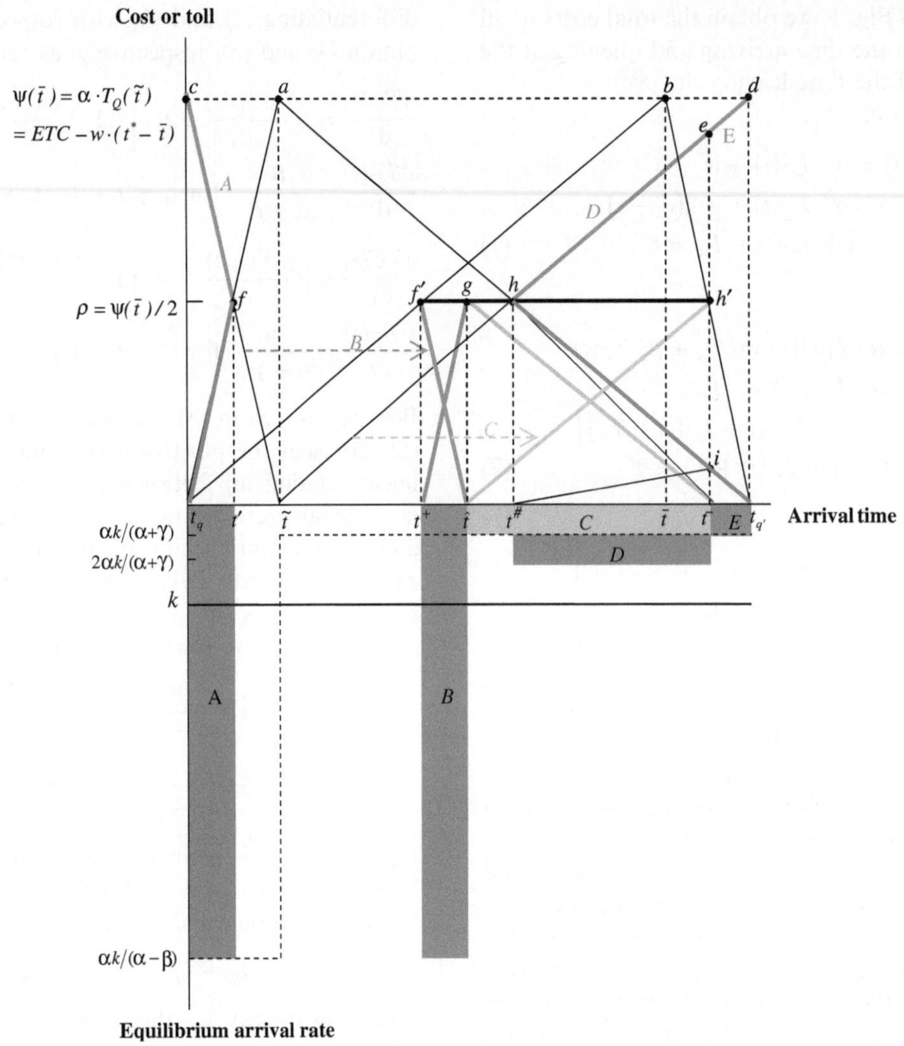


**Fig. 2. Equilibrium costs and arrival rate distributions under the optimal single step toll scheme**

Next we consider the optimal time-varying toll scheme to bulk ships for a queuing port. The optimal time-varying toll is defined as a series of tolls that will completely eliminate the loss of queuing times without making ship owners worse off than they would be in the nontoll equilibrium. In order to attain such an objective, it is necessary to impose a series of tolls, $\psi(t)$, that results in $T_Q(t)=0$ and $TC(t)=ETC$ for all $t$ in (1), (2) and (3). Then we obtain a series of the optimal time-varying toll as

$$TC(\tilde{t}) = \alpha \cdot T_Q(\tilde{t}) + w \cdot (t^* - \tilde{t}) + \psi(\tilde{t}) = ETC$$

$$\psi(\tilde{t}) = ETC - w \cdot (t^* - \tilde{t}) = \frac{\beta \cdot \gamma}{\beta + \gamma} \cdot T_w \cdot (N-1) \quad (13)$$

$$TC(t) = \alpha \cdot T_Q(t) + w \cdot \left(t^* - \tilde{t}\right) + \beta \cdot [t^* - (t + T_Q(t) + (t^* - \tilde{t}))] + \psi(t) = ETC$$

$$\psi(t) = ETC - w \cdot \left(t^* - \tilde{t}\right) - \beta \cdot (\tilde{t} - t) = \frac{\beta \cdot \gamma}{\beta + \gamma} \cdot T_w \cdot (N-1) - \beta \cdot (\tilde{t} - t),$$

$$\text{for } t_q \le t < \tilde{t} \quad (14)$$

$$TC(t) = \alpha \cdot T_Q(t) + w \cdot \left(t^* - \tilde{t}\right) + \gamma \cdot [(t + T_Q(t) + (t^* - \tilde{t})) - t^*] + \psi(t) = ETC$$

$$\psi(t) = ETC - w \cdot \left(t^* - \tilde{t}\right) - \gamma \cdot (t - \tilde{t}) = \frac{\beta \cdot \gamma}{\beta + \gamma} \cdot T_w \cdot (N-1) - \gamma \cdot (t - \tilde{t}),$$

$$\text{for } \tilde{t} \le t < t_{q'} \quad (15)$$

The shape of the optimal time-varying toll scheme, $\psi(t)$, is shown as $\Delta t_q b t_{q'}$ in Fig. 2. Based on (14) and (15), slopes of $\overline{t_q b}$ and $\overline{b t_{q'}}$ are $\beta$ and $-\gamma$, respectively. The optimal time-varying toll scheme has continuously changeable charges throughout the queuing period $[t_q, t_{q'}]$. The maximum optimal time-varying toll is located at $\bar{t}(=\text{ETA})$ as shown in (13). This is reasonable because ship owners are willing to pay the highest optimal time-varying toll to match the on-time schedule (ETA and ETD) without incurring any early or late costs. Since the two triangles ($\Delta t_q a t_{q'}$ and $\Delta t_q b t_{q'}$) in Fig. 2 have the same area, the total optimal time varying toll completely replace all bulk ships' queuing costs in the nontoll equilibrium.

## III. The Optimal Single Step Toll Scheme

The optimal time-varying toll is capable of eliminating queuing time completely, but has practical difficulties because it requires continuously changeable charges. Therefore a step toll scheme, which is first developed by Laih (1994), has been considered as an alternative to reduce queuing time. The step toll scheme, inscribed in the optimal time-varying toll triangle, is designed to make the toll payers no worse off than they would be in the nontoll equilibrium. As shown in Fig. 2, the optimal single step toll, $\rho=\psi(\bar{t})/2$, inscribed within the optimal time-varying toll, $t_q b t_{q'}$, is applied at $t^+$ and lifted at $t^-$, and the toll revenue is shaped as $t^+ f h' t^-$. This is the maximum toll revenue in all single step toll cases because the toll level is just half of the highest optimal time-varying toll. Therefore the optimal single step toll scheme removes the largest proportion of the total queuing time in all single step toll cases and make ship owners no worse off than they would be in the nontoll equilibrium. Under this optimal single step toll scheme, $\hat{t}$ in Fig. 2 is defined as a bulk ship's arrival time at the anchorage which allows the berthing time just the same as ETA after queuing. It is reasonable that $\hat{t}$ under the optimal single step toll scheme is later than $\tilde{t}$ under the nontoll equilibrium.

In Fig. 2, $t'$ is defined as the start time when no bulk ship arrives at the anchorage until $t^+$ under the optimal single step toll scheme. According to this pricing scheme, the queuing cost to the first bulk ship that will pay the toll, $\rho$, at $t^+$ is zero. It is then clear that no bulk ship arrives at the anchorage from $t'$ until $t^+$, and the length of the time period $[t', t^+)$ is equal to $\rho/\alpha$. Consequently the last untolled bulk ship before $t^+$ must arrive at the anchorage $\rho/\alpha$ earlier than the first tolled bulk ship at $t^+$.

On the other hand, $t^\#$ in Fig. 2 is defined as the start time when the first bulk ships arrive at the anchorage but decide not to notify the port officer for berthing until $t^-$ in order to avoid paying the toll. Also according to this pricing scheme, the queuing cost to the last bulk ship that will pay the toll $\rho$ before $t^-$ is zero. This is impossible unless there are a mass of arrived bulk ships waited willingly at the anchorage from $t^\#$ until $t^-$ to avoid being tolled. These speculators are ready to enter the berth free once the toll is lifted on $t^-$. Consequently, the length of the time period $[t^\#, t^-]$must be equal to $\rho/\alpha$.

Note that $t_q$ is now assumed to locate on the origin (i.e. $t_q=0$) in Fig. 2 for the purpose of simplifying computation to all arrival time values without losing the generality. Detailed computations to the toll level and arrival times values appeared in Fig. 2 are shown as follows:

$$\rho=\frac{1}{2}\psi(\bar{t})=\frac{1}{2}\frac{\beta\cdot\gamma}{(\beta+\gamma)}\cdot T_w\cdot(N-1),$$

$$t_{q'}=t_q+T_w\cdot(N-1)=T_w\cdot(N-1)$$

$$\tilde{t}=t_q+\overline{t_q\tilde{t}}=0+\frac{ETC-w\cdot(t^*-\bar{t})}{\frac{\alpha\cdot\beta}{\alpha-\beta}}$$

$$=\frac{\gamma\cdot(\alpha-\beta)}{\alpha\cdot(\beta+\gamma)}\cdot T_w\cdot(N-1)$$

$$\bar{t}=\tilde{t}+T_Q(\tilde{t})=\tilde{t}+\frac{ETC-w\cdot(t^*-\bar{t})}{\alpha}$$

$$=\frac{\gamma}{\beta+\gamma}\cdot T_w\cdot(N-1)$$

$$\hat{t}=\bar{t}-T_Q(\hat{t})=\bar{t}-\frac{\rho}{\alpha}=\frac{\gamma\cdot(2\alpha-\beta)}{2\alpha\cdot(\beta+\gamma)}\cdot T_w\cdot(N-1),$$

$$t^+=t_q+\overline{t_q t^+}=0+\frac{\rho}{\beta}=\frac{\gamma}{2(\beta+\gamma)}\cdot T_w\cdot(N-1)$$

$$t'=t^+-\frac{\rho}{\alpha}=\frac{\gamma\cdot(\alpha-\beta)}{2\alpha\cdot(\beta+\gamma)}\cdot T_w\cdot(N-1),$$

$$t^-=t_{q'}-\overline{t^-t_{q'}}=t_{q'}-\frac{\rho}{\gamma}=\frac{\beta+2\gamma}{2(\beta+\gamma)}\cdot T_w\cdot(N-1)$$

$$t^\#=t^--\overline{t^\#t^-}=t^--\frac{\rho}{\alpha}$$

$$=\frac{2\alpha\gamma+\alpha\beta-\beta\gamma}{2\alpha(\beta+\gamma)}\cdot T_w\cdot(N-1)$$

## IV. Equilibrium Results Under the Optimal Single Step Toll Scheme

This section illustrates some equilibrium results, as shown in columns [1]–[5] of Table 1, for all arrival intervals under the optimal single step toll scheme to bulk ships. Note that a blanket arrival time interval

**Table 1. Equilibrium results and arrival time adjustments under the optimal single step toll scheme**

| [1] Groups (Arrival times at the anchorage) | [2] Types (a)Toll payers or not (b)Departure patterns | [3] EQC: $\alpha \cdot T_Q(t)$ *EOC*: $ETC - EQC - \rho$ | [4] EAR : $k + \frac{d(k \cdot T_Q(t))}{t}$ | [5]=[4]×[1] Number of arrivals at the anchorage | [6] Arrival time adjustments |
|---|---|---|---|---|---|
| A, $t \in [t_q, t']$ (No Toll Period) | (a)Toll free (b)Early departures | $(\overline{t_q f})\, \frac{\alpha\beta \cdot t}{\alpha - \beta}$ | $\frac{\alpha k}{\alpha - \beta}$ | $\frac{\gamma k}{2(\beta+\gamma)} \cdot \varepsilon$ | $[t_q, t')\ (\because \overline{cf} = \overline{cf})$ |
| | | $(\overline{cf})\, \frac{-\alpha\beta \cdot t}{\alpha - \beta} + \frac{\beta\gamma}{\beta+\gamma} \cdot \varepsilon$ | | | |
| $t \in [t', t^{+}]$ (No Toll Period) | None | 0 | 0 | 0 | None |
| B, $t \in [t^{+}, \hat{t}]$ (Tolled Period) | (a).Toll payers (b).Early departures | $(\overline{t^{+}g})\, \frac{\alpha\beta \cdot t}{\alpha - \beta} - \frac{\alpha\beta\gamma}{2(\alpha-\beta)(\beta+\gamma)} \cdot \varepsilon$ | $\frac{\alpha k}{\alpha - \beta}$ | $\frac{\gamma k}{2(\beta+\gamma)} \cdot \varepsilon$ | $[t', \tilde{t}) \to [t^{+}, \hat{t})\ (\because \overline{f\tilde{t}} = \overline{f'\hat{t}})$ |
| | | $(\overline{f'\hat{t}})\, \frac{-\alpha\beta \cdot t}{\alpha - \beta} + \frac{\beta\gamma(2\alpha-\beta)}{2(\alpha-\beta)(\beta+\gamma)} \cdot \varepsilon$ | | | |
| C, $t \in (\hat{t}, t^{-})$ (Tolled Period) | (a)Toll payers (b)Late departures | $(\overline{gt^{-}})\, \frac{-\alpha\gamma \cdot t}{\alpha+\gamma} + \frac{\alpha\gamma(\beta+2\gamma)}{2(\alpha+\gamma)(\beta+\gamma)} \cdot \varepsilon$ | $\frac{\alpha k}{\alpha+\gamma}$ | $\frac{\beta k}{2(\beta+\gamma)} \cdot \varepsilon$ | $[\tilde{t}, t^{\#}) \to [\hat{t}, t^{-})$ $(\because \overline{\tilde{t}h} = \overline{\hat{t}h'})$ |
| | | $(\overline{\hat{t}h'})\, \frac{\alpha\gamma \cdot t}{\alpha+\gamma} - \frac{\gamma^2(2\alpha-\beta)}{2(\alpha+\gamma)(\beta+\gamma)} \cdot \varepsilon$ | | | |
| D, $t \in (t^{\#}, t^{-})$ (Tolled Period) | (a)Toll free (speculators) (b)Late departures | $(\overline{hi})\, \frac{-\alpha\gamma \cdot t}{\alpha+\gamma} + \frac{\alpha\gamma}{\alpha+\gamma} \cdot \varepsilon$ | $\frac{\alpha k}{\alpha+\gamma}$ | $\frac{\beta\gamma \cdot k}{2(\alpha+\gamma)(\beta+\gamma)} \cdot \varepsilon$ | $[t^{\#}, t^{-})\ (\because \overline{he} = \overline{he})$ |
| | | $(\overline{he})\, \frac{\alpha\gamma \cdot t}{\alpha+\gamma} - \frac{\gamma^2(\alpha-\beta)}{\alpha+\gamma} \cdot \varepsilon$ | | | |
| E, $t \in (t^{-}, t_{q'})$ (No Toll Period) | (a)Toll free (b)Late departures | $(\overline{it_{q'}})\, \frac{-\alpha\gamma \cdot t}{\alpha+\gamma} + \frac{\alpha\gamma}{\alpha+\gamma} \cdot \varepsilon$ | $\frac{\alpha k}{\alpha+\gamma}$ | $\frac{\alpha\beta k}{2(\alpha+\gamma)(\beta+\gamma)} \cdot \varepsilon$ | $[t^{-}, t_{q'})\ (\because \overline{ed} = \overline{ed})$ |
| | | $(\overline{ed})\, \frac{\alpha\gamma \cdot t}{\alpha+\gamma} - \frac{\gamma^2(\alpha-\beta)}{\alpha+\gamma} \cdot \varepsilon$ | | | |

*Note*: $\varepsilon = T_w \cdot (N-1), k = N/T_w \cdot (N-1)$.

$[t', t^+)$ is existed in Table 1 because no bulk ship arrives at the anchorage during this time period that mentioned before. Bulk ships of groups B, C and D arrive at the anchorage during the tolled period $[t^+, t^-)$. Except for group D, speculators, escaping from being tolled, groups B and C pay the toll to enter the berth. Groups A and E do not need to pay the toll because they arrive at the anchorage during the no toll periods. In addition, only groups A and B will be alongside the berth earlier than ETA because they arrive at the anchorage before $\hat{t}$. Consequently only groups A and B are early departures because they will leave the berth (depart from the queuing port) earlier than ETD. These results are arranged as columns [1]–[2] in Table 1.

Since equilibrium will be achieved as long as all bulk ships have the same total cost throughout the queuing period, there are two kinds of equilibrium conditions for the early and late departures. One is $TC(t) = TC(t_q)$ for groups A and B of the early departure, and the other is $TC(t) = TC(t_{q'})$ for groups C, D and E of the late departure. These equilibrium conditions then can be expressed as follows:

$$\alpha \cdot T_Q(t) + w \cdot T_w + \beta \cdot [t^* - (t + T_Q(t) + T_w)] = \beta \cdot \bar{t} + w \cdot (t^* - \bar{t}), \quad t_q \le t \le t' \tag{16}$$

$$\alpha \cdot T_Q(t) + w \cdot T_w + \beta \cdot [t^* - (t + T_Q(t) + T_w)] + \rho = \beta \cdot \bar{t} + w \cdot (t^* - \bar{t}), \quad t^+ \le t < \hat{t} \tag{17}$$

$$\alpha \cdot T_Q(t) + w \cdot T_w + \gamma \cdot [(t + T_Q(t) + T_w) - t^*] + \rho = \gamma \cdot (t_{q'} - \bar{t}) + w \cdot (t^* - \bar{t}), \quad \hat{t} < t < t^- \tag{18}$$

$$\alpha \cdot T_Q(t) + w \cdot T_w + \gamma \cdot [(t + T_Q(t) + T_w) - t^*] = \gamma \cdot (t_{q'} - \bar{t}) + w \cdot (t^* - \bar{t}), \quad t^\# \le t < t^- \text{ or } t^- \le t \le t_{q'} \tag{19}$$

The above equilibrium conditions (16)–(19) are established to groups A, B, C and D (=E), respectively. The values of $TC(t_q)$ and $TC(t_{q'})$ are $\beta \cdot \bar{t} + w \cdot (t^* - \bar{t})$ and $\gamma \cdot (t_{q'} - \bar{t}) + w \cdot (t^* - \bar{t})$, respectively, because $t_q = 0$ and $T_Q(t_q) = T_Q(t_{q'}) = 0$.

Equilibrium queuing costs at the anchorage $(EQC : \alpha \cdot T_Q(t))$ to groups A–E, listed in column [3] of Table 1 are obtained based on (16)–(19). As shown in Fig. 2, the equilibrium queuing costs to groups A–E under the optimal step toll scheme are green lines $\overline{t_qf}$, $\overline{t^+g}$, $\overline{gt^-}$, $\overline{hi}$ and $\overline{it_{q'}}$, respectively. The slope of $\overline{t_qf}$ and $\overline{t^+g}$ for all early departures is $\alpha\beta/(\alpha - \beta)$, which is the same as the slope of the equilibrium queuing cost $(\overline{t_qa})$ to all early departures in the nontoll case. Note that there is no green lines of equilibrium queuing costs through the arrival period $[t', t^+)$ since no bulk ship arrives at the anchorage during this period. In addition, the length of the queue will be reduced to zero at $t^+$ because of $T_Q(t') = \rho/\alpha = t^+ - t'$. On the other hand, the slope of $\overline{gt^-}$, $\overline{hi}$ and $\overline{it_{q'}}$ for all late departures is $-\alpha\gamma/(\alpha + \gamma)$, which is the same as the slope of the equilibrium queuing cost $(\overline{at_{q'}})$ to all late departures in the nontoll case. Note that group D ships' equilibrium queuing costs incurred before and after $t^-$ in Fig. 2 are $\overline{ht^-}$ and $\overline{t^\# i}$, respectively. The former is the decreasing equilibrium queuing costs, from $h$ to zero, to those speculators who avoid paying the toll during the tolled period $[t^\#, t^-)$. The latter is their increasing equilibrium queuing costs, from zero to $i$. Consequently, the total equilibrium queuing cost for group D ships is $\overline{hi}(= \overline{ht^-} + \overline{t^\# i})$.

In Fig. 2, the total equilibrium queuing cost in the original nontoll case is $\Delta t_q a t_{q'}$, and the total equilibrium queuing cost under the optimal single step toll scheme is composed of $\Delta t_q f t'$, $\Delta t^+ g t^-$ and $\Delta t^\# h t_{q'}$. Because $\Delta t^+ g t^-$ can be moved to $\Delta fah$ due to the same area, it is then clear that the effect of the optimal Single step toll on queuing reduction is just half of the total queuing cost in the nontoll equilibrium.

The equilibrium arrival rates (EAR) for groups A–E in column [4] of Table 1 are obtained by using the corresponding equilibrium queuing time $(T_Q(t))$. The lower part of Fig. 2 shows the EAR distributions varying with arrival times for the nontoll, optimal time-varying toll and optimal single step toll cases. These cases are shown as the dotted line, straight line and the shadowed areas, respectively.

In the nontoll case, the equilibrium queuing costs $(\alpha \cdot T_Q(t))$ for all early and late arrivals in Fig. 2 are $\overline{t_qa}$ and $\overline{at_{q'}}$, respectively, and the slopes for the former and latter are $\alpha\beta/(\alpha - \beta)$ and $-\alpha\gamma/(\alpha + \gamma)$, respectively. Accordingly, the marginal arrival rate $(= \mathrm{d}(k \cdot T_Q(t))/\mathrm{d}k)$ for the early and late arrivals are $\beta k/(\alpha - \beta)$ and $-\gamma k/(\alpha + \gamma)$, respectively. Where $k$ is defined as the average number of arrived bulk ships at the anchorage per hour during the queuing period $[t_q, t_{q'}]$. Then $k = N/(T_w \cdot (N - 1))$. The EAR for the early and late arrivals in the nontoll case are therefore equal to $\alpha k/(\alpha - \beta)(= k + (\beta k)/(\alpha - \beta))$ during $[t_q, \tilde{t})$ and $\alpha k/(\alpha + \gamma)(= k - (\gamma k)/(\alpha + \gamma))$ during $[\tilde{t}, t_{q'})$, respectively. (see the dotted line area in Fig. 2). Next, the EAR in the optimal time-varying case is always equal to $k$ because $T_Q(t) = 0$ for all $t$. (see the straight line area in Fig. 2).

Equilibrium arrival rates in the optimal step toll case is somewhat more complicated than the previous two cases. First, because the equilibrium queuing cost $\overline{t_qf}$ for group A coincides $\overline{t_qa}$ during $[t_q, t')$ in Fig. 2, EAR for group A during this arrival time period is the same as that in the nontoll case, and shown as the shadowed area A. Secondly, since there are no arrivals during $[t', t^{+})$, EAR is zero for this time period. Thirdly, because the slopes of equilibrium queuing costs $\overline{t^{+}g}$ for group B and $\overline{gt^{-}}$ for group C in Fig. 2 are the same as the slope of $\overline{t_q a}$ and $\overline{at_{q'}}$, respectively, EAR for group B during $[t^{+}, \hat{t})$ and EAR for group C during $[\hat{t}, t^{-})$ are $\alpha k/(\alpha - \beta)$ and $\alpha k/(\alpha + \gamma)$, respectively. The former is shown as the shadowed area B, and the latter is shown as the shadowed area C. Note that there exist group D bulk ships that arrived during the tolled period $[t^{\#}, t^{-})$ but decided to enter the berth free after $t^{-}$. It is clear that their arrival time period $[t^{\#}, t^{-})$ overlaps with group C. Because the equilibrium queuing cost $\overline{hi}(= \overline{ht^{-}} + \overline{t^{\#}i})$ for group D has the same slope with $\overline{at_{q'}}$, EAR for group D during $[t^{\#}, t^{-})$ is also equal to $\alpha k/(\alpha + \gamma)$. The total EAR for both groups C and D during $[t^{\#}, t^{-})$ in Fig. 2 therefore becomes $2\alpha k/(\alpha + \gamma)$. Finally, since the equilibrium queuing cost $\overline{it_{q'}}$ for group E coincides $\overline{at_{q'}}$ during $[t^{-}, t_{q'}]$, EAR for group E during this arrival time period is also $\alpha k/(\alpha + \gamma)$.

The numbers of arrived bulk ships listed in column [5] of Table 1 are computed by multiplying the lengths of arrival time intervals and corresponding values of EAR together. Arrival time intervals are shown as column [1], and the lengths for these intervals can be obtained by using the related departure time values shown in the end of Section III. Values of EAR for these intervals have already shown in column [4]. From column [5], it is clear that numbers of the early (groups A and B) and late (groups C, D and E) arrived bulk ships are equal to $[(\gamma k)/(\beta + \gamma)] \cdot T_w \cdot (N - 1)$ and $[(\beta k)/(\beta + \gamma)] \cdot T_w \cdot (N - 1)$, respectively, and both are independent of $\alpha$.

## V. Bulk Ship Owners' Decisions of Arrival Time Adjustments

Other equilibrium costs for a bulk ship staying at the berth ($EOC = ETC - EQC - \rho$) in the optimal single step toll case must be the same as that in the original nontoll case to maintain the equilibrium total cost, $ETC = [(\beta \cdot \gamma)/(\beta + \gamma)] \cdot T_w \cdot (N - 1) + w \cdot (t^{*} - \tilde{t}) = \psi(\tilde{t})$ because the optimal step toll derived from our model is simply the money cost to the tolled bulk ships that require to save the same amount of queuing costs. For this purpose, bulk ship owners' decisions of arrival time adjustment can be investigated by '*the invariant EOC principle*'.

In Table 1, the contents of the equilibrium total cost to groups A–D(= E) bulk ships under the optimal step toll scheme can be shown as $\alpha \cdot T_Q(t) + w \cdot T_w + \beta \cdot [t^{*} - (t + T_Q(t) + T_w)]$, $\alpha \cdot T_Q(t) + w \cdot T_w + \beta \cdot [t^{*} - (t + T_Q(t) + T_w)] + \rho$, $\alpha \cdot T_Q(t) + w \cdot T_w + \gamma \cdot [(t + T_Q(t) + T_w) - t^{*})] + \rho$ and $\alpha \cdot T_Q(t) + w \cdot T_w + \gamma \cdot [(t + T_Q(t) + T_w) - t^{*})]$, respectively. Since all results of equilibrium queuing costs to bulk ships at the anchorage ($EQC$) under the optimal single step toll scheme have been shown in column [3] of Table 1, other equilibrium costs to bulk ships staying at the berth ($EOC$) required to achieve the equilibrium total cost, $ETC$, can be easily obtained as shown in the same column. $EOC$ to groups A–E bulk ships under the optimal single step toll scheme are drawn as the red lines $\overline{cf}$, $\overline{f'\hat{t}}$, $\overline{\hat{t}h'}$, $\overline{he}$ and $\overline{ed}$, respectively in Fig. 2. The slope of $\overline{cf}$ and $\overline{f'\hat{t}}$ to all early departures is identical and equal to $-\alpha\beta/(\alpha - \beta)$. This is the same as the slope of $\overline{c\tilde{t}}$ that represents all early departures' $EOC$ in the nontoll case. On the other hand, the slope of $\overline{\hat{t}h'}$, $\overline{he}$ and $\overline{ed}$ to all late departures is identical and equal to $\alpha\gamma/(\alpha + \gamma)$. This is also the same as the slope of $\overline{\tilde{t}d}$ that represents all late departures' $EOC$ in the nontoll case.

Bulk ship owners' decisions of arrival time adjustments under the optimal step toll scheme are shown as column [6] in Table 1. First, group A ships will not adjust their original arrival times in the nontoll case when the port is priced with the optimal single step toll, because $\overline{cf}$ in both the nontoll and optimal single step toll cases coincide during the arrival period $[t_q, t')$. Secondly, because $\overline{f'\hat{t}}$ in the optimal single step toll case and $\overline{f\tilde{t}}$ in the nontoll case are two identical and parallel lines, all group B ships that originally arrive during the period $[t', \tilde{t})$ in the nontoll case will adjust their arrivals to the period $[t^{+}, \hat{t})$ in the optimal single step toll case. Similarly, because $\overline{\hat{t}h'}$ in the optimal single step toll case and $\overline{\tilde{t}h}$ in the nontoll case are two identical and parallel lines, all group C ships that originally arrive during the period $[\tilde{t}, t^{\#})$ in the nontoll case will adjust their arrivals to the period $[\hat{t}, t^{-})$ in the optimal single step toll case. Thirdly, because $\overline{he}$ in both the nontoll and optimal single step toll cases coincide during the arrival time period $[t^{\#}, t^{-})$, group D ships will not change their original arrival times in the nontoll case when the port is priced with the optimal single step toll. Since $[t^{\#}, t^{-})$ exists within $[\hat{t}, t^{-})$, groups C and D ships arrive simultaneously during $[t^{\#}, t^{-})$. Finally, because $\overline{ed}$ in both the nontoll and optimal single step toll cases coincide during the arrival time period $[t^{-}, t_{q'}]$, group E ships will not change their original arrival times in the nontoll case when the port is priced with the optimal single step toll.

It is clear from the above outcomes that bulk ship owners who choose the same arrival times at the anchorage as they did in the original nontoll equilibrium case are not the toll payers in the tolled case. As shown in Fig. 2, these bulk ships are groups A, D and E. On the other hand, other groups of bulk ships that postpone their original arrival times at the anchorage are the toll payers. As shown in Fig. 2, $[t', \tilde{t}) \rightarrow [t^{+}, \hat{t})$ for group B ships, and $[\tilde{t}, t^{\#}) \rightarrow [\hat{t}, t^{-})$ for group C ships.

## VI. Conclusions

This paper considered a pricing model for bulk ships anchoring a queuing port. According to bulk ships' departure patterns at a queuing port, we derived the non-toll equilibrium total cost (*ETC*) per bulk ship during the queuing period. We also developed a series of optimal time-varying tolls that eliminate the loss of queuing times without making ship owners worse off than they would be in the non-toll equilibrium. Because the optimal time-varying toll scheme has practical difficulties, the optimal single step toll inscribed in the optimal time-varying toll is established in this paper as an alternative pricing scheme to bulk ships at a queuing port.

This paper has shown all arrival time values, equilibrium conditions, equilibrium queuing costs at the anchorage (*EQC*), equilibrium arrival rates (EAR) and other equilibrium costs for a bulk ship staying at a berth (*EOC*) under the optimal single step toll scheme. By following the invariant *EOC* principle to achieve the equilibrium purpose, this paper provided a framework to predict bulk ship owners' decisions of arrival time adjustment under the optimal single step toll scheme. We have found that bulk ship owners who choose the same arrival times at the anchorage as they did in the original non-toll equilibrium case are not the toll payers under the optimal single step toll scheme. The other part of bulk ships that postpone their original arrival times at the anchorage are the toll payers under the optimal single step toll scheme.

## References

Laih, C. -H. (1994) Queuing at a bottleneck with single- and multi-step tolls, *Transportation Research*, **28A**, 197–208.

Laih, C. -H. (2004) Effects of the optimal single step toll scheme on equilibrium commuter behavior, *Applied Economics*, **36**, 59–81.

Laih, C. -H., Lin, B and Chen, K. Y. (2007) Effects of the optimal port queuing pricing on arrival decisions for container ships, *Applied Economics*, **39**, 1855–65.

Laih, C. -H. and Chen, K. Y. (2008) Economics on the optimal *n*-step toll scheme for aqueuing port, *Applied Economics*, **40**, 209–28.

Small, K. (1982) The scheduling of consumer activities, *American Economic Review*, **72**, 467–79.

Vickrey, W. S. (1969) Congestion theory and transport investment, *American Economic Review*, **59**, 251–61.

# The determinants of efficiency and productivity in European railways

Antonio Couto and Daniel J. Graham

This article evaluates the economic performance of European railways over the period 1972 to 1999. The cost structure of the railway industry is analysed using a stochastic frontier approach estimated within the framework of a translog cost system. The results confirm that European railways experience significant cost increases due to inefficient behaviour. In contrast to previous studies, however, the estimates indicate a much greater role for allocative rather than technical inefficiency. Overall, inefficiencies can essentially be explained by the supply of excess capacity and by the over-employment of labour inputs. Regarding productivity, it appears to be technological progress, and not levels of efficiency or scale economies, that provide the most convincing explanation for variance in growth rates within the sample.

## I. Introduction

In the last decade, a significant number of European Union directives have proposed vertical separation of rail infrastructure management from the operation of rail services and have also promoted open access to new operators (e.g. Council Directive 91/440/EEC, 95/18/EC, 95/19/EC and 2001/13/EC). The aim of these directives has been to encourage internal competition in the European railway market and to address the trends over recent decades that have culminated in a falling market share of European railways and an increasing need for subsidies.

The EU proposals were based on the conviction that competitive pressure, and the competitive strategy of railway firms, would result in a reduction of subsidies and operation costs by eliminating inefficiencies and encouraging revenue maximization. However, if there has been some consensus in the last decade about the need to stimulate contestable markets, it seems that recent difficulties in implementation and in the actual process of reform have raised the possibility that we may be able to achieve only marginal and temporary contestability (Bognetti and Fazioli, 1999). Issues such as these have motivated research into the economic characteristics of the railway industry, aiming to predict which policy environments and production structures can give rise to increased efficiency and productivity and allow the railway sector to become more competitive.

While there is extensive literature on rail productivity and efficiency, most studies to date have concentrated on identifying particular sources of productivity. In this article we estimate the sources of efficiency and productivity within the European railway industry, and also identify their main determinants including firm and country specifics effects and the influence of policy restructuring processes. The analysis makes use of recent developments in econometrics to estimate a cost frontier that isolates three main sources of productivity: firm efficiency, returns to scale and technological progress.

Using two alternative assumptions regarding the nature of allocative inefficiency, the cost frontier analysis allows us to identify the relative contributions of allocative and technical inefficiencies in the cost performance of firms. Following the methodology set out in Bauer (1990a), the growth rate of Total Factor Productivity (TFP) is then calculated allowing us to distinguish movements of the cost function that are due to embodied and disembodied technological progress, changes in efficiency of firms and movements along the cost function due to economies of scale.

In addition to these substantive contributions the article also makes methodological innovations through the choice and measurement of the variables used for estimation. In addition to the variables typically used in railway econometric studies, this article provides a re-evaluation of capital stock and introduces new exogenous variables such as environmental characteristics and quality of service variables, which were developed to improve model specification and to allow for the analysis of firm specific and technological effects.

The article is organized as follows. Section II describes the stochastic approach to minimum cost function estimation and efficiency analysis. Section III describes the data and the variables used in our model. Econometric results and analyses of cost inefficiencies and the growth of TFP are provided in Section IV. Conclusions are drawn in the final section.

## II. The Stochastic Frontier Approach

The traditional cost function approach assumes that the producer is efficient in reaching the cost minimization objective. The only error in this model is white noise and possible model misspecification. The stochastic cost function recognizes that a cost-minimizing firm may not be able to produce a given level of output, with given input prices, at a minimum cost due to the existence of technical and allocative inefficiencies which cause deviations from the cost frontier. Technical inefficiency is the failure to produce the maximum possible output with some given set of inputs. Allocative inefficiency arises from adopting a wrong, or sub-optimal, choice of input-proportions given input prices. Both types of inefficiencies increase total cost.

The cost frontier is rendered stochastic through the inclusion of white noise error, which could represent exogenous shocks that are outside the control of firms, the use of inappropriate data, measurement error and sources of model misspecification. White noise may increase or decrease cost and give rise to the following specification of the cost function:

$$\ln C = \ln C^* + \varepsilon \tag{1}$$

where $C$ is the total or variable cost, $C^*$ defines the deterministic cost frontier and $\varepsilon$ comprises technical ($C_\tau$) and allocative ($C_a$) inefficiencies as well as a random term. Thus the cost Equation 1 can be rewritten as:

$$\ln C = \ln C^* + \ln C_\tau + \ln C_a + \upsilon \tag{2}$$

The appearance of $C_\tau$ and $C_a$ in log-linear form allows one to express the actual costs (discarding the white noise component) supported by firms as the product of three impendent elements: the minimum or frontier cost ($C^*$), the cost of allocative inefficiency ($C_a$) and the cost of technical inefficiency ($C_t$) (Farrell, 1957).

The factor shares can be obtained by differentiating the previous expression of the logarithm cost with respect to the logarithm of each factor price ($w_i$), as follows:

$$S_i = \frac{\partial \ln C}{\partial \ln w_i} = \frac{\partial \ln C^*}{\partial \ln w_i} + \frac{\partial \ln C_a}{\partial \ln w_i} + \alpha_i \tag{3}$$

where $\alpha_i$ indicates a component error term. Since the cost of technical inefficiency is, by definition, independent of input prices, there is no explicit term of technical inefficiency in cost-share equations.

Brown and Walker (1995) argue that in a model consisting of the share equations and the cost function, the share residuals should not contain the additive functionally independent errors, that is, the noise component $\alpha_i$. They found that the use of an additive, homoscedastic error structure, functionally independent of input prices and output levels, for a complete system of equations derived from cost minimization, either violates the basic restriction from production theory or restricts the form of the underlying technology. Thus, based on this theoretical view, the share equations, as ancillary functions, only reproduce the piece of information contained in the cost function that depends on input prices, and, as a consequence, the deviations from each optimal share equation are exclusively due to an over or underutilization of the input considered (the allocative inefficiency). However, we can also argue that the actual share observations $S_i$, by their own empirical nature, incorporate stochastic terms that are clearly independent of the model, and as such potentially include measurement errors that could bias the residual based measure of allocative inefficiency.

The development of a consistent model of the cost-share system, which incorporates the heteroskedastic term in the cost function (resulting from the additive error term of share equations), is an extremely difficult task (Brown and Walker, 1995). We approach this problem by specifying alternative estimation models corresponding to both hypotheses: one with and one without, the stochastic noise term $\alpha_i$ in the cost-share equations.

Thus, generically the share equation presented above can be written in the following form:

$$S_i = \frac{\partial \ln C}{\partial \ln w_i} = \frac{\partial \ln C^*}{\partial \ln w_i} + u_i \tag{4}$$

where $u_i$ represents the random deviation term to optimal input shares, and which, depending on the hypothesis considered, includes or does not include the stochastic noise term.

The cost function can be estimated after specifying a functional form for ln $C^*$ and making some distributional assumptions regarding $\ln C_\tau$ and $\ln C_a$. However, since the cost of allocative inefficiency is not independent of input prices, then in order to obtain consistent parameter estimates, it is necessary to separate the costs of technical and allocative inefficiencies through some additional assumptions. Specifically, we need to link allocative inefficiency as indirectly measured by the cost-share equation residuals $u_i$, and the cost of allocative inefficiency ($\ln C_a$) in the cost function.

We model the deterministic component of the cost function using the translog form:

$$\begin{aligned}\ln C^* &= \alpha_0 + \gamma' \ln y + \alpha' \ln w + \eta' \ln q \\ &+ \ln y \Omega \ln w + \ln w \Phi \ln q + \ln y \Psi \ln q \\ &+ \frac{1}{2} \ln y \Pi \ln y + \frac{1}{2} \ln w \mathrm{B} \ln w + \frac{1}{2} \ln q \Delta \ln q\end{aligned} \tag{5}$$

where $y$ is a vector of outputs, $w$ is a vector of input prices and $q$ is a vector of exogenous variables, which include a time trend, firm-specific technical attributes, the characteristics of the general operational environment characteristics and the nature of quasi-fixed factors.

The dependent variable $\ln C^*$ is defined as the firms' variable cost.[1] In addition to the symmetry restrictions on the parameter matrices B, Π and Δ, we impose the following restrictions: $\alpha' l = 1$, $\mathrm{B}' l = 0$, $\Omega' l = 0$, $\Phi' l = 0$, where $l$ is a vector of ones. These restrictions on parameter vectors make the cost function in Equation 5 a linear homogeneous in input prices. By applying Shephard's lemma to Equation 5, we derive the deterministic part of cost-shares equations:

$$\begin{aligned}S_i^* &= \alpha_i + \sum_{j=1}^{n} \beta_{ij} \ln w_j + \sum_{k=1}^{m} \omega_{ik} \ln y_k \\ &+ \sum_{l=1}^{r} \varphi_{il} \ln q_l, \quad i = 1, \ldots, n\end{aligned} \tag{6}$$

Estimation of the model given in Equations 2 and 4 requires some specification of distributional assumptions for $\ln C_\tau$, $\ln C_a$ and $u_i$. Regarding distribution of the composite error vector $\varepsilon$ (Equation 1) we assume that:

(i) $u_i$ is distributed independently and identically through firms as multivariate normal with zero mean and constant covariance Σ,
(ii) ln $C_\tau$ is independently and identically distributed following a Half-Normal distribution $N(0,\sigma_\tau)$ – corresponding to the absolute value of a normally distributed variable with mean zero and SD $\sigma_\tau$,
(iii) the random noise, $n$, is independently and identically distributed according to a normal distribution – $N(0,\sigma_\upsilon)$,
(iv) the error components ln $C_\tau$, $u_i$ and $\upsilon$ are assumed to be mutually independent over years and across firms.

With these distributional assumptions, the concentrated log-likelihood function $L$ for a sample of $F$ firms observed over $T$ years, following the same derivation used by Kumbhakar (1991) and Parisio (1999), is given by:

$$\begin{aligned}L_c &= \text{const.} - \frac{1}{2} FT \ln|\Sigma| - FT \ln \sigma \\ &- \frac{\sum_{f=1}^{F} \sum_{t=1}^{T} \zeta_{ft}^2}{2\sigma^2} + \sum_{f=1}^{F} \sum_{t=1}^{T} \ln\left[1 - \Phi\left(-\frac{\lambda \zeta_{ft}}{\sigma}\right)\right]\end{aligned} \tag{7}$$

where, $f$ and $t$ index firm and time ($f = 1, \ldots F$, $t = 1, \ldots, T$), $\zeta_{ft} = (\varepsilon_{ft} - \ln C_{a_{ft}})$, $\sigma^2 = (\sigma_\upsilon^2 + \sigma_\tau^2)$,

[1] The short-run perspective is justified by the fact that the railways operate in a heavy-regulated environment where decisions on the economic adjustment of 'way and structures' capital factor cannot be based on static cost minimization criteria. For this reason, a quasi-fixed capital factor is introduced in the model as an exogenous variable.

$\lambda = \sigma_\tau/\sigma_\upsilon$, (.) is the standard normal distribution function and the $(i,j)$ element of $\Sigma$, $\sigma_{ij}$, is:

$$\sigma_{ij} = \frac{1}{FT}\sum_f\sum_t u_{ift}u_{jft}$$
$$= \frac{1}{FT}\sum_f\sum_t \left(S_{ift} - S^*_{ift}\right)\left(S_{jft} - S^*_{jft}\right) \quad (8)$$

Given the relationship between random terms and allocative inefficiency, the maximum-likelihood estimates of the parameters in Equations 5 and 6 can be obtained by maximizing the log-likelihood function $L_c$, where the elements of $\Sigma$ are given by relation Equation 8.

The relationship between the allocative inefficiency component in the cost equation and the deviations to optimal cost shares in Equation 4 can be explicitly modelled for the translog system by means of alternative specifications taking into account the differentiability condition and the fact that ln $C_a(u_i) \geq 0$. The specification choice depends on the nature of the assumptions made about the structure of the error terms $u_i$ and the level of flexibility imposed on the system. Specifically, it depends on the possible pre-violation of the regularity and of the integrability conditions, which we are willing to tolerate in order to benefit from the empirical advantages that arise from use of a more flexible estimation technique.

In this context, we propose two alternative models establishing the relationship through an approximating function imposing all the structure we know *a priori*. These models are based on the Schmidt and Sickles (1984) proposed specification where ln $C_a$ is formulated as:

$$\ln C_a = U'KU \quad (9)$$

where $K$ is a pre-specified positive matrix and $U = (u_1, u_2, \ldots, u_{n-1})$. In this specification, the cost of allocative inefficiency is a weighted average of the squared cost-share errors. Thus, the cost is increased as the magnitude of the absolute cost-share errors increase, always being positive if at least one $u_i$ is different from zero. In this study the pre-specific matrix $K$ requires a simplification relative to Schmidt's specification to obtain a more tractable maximum-likelihood procedure. Following the suggestion proposed by Bauer (1990b), we set the matrix $K$ to be a symmetric matrix where its elements are separate parameters to be estimated. Under this specification, no regularity conditions are imposed *a priori* and, moreover, the integrability condition associated with the application of Shepard's Lemma to the allocative cost term and to Equation 3 or 4 is not satisfied.

The two models used to estimate the allocative inefficiency are as follows.

(i) Model I gives a solution with the cost-share error term exclusively indexed to allocative errors. In this model the allocative inefficiency is calculated from the relation Equation 4, where the matrix $K$ is assumed to be a diagonal matrix and the parameters of this diagonal matrix are to be jointly estimated with the remaining parameters of the cost function. In this approximation method, the allocative inefficiency of the cost term appears in the cost function as a linear function of the error terms $u_i$ of the cost-share equation and can be expressed as:

$$\ln C_a = \sum_{i=1}^{n-1} C_i\left(u_i^2\right) \quad (10)$$

where $C_i$ are the parameters to be estimated and $u_i$ is the error term of the $i$th input cost-share equation.

(ii) Model II gives a solution with the cost-share term including allocative and noise errors. The second approximate solution model has been formulated on the basis that the error term in the cost-share equations is composed of a functionally dependent error term, the $\alpha_i^a$, and the noise term $\alpha_i$. The allocative error term, $\alpha_i^a$, is considered to be a linearly dependent function of the input prices, a time-trend variable and a firm-specific effect variable. Thus, as in the first model, assuming the cost of allocative inefficiency given by the relation Equation 9, where the matrix $K$ was pre-specified as a symmetric matrix, the term ln $C_a$ would be given by the following formulation:

$$\ln C_a = \sum_{i=1}^{n-1}\sum_{j=1}^{n-1} k_{ij}\alpha_i^a\alpha_j^a \quad (11)$$

where $k_{ij}$ are the elements of matrix $K$ to be estimated with $k_{ij} = k_{ji}$; $\alpha_i^a$ is given by:

$$\alpha_i^a(w_j, t, D_f) = \sum_{j=1}^{n} \omega_{ij}w_j + \sum_{f=1}^{F} \varpi_{if}D_f \times (1 + \log t)^{-1} + \sum_{f=1}^{F} \delta_{if}D_f \quad (12)$$

where the parameters $\omega_{ij}$, $\bar{\omega}_{if}$ and $\delta_{if}$ are parameters to be estimated. Note that the time-trend formulation $[1+\log(t)]^{-1}$ has been used instead of a linear one. The reason for this is that since efficiency gains are not a continuous source of productivity, gains from correcting allocative inefficiency (implying decreasing inefficiency over time) become increasingly more difficult after previous years, and consequently, a constant marginal efficiency gain over time would not characterize this effect. The $D_f$ variables are firm-specific dummy variables.

Finally in this section, we turn to the calculation of technical efficiency. Since the cost of technical inefficiency is independent of input prices in a cost-minimization framework, the random term characterizing the cost of technical inefficiency ($\ln C_\tau$) gives the maximum rate at which the use of all the input can be reduced without reducing output. Thus $\ln C_\tau$ ($\geq 0$) measures input-saving technical inefficiency. Ideally, we would estimate $\ln C_\tau$ for each firm in the sample to compare them on the basis of their productivity inefficiency. Unfortunately, this is not directly estimable since, with parameters estimate in hand, we are only able to compute a direct estimate of $(\ln C_\tau + \upsilon)$. Jowdrow *et al.* (1982), however, have derived a useful approximation that is now the standard measure in these settings, and which will be applied here.[2] Using the maximum-likelihood estimates of the structural parameters in the model and the assumed half-normal distribution for the random variable ($\tau = \ln C_\tau$), the proposed approximation for technical inefficiency measure is given by:

$$E[\tau|\varsigma] = \frac{\sigma\lambda}{1+\lambda^2}\left[\frac{\phi(z)}{1-\Phi(z)} - z\right], \quad \text{with } z = \frac{\varsigma\lambda}{\sigma} \qquad (13)$$

where $\zeta = (\varepsilon - \ln C_a)$, $\phi(\cdot)$ and $(\cdot)$ are respectively the standard normal density and distribution function, $\sigma^2 = (\sigma_\upsilon^2 + \sigma_\tau^2)$ and $\lambda = \sigma_\tau/\sigma_\upsilon$ as defined above.

## III. Data

The cost system that we have derived is composed in its deterministic part by three different types of exogenous variables:[3] output, input prices and the operational attribute variables. The data that are available to represent this cost system are for 27 firms of European countries over the period 1972 to 1999 (Table 1) (Appendix).[4] These data were obtained from the International Union of Railways (UIC) (1972–1999) and additionally supplemented with information from Jane's World Railways (1995), ECIS (1996), Uden (2001) and firm annual reports.

As mentioned previously, the dependent variable is the short-run variable cost. The infrastructure capital stock variable enters the function as an exogenous and fixed quantity (in a short-run perspective) and includes the 'land and fixed installations' as defined in reported UIC data. The cost, prices and productive capital stock of infrastructure were estimated following the criteria defined in Organization for Economic Cooperation and Development (OECD) Statistics (2001c) and OECD-Statistics (2001a), where the cost of capital was estimated as a user cost, defined as the sum of depreciation[5] and interest costs. The productive capital stock ($K_t$) is the stock of a particular asset, after assets of different ages have been converted into standard efficiency units, thus adjusting the older assets in the stock to account for their reduced efficiency in producing capital services. Productive capital stock is a proxy for the quantity of capital services produced by the asset, not directly observable, and thus assumed to be in proportion to the stock

[2] As Bauer (1990b) notes, unfortunately, these estimates cannot be shown to be consistent estimates of $\ln C_\tau$, since the variability of the conditional distribution $\ln C_\tau$ given $\zeta$ is independent of the sample size (i.e. $\zeta$ contains only imperfect information about $\ln C_\tau$).

[3] See Couto (2005) for full descriptions and treatments of these variables. The choice of variables was very constrained by the unavailability of reliable variable measures for the whole period.

[4] Due to a lack of quality data over the whole period and for all firms, cross-section data is unbalanced with yearly observations covering the whole period for some firms but other firms with reduced number of observations, mainly those from the Eastern countries. For this reason, and attending that the reliability of the data for these countries, corresponding to a period of political and economic system transition, can be questioned in the presence of high levels of inflation, any conclusions relative to these country companies should be taken with cautions.

[5] The traditional application of the perpetual inventory method requires the direct estimation of depreciation from which the net capital stock is obtained indirectly. The alternative approach, which was used in this study, is to use the age price profiles to directly estimate the net capital stock from which depreciation is obtained indirectly. This alternative method has the advantage of all stock data being necessarily consistent with each other because the age-efficiency profiles (used to estimate the productive capital stock) determine the age-price profiles (used to estimate the net capital stock and depreciation).

**Table 1. Data for cost system estimation**

| Firms | Data period | Firms | Data period |
|---|---|---|---|
| CFF (SBB/CFF/FFS) | 1972–1999 | NSB | 1972–1993 |
| CFL | 1972–1999 | BR | 1972–1994 |
| CH | 1972–1999 | DSB | 1972–1996 |
| CIE | 1972–1999 | CD (CSD) | 1990–1999 |
| CP (CP/REFER) | 1972–1999 | PKP | 1991–1999 |
| DB (DBAG) | 1972–1999 | MÁV | 1991–1999 |
| FS (FS SpA) | 1972–1999 | BC | 1992–1999 |
| NS (NS B.V./N.V.) | 1972–1999 | BDZ | 1992–1999 |
| ÖBB | 1972–1999 | CFR | 1992–1999 |
| RENFE | 1972–1999 | EVR | 1992–1999 |
| SJ (SJ/BV) | 1972–1999 | SZ | 1992–1999 |
| SNCB (SNCB/NMBS) | 1972–1999 | ZSR | 1993–1999 |
| SNCF (SNCF/RFF) | 1972–1999 | | |
| TCDD | 1972–1999 | | |
| VR (VR/RHK) | 1972–1999 | | |

of assets after each vintage has been converted into standard efficiency units.

Thus, productive capital stock was given by the following expression:

$$K_t = \sum_{\tau=0}^{T} h_\tau \cdot F_\tau \frac{IN_{t-\tau}}{q_{t-\tau,0}} \tag{14}$$

where $IN$ is the nominal investment expenditure[6] on the asset at time $t$, $q_{t,0}$ is the price index deflator for the asset of age zero (a new asset) in year $t$, $F_t$ is a retirement function that spells out the share of asset of age $t$ that is still in service, $T$ is the maximum service life of asset and $h_t$ is an age-efficiency profile, tracing the loss in productive efficiency as an asset ages.[7]

The variable input prices used in this study are Labour (LB), services rendered by third parties (EM), which include Energy and Materials consumption and Equipment capital stock (EQ). The use of aggregated inputs was necessary due to the lack of available homogeneous disaggregate input data. Constant cost and price data for the sample have been calculated using the World Bank country price deflators and the OECD country Purchasing Power Parities (PPPs). The variable definitions are as follows.

(i) The labour input price variable is measured, as is common in the literature, by the ratio of staff charges to annual mean staff. Staff charges are the sum of expenses from salaries plus pensions and various social charges.
(ii) Ideally, materials and energy would be constructed as two distinct variables. However, for this study, disaggregate data on both inputs are not available and instead we use the ratio of materials and energy costs over the total train-kilometres supplied by each company. This approximation of the prices of material and energy inputs is similar to that proposed by Preston (1994) and Sánchez and Villarroya (2000). The use of an aggregate measure is less problematic due to the empirical proportionality that is typically found between material and energy consumption and train-kilometres supplied.

[6] Investments expenditures were obtained by first differencing the reported nondepreciated value of stocks between each year. Due to the lack of some year/firm's observations or misleading capital stock observations reported in UIC data, investment expenditures for these years and firms were obtained from figures reported in ECIS (1996) and firm annual reports. Additionally, for companies with several capital stock revaluations or accounting changes in the period, the firm's revaluation capital stock and the following year observations were interpreted as *new firm* observations.

[7] The hyperbolic age-efficiency profile has been calculated by a function of the form, $h_\tau = T - (\tau - 1)/T - \beta(\tau - 1)$, where $T$, the duration of the asset, was set at 50 years and $\beta$ was set 0.75 according to the values given in OECD-Statistics (2001b) for infrastructure assets. The function assumed for retirement patterns, $F_t$, was the simultaneous exit function, which means that any investment produced at a certain point in time will be completely discarded at a certain future time. Railway infrastructures have, as physical characteristics, their long-life duration, which means that infrastructures have the capacity of being able to produce until they reach their service life and are then discarded/abandoned from service, which usually happens in block (i.e. there is a reduced number of infrastructures which have the ability of being partially discarded and still continuing in service; nevertheless, even in the cases where this is possible, due to its long-life duration, this would occur far from the period in study, more than 30 years). Productive capital stocks were converted in constant 1995 US$ throughout the use of PPP's 1995 deflators.

(iii) Capital stock equipment includes the transport stock and other equipment fixed assets. The cost, prices and productive capital stock[8] of 'capital stock equipment' were estimated following the same procedure used to derive the capital stock infrastructure. The rate of depreciation ($d_t$) was calculated as the change of the net capital stock at constant prices[9] and the real cost of financial capital ($r_t$) was measured as a return on government bonds given by the long-term real interest rates for government bonds reported in IMF (2001), World Bank (2002) and OECD (2002).

For the vector of aggregated output representing the production of the passenger (PKM) and freight services (TKM), either passenger-kilometres and ton-kilometres- or passenger train-kilometres and freight train-kilometres could be used. Here we use both alternative output vectors to provide a comparison of productive efficiency results. Using passenger-kilometres and ton-kilometres as output ($Y_{\mathrm{I}}$), the inefficiency results include, apart from managerial inefficiency, the inefficiency that arises through effects such as subsidies, governmental and/or regulatory control. The other model group ($Y_{\mathrm{II}}$) uses passenger train-kilometres and freight train-kilometres and consequently the empirical inefficiency results can be interpreted exclusively as firm managerial efficiency effects.

The operational attribute variables ($q$) in the system of Equations 5 and 6 represent a variety of exogenous variables related to the geographical environment of the firm and the characteristics of firm technology.

The variables we use to characterize the physical environment where the firms operate are: the length of network (NET), the population density of the country (DENS) (World Bank, 2002), the number of metropolitan cities potentially served by the firm network with more than one million inhabitants (AGM) (Brinkhoff, 2002), the average number of days per year that have snow in each country (SNOW) (ESRI, 2002) and the weighted average of the gradient level that characterizes the differences in terrain in each country (SURVEY) (Maps.com, 1999).

The variables that characterize the technological differences between firms and over time are:

(i) a linear time trend that captures technical progress from the shift in the cost function over time (TIME);
(ii) a set of dummy variables capturing the effects of introduction and use of high-speed lines (HS220, TT, DHS, DTT)[10] and
(iii) a proxy index number variable quantifying the operational quality level provided by firms. This variable ($QV_{max}$) mainly takes into account factors related to the potential 'network' velocity and works out as a complement velocity effect not captured by high-speed dummy variables. Specifically, we collect information on the potential maximum velocity of tractive stock, the frequency of service, the percentage of electrified network and the percentage of double track. To overcome potential problems of multicollinearity, the $QV_{max}$ variable was calculated as the first principal component of these four original variables after they have been standardized to have unit variance. Use of the method of principal components means that the service quality variable is an index without units of measurement.

Table 2 gives a summary of some basic characteristics of the companies that comprise our sample of European railways.

[8] The average life service for railway transport equipment considered in this study was 25 years. A delayed linear retirement pattern was used as the distribution function $F_t$ characterizing discards occurrences, and the hyperbolic age-efficiency profile $h_t$ was calculated assuming $T=30$ years and $b=0.5$, the value used by ABS and BLS for most types of machinery and equipment.

[9] The rate of depreciation was calculated as the ratio between the real depreciation ($D_t$) and the real net capital stock ($K_t$) at constant prices. $D_t$ is the real depreciation term, which is given by: $D_t = \sum_\tau (z_\tau F_\tau - z_{\tau+1} F_{\tau+1})(IN_{t-\tau-1}/q_{t-\tau-1})$, where $IN_t$ is the nominal investment expenditure on the asset at time $t$, for $q_t$ (the price index deflator for the asset of age zero in year $t$) the GDP deflator was used, the age-price profile ($Z_s$) was derived from the age-efficiency profile ($h_s$) and the retirement profile ($F_s$) and assuming a 'real discount rate' of 4% (as usual in empirical applications).

[10] Since these alternative options to increase passenger rail traffic velocity are very distinct in technology as well as in the magnitude of investment expenses, two distinct dummy variables were introduced, one which detects the presence of high-speed technology which allows running vehicles with maximum speed above 220 km/h, labelled DHS, and the other dummy variable which assumes the value one when firms own titling trains vehicles and the value zero otherwise, this dummy variable was labelled DTT. To capture the effect on costs of expanding investment on high-speed technology besides the dummy variables described above, two more variables HS220 and TT were introduced, which were defined as the product of initial dummy variables by the respective logarithm of the number of vehicles existent in each technology. This way it is possible to analyse the effect of the increment in this type of technologies in costs and consequently in productivity.

**Table 2. Basic characteristics of the European railway systems**

| | Basic network characteristics (Mean value during sample period) | | | | | | | | Basic cost characteristics (Mean value during sample period) | | | | |
|---|---|---|---|---|---|---|---|---|---|---|---|---|---|
| Firms | NET (km) | APTD | AFTD | PTRD (*1000) | FTRD (*1000) | ALT (km) | ALH (km) | $QV_{max}$ (Index) | VC_TK (US$/km) | SHLB (%) | SHEM (%) | SHEQ (%) | TK_S (km/empl.) |
| BR | 17 303 | 20.0 | 4.4 | 1802.4 | 1036.7 | 42.7 | 121.6 | 4.2 | 19.3 | 56.73 | 36.74 | 6.52 | 2.52 |
| CD* | 9417 | 10.6 | 5.0 | 818.6 | 2181.2 | 37.6 | 203.3 | 1.5 | 23.9 | 37.73 | 44.53 | 17.75 | 1.51 |
| CFF | 2951 | 26.9 | 9.4 | 3409.8 | 2456.9 | 42.1 | 159.3 | 5.1 | 24.4 | 61.09 | 23.32 | 15.59 | 3.00 |
| CFL | 272 | 13.9 | 5.3 | 900.3 | 2366.0 | 22.2 | 37.8 | 4.2 | 51.5 | 78.14 | 14.73 | 7.14 | 1.59 |
| CH | 2467 | 5.6 | 1.1 | 686.3 | 259.1 | 144.0 | 195.8 | 0.4 | 30.9 | 59.70 | 20.77 | 19.53 | 1.40 |
| CIE | 1984 | 4.5 | 2.1 | 552.1 | 293.5 | 55.2 | 176.3 | 1.5 | 45.8 | 57.19 | 32.57 | 10.24 | 2.13 |
| CP | 3393 | 8.4 | 2.0 | 1513.3 | 407.4 | 26.7 | 237.5 | 1.1 | 22.2 | 58.81 | 25.22 | 15.97 | 1.70 |
| CP/REFER* | 2821 | 13.8 | 2.8 | 1594.6 | 889.9 | 26.0 | 238.5 | 2.2 | 16.8 | 44.44 | 41.24 | 14.32 | 3.61 |
| DB* | 27 988 | 14.4 | 7.0 | 1456.7 | 2135.2 | 39.1 | 206.7 | 3.0 | 31.3 | 72.66 | 21.15 | 6.19 | 2.09 |
| DB AG | 39 674 | 16.8 | 5.2 | 1571.4 | 1790.4 | 43.9 | 241.7 | 3.6 | 15.5 | 49.40 | 46.66 | 3.94 | 3.38 |
| DSB | 2223 | 18.9 | 3.5 | 1832.0 | 809.7 | 33.9 | 234.8 | 2.6 | 22.3 | 48.31 | 31.31 | 20.38 | 3.00 |
| EVR* | 1001 | 4.7 | 3.5 | 454.9 | 4468.8 | 45.1 | 158.3 | 0.4 | 24.0 | 37.74 | 56.53 | 5.73 | 1.16 |
| FS | 16 114 | 14.5 | 3.8 | 2601.9 | 1211.1 | 102.5 | 325.1 | 3.2 | 39.1 | 60.74 | 27.89 | 11.38 | 1.66 |
| MAV* | 7665 | 9.4 | 2.6 | 856.6 | 1072.8 | 51.1 | 173.2 | 1.4 | 21.2 | 41.71 | 34.58 | 23.72 | 1.44 |
| NS | 2832 | 35.6 | 4.5 | 3624.8 | 1078.0 | 44.9 | 157.1 | 5.6 | 14.8 | 54.21 | 29.26 | 16.53 | 4.19 |
| NS (B.V./N.V.)* | 2807 | 41.0 | 2.3 | 5220.7 | 1279.9 | 46.0 | 151.2 | 6.9 | 24.9 | 32.66 | 57.58 | 9.76 | 4.65 |
| NSB | 4187 | 5.5 | 2.5 | 506.1 | 642.0 | 61.0 | 110.2 | 1.0 | 19.6 | 63.83 | 23.90 | 12.27 | 2.49 |
| OBB | 5740 | 12.4 | 6.6 | 1352.8 | 2041.8 | 44.9 | 203.0 | 2.8 | 29.7 | 51.65 | 27.09 | 21.26 | 1.71 |
| PKP* | 24 131 | 7.5 | 4.2 | 1014.3 | 2620.5 | 59.2 | 301.3 | 2.3 | 29.6 | 34.20 | 30.25 | 35.55 | 1.22 |
| RENFE | 12 997 | 8.3 | 3.4 | 1212.7 | 898.2 | 68.0 | 363.8 | 2.2 | 24.0 | 51.12 | 30.20 | 18.69 | 2.85 |
| SJ | 11 389 | 5.3 | 3.6 | 515.3 | 1407.7 | 83.7 | 305.7 | 1.6 | 17.1 | 65.03 | 22.12 | 12.86 | 3.07 |
| SJ/BV | 10 230 | 6.0 | 3.6 | 603.9 | 1733.6 | 67.2 | 394.9 | 2.5 | 18.7 | 40.68 | 47.99 | 11.33 | 4.84 |
| SNCB | 3711 | 19.1 | 5.6 | 1865.6 | 2250.4 | 43.9 | 114.9 | 5.0 | 37.2 | 60.96 | 25.13 | 13.91 | 1.97 |
| SNCF | 33 958 | 8.8 | 5.4 | 1659.6 | 1737.3 | 77.2 | 336.7 | 3.2 | 26.5 | 55.58 | 27.54 | 16.88 | 2.19 |
| SNCF/RFF* | 31 715 | 11.1 | 4.9 | 2018.8 | 1934.5 | 78.1 | 384.8 | 4.1 | 29.3 | 43.52 | 50.51 | 5.97 | 3.03 |
| SZ* | 1201 | 9.3 | 6.0 | 499.0 | 2207.4 | 45.1 | 196.4 | 2.1 | 25.7 | 45.59 | 36.61 | 17.80 | 1.86 |

| | | | | | | | | | | | | | |
|---|---|---|---|---|---|---|---|---|---|---|---|---|---|
| TCDD | 8297 | 2.8 | 2.2 | 715.9 | 877.9 | 49.0 | 509.2 | 0.6 | 35.7 | 54.56 | 33.10 | 12.33 | 0.93 |
| VR | 5961 | 4.2 | 3.1 | 517.7 | 1285.1 | 78.4 | 264.8 | 1.2 | 18.4 | 69.77 | 21.54 | 8.56 | 1.98 |
| VR/RHK* | 5857 | 4.5 | 2.9 | 572.9 | 1634.9 | 66.7 | 241.1 | 1.7 | 16.2 | 45.88 | 47.31 | 6.81 | 4.43 |
| ZSR* | 3666 | 10.3 | 6.3 | 1023.2 | 3345.5 | 46.5 | 210.6 | 2.0 | 24.1 | 41.44 | 46.96 | 11.60 | 1.24 |

*Notes*: NET: Network length (kilometres).
APTD: Average passenger train density (passenger train-kilometres per route kilometres).
AFTD: Average freight train density (freight train- kilometres per route kilometres).
PTRD: Passenger traffic density (passenger-kilometres per route kilometres).
FTRD: Freight traffic density (tonne-kilometres per route kilometres).
ALT: Average passenger trip length (passenger-kilometres per passenger).
ALH: Average freight length of haul (tonne-kilometres per tonne).
$QV_{max}$: Quality of service index.
VC_TK: Variable costs per train kilometres.
SHLB: Average labour cost shares (%).
SHEM: Average energy and materials cost share (%).
SHEQ: Average equipment cost share (%).
TK_S: Train-kilometres per number of employees.
*Mean firm values from a sample with <10 years observations.

## IV. Results

The results section is organized as follows. First we present parameter estimates from cost-function estimation for our two models using two separate output vectors. Next, we use the estimates to construct measures of technical and allocative inefficiencies for the railways. We then present the results of some further regressions to identify the sources of cost inefficiencies. Finally, we present a decomposition of TFP growth.

### *Parameter estimates from the cost functions*

Initial estimation of the general cost function Equation 5 revealed evidence of severe multicollinearity. Following Klein (1962), the correlation matrix of all terms in the deterministic cost function was calculated, and the variable terms with high levels of correlation were excluded. The exclusion of these variables did not imply restrictions either in the flexibility of the function (still allowing variable elasticity of substitution) nor in the theoretical properties of the cost function.

Preliminary estimation results using the standard infrastructure productive capital stock, KQ, showed frequent violations of curvature conditions, with positive estimates for the parameter associated with the second-order quadratic KQ term, directly contradicting cost theory. To solve this problem, quasi-fixed capital stock, KQ, was replaced by a measure of the service flow from capital as the argument in the variable cost function, as suggested by Oum and Zhang (1991). To compute infrastructure capital stock service flow, KQ*, we need to multiply the infrastructure productive capital stock (KQ) by its utilization rate. Since the utilization rate of infrastructure-productive capital stock is not directly observable, some proxy must be constructed. Therefore the utilization rate (CUK) was defined as the ratio of total train-kilometres run (per year) per kilometre of line to the maximum value of total train-kilometres run (per year) per kilometre of line observed in the present sample.

The restriction of linear homogeneity in the input prices was imposed by normalizing variable costs and the other prices by the price of materials and energy input (PEM). To avoid singularity in the disturbance variance-covariance matrix, the materials and energy input cost–share equation was dropped from estimation. It is well known that the maximum-likelihood estimates are invariant to the choice of the share equation dropped.

Thus, the final system for estimation comprising a variable cost functions and input cost shares is:

$$
\begin{aligned}
\ln\left(\frac{VC}{PEM}\right) &= \alpha_0 + \alpha_{LB}\ln\left(\frac{PLB}{PEM}\right) \\
&+ \alpha_{EQ}\ln\left(\frac{PEQ}{PEM}\right) + \gamma_{PKM}\ln(PKM) \\
&+ \gamma_{TKM}\ln(TKM) + \eta_{QV_{max}}\ln(QV_{max}) \\
&+ \eta_{Net}\ln(NET) + \eta_{KQ}\ln(KQ^*) \\
&+ \eta_{Time}(TIME) + \omega_{LBPKM}\ln\left(\frac{PLB}{PEM}\right) \\
&\times \ln(PKM) + \omega_{EQPKM}\ln\left(\frac{PEQ}{PEM}\right) \\
&\times \ln(PKM) + \omega_{EQTKM}\ln\left(\frac{PEQ}{PEM}\right) \\
&\times \ln(TKM) + \phi_{LBTime}\ln\left(\frac{PLB}{PEM}\right)\cdot(TIME) \\
&+ \phi_{LBQV max}\ln\left(\frac{PLB}{PEM}\right)\cdot\ln(QV_{max}) \\
&+ \phi_{EQKQ}\ln\left(\frac{PEQ}{PEM}\right)\cdot\ln(KQ^*) \\
&+ \psi_{PKMKQ}\ln(PKM)\cdot\ln(KQ^*) \\
&+ \psi_{YKMKQ}\cdot\ln(TKM).\ln(KQ^*) \\
&+ \frac{1}{2}\beta_{LBLB}\left[\ln\left(\frac{PLB}{PEM}\right)\right]^2 \\
&+ \beta_{LBEQ}\ln\left(\frac{PLB}{PEM}\right)\cdot\ln\left(\frac{PEQ}{PEM}\right) \\
&+ \frac{1}{2}\lambda_{QVQV}[\ln(QV_{max})]^2 \\
&+ \lambda_{QVTime}\ln(QV_{max})\cdot(TIME) \\
&+ \lambda_{KQKQ}\left[\ln(\frac{KQ^*}{NET})\right]^2 + \kappa_{Snow}\ln(SNOW) \\
&+ \kappa_{Survey}\ln(SURVEY) + \kappa_{DENS}\ln(DENS) \\
&+ \kappa_{AGM}\ln(AGM) + \delta_{HS220}(HS220) \\
&+ \delta_{TT}(TT) + \delta_{DHS}(DHS) + \delta_{DTT}(DTT) \\
&+ \tau + \upsilon \qquad (15.1)
\end{aligned}
$$

$$
\begin{aligned}
SHLB &= \alpha_{LB} + \beta_{LBLB}\cdot\ln\left(\frac{PLB}{PEM}\right) \\
&+ \beta_{LBEQ}\cdot\ln\left(\frac{PEQ}{PEM}\right) \\
&+ \omega_{LBPKM}\cdot\ln(PKM) \\
&+ \phi_{LBTime}(TIME) + \phi_{LBQV_{max}} \\
&\times \ln(QV_{max}) + u_{LB} \qquad (15.2)
\end{aligned}
$$

$$\text{SHEQ} = \alpha_{\text{EQ}} + \beta_{\text{LBEQ}} \cdot \ln\left(\frac{\text{PLB}}{\text{PEM}}\right) + \omega_{\text{EQPKM}} \cdot \ln(\text{PKM}) + \omega_{\text{EQTKM}} \cdot \ln(\text{TKM}) + \phi_{\text{EQKQ}} \cdot \ln(\text{KQ}^*) + u_{\text{EQ}} \quad (15.3)$$

where SHLB and SHEQ are the input cost shares for labour and transport equipment capital stock.

The two model specifications (Model I and Model II) were applied to the sample dataset, and they were run for the two alternative output specifications $Y_{\text{I}}$ and $Y_{\text{II}}$. Table 3 displays the parameter estimates of the cost frontier functions. Overall, the parameter values indicate that the estimated cost function performs fairly well in both models. For instance, we can see that the values of the log-likelihood function are high, the majority of parameter estimates have the intuitively expected signs, and most importantly, the regularity conditions requiring global concavity of the cost function are confirmed by the estimation of the Hicks–Allen own partial elasticities of substitution, which are all negative at the mean sample and practically negative at all points. To ensure that the cost functions are monotonically increasing in prices, the fitted shares were checked and confirmed to be all positive for both models. Additionally, they are found to be increasing in $Y$, and therefore, all the theoretical properties of the cost function are satisfied.

The model that provides elasticities of substitution values with less variability is Model II using the output set $Y_{\text{II}}$.[11] The sample mean values of the own partial elasticities of substitution are for labour $\sigma_{\text{LBLB}} = -1.10$, for transport equipment $\sigma_{\text{EQEQ}} = -4.91$ and for materials and energy $\sigma_{\text{EMEM}} = -0.32$ and the cross partial elasticities of substitution are $\sigma_{\text{LBEQ}} = 1.78$, $\sigma_{\text{EQEM}} = 0.41$ and $\sigma_{\text{EMLB}}$ 0.11. The cross partial elasticities of substitution mean values, with the exception of $\sigma_{\text{LBEQ}}$ (mean value of $\sigma_{\text{LBEQ}}$, around 1.8), are not significantly different from zero by the $t$-test, at a probability level of 5%. So these mean sample values show that input-substitutability prevails among inputs but only labour and transport equipment inputs appear to be truly viable substitutes.

The external factor parameters estimates, such as weather and terrain, have, the expected positive signs and are statistically significant at the 1% probability level for the majority of models. This implies that countries with worse terrain and weather conditions have an increase in operational costs. Parameters related to population density (DENS) are all significant at the 1% probability level for each model. However, the elasticity of this variable is dependent on the output chosen. Likewise, the parameters related to the number of agglomeration cities (AGM) are mostly significant at the 1% probability level, but again vary considerably from model to model. The reason for the differences between model parameter values for the DENS and AGM variables can be explained by the fact that they have an implicit relationship with output which depends on the nature of the individual output measures used.

Two types of variables were introduced in the cost functions to explicitly characterize the quality of service effects: $\text{QV}_{\text{max}}$ and the set of high-speed dummy variables. For Model II, the mean values of the cost elasticity of the quality of service $\text{QV}_{\text{max}}$ are $-0.05$ and of $-0.02$, respectively for the output set given by $Y_{\text{I}}$ and $Y_{\text{II}}$. Thus, at the point of means, an increase in the quality of service is associated with an increase in operational costs. Regarding the results relating to the high-speed dummy variables (HS220, DHS, TT, DTT), three main observations can be made. The first is that we do not find evidence of a significant effect on operational costs from the introduction of a high-speed network: the elasticity associated with the DHS variable is statistically insignificant in all models. Second, the dummy variable which accounts for the increment of high-speed usage (HS220) has a negative effect significant at the 1% probability level. Third, for the tilting train technology, gains on operational cost come not from the increment of traffic density of tilting trains technology but from impact of introducing this technology into the network.

### *Estimates of technical and allocative inefficiencies*

In this section, sources of inefficiency are analysed using the cost structure results presented above. To avoid excessive and repetitive analysis, we concentrate our discussion on the model that yields the most reliable measures for the railway cost structure based on the following criteria:

(i) has the highest number of observations in the sample with correct (negative) estimated own elasticities of substitution signs;
(ii) has nonnegative measures of technical and allocative cost inefficiencies for all observations in the sample;

[11] All models gave elasticities of substitution with similar values for the majority of observations; however, in some models for a restricted number of data points the figures of these elasticities are extremely high in comparison with the remaining observations, which consequently yielded, for these models, higher values of SDs.

**Table 3. Cost function parameters' estimates**

| | Model I | | | | Model II | | | |
|---|---|---|---|---|---|---|---|---|
| | Output set $Y_I$ | | Output set $Y_{II}$ | | Output set $Y_I$ | | Output set $Y_{II}$ | |
| Parameters | Coeff. | SE | Coeff. | SE | Coeff. | SE | Coeff. | SE |
| $\alpha_0$ | −4.63169 | 0.5898*** | 3.19616 | 0.401728*** | −4.844440 | 0.525708*** | 5.239590 | 0.363599*** |
| $\alpha_{LB}$ | 1.65855 | 0.1278*** | 0.82500 | 0.0937162*** | 1.70230 | 0.119958*** | 0.773276 | 0.080305*** |
| $\alpha_{EQ}$ | −0.560832 | 0.0361*** | −0.378212 | 0.0368914*** | −0.540094 | 0.034551*** | −0.214595 | 0.030771*** |
| $\eta_{KQ}$ | 0.675204 | 0.0522*** | 0.28364 | 0.0527012*** | 0.683179 | 0.045825*** | 0.180675 | 0.046927*** |
| $\eta_{QVmax}$ | 0.117955 | 0.0291*** | 0.0580194 | 0.0362897 | 0.110436 | 0.027362*** | 0.044138 | 0.035539 |
| $\gamma_{PKM}$ | −0.212865 | 0.0994** | −0.37727 | 0.153247** | −0.197686 | 0.093003** | −0.517170 | 0.163849*** |
| $\gamma_{tkm}$ | 0.786782 | 0.0902*** | 0.956365 | 0.15451*** | 0.812507 | 0.086550*** | 1.051800 | 0.153613*** |
| $\delta_{HS220}$ | −0.036211 | 0.0094*** | −0.021871 | 0.0096724** | −0.044664 | 0.009298*** | −0.007025 | 0.010554 |
| $\Delta_{TT}$ | 0.033768 | 0.0113*** | 0.0132182 | 0.0093127 | 0.023206 | 0.010346** | 0.014572 | 0.009394 |
| $\delta_{DHS}$ | 0.038389 | 0.0341 | 0.0007219 | 0.0379293 | 0.053490 | 0.034433 | −0.026912 | 0.039429 |
| $\delta_{DTT}$ | −0.229561 | 0.0333*** | −0.144623 | 0.0278596*** | −0.194635 | 0.026556*** | −0.113963 | 0.023740*** |
| $\kappa_{Snow}$ | 0.041655 | 0.0057*** | 0.0079092 | 0.0058846 | 0.056098 | 0.004609*** | 0.007905 | 0.004894 |
| $\kappa_{Survey}$ | 0.075432 | 0.009*** | 0.0657955 | 0.009157*** | 0.065464 | 0.007650*** | 0.059189 | 0.008297*** |
| $\eta_{Time}$ | −0.00375 | 0.0022* | −0.008059 | 0.0025314*** | −0.005065 | 0.001984** | −0.007672 | 0.001988*** |
| $\beta_{LBLB}$ | 0.011116 | 0.0305 | 0.106963 | 0.0321414*** | −0.004376 | 0.027623 | 0.083330 | 0.029121*** |
| $\beta_{LBEQ}$ | 0.012529 | 0.0079 | 0.0285687 | 0.0068408*** | 0.019656 | 0.006883*** | 0.041006 | 0.005729*** |
| $\omega_{LBPKM}$ | −0.126063 | 0.0107*** | −0.116246 | 0.0093441*** | −0.124200 | 0.009847*** | −0.069951 | 0.010422*** |
| $\omega_{EQPKM}$ | −0.039599 | 0.0055*** | −0.007066 | 0.0102923 | −0.047478 | 0.005234*** | −0.026919 | 0.008001*** |
| $\omega_{EQTKM}$ | 0.009174 | 0.0054* | 0.0165605 | 0.0087077* | 0.019473 | 0.004737*** | 0.032142 | 0.006497*** |
| $\Psi_{PKMKQ}$ | 0.026149 | 0.0059*** | 0.0572752 | 0.0098321*** | 0.020716 | 0.005365*** | 0.059461 | 0.010168*** |
| $\Psi_{TKMKQ}$ | −0.042407 | 0.006*** | −0.055671 | 0.009662*** | −0.042111 | 0.005864*** | −0.052318 | 0.009626*** |
| $\phi_{EQKQ}$ | 0.069316 | 0.0041*** | 0.0329679 | 0.0040203*** | 0.064134 | 0.004034*** | 0.025254 | 0.003103*** |
| $\phi_{LBTime}$ | −0.006691 | 0.0016* | −0.002549 | 0.0017877 | −0.007364 | 0.001440*** | −0.002763 | 0.001463* |
| $\phi_{LBQVmax}$ | −0.085278 | 0.0154*** | −0.000473 | 0.0198758 | −0.092689 | 0.013980*** | −0.025189 | 0.021106 |
| $\lambda_{QVTime}$ | 0.000265 | 0.0011 | −0.001585 | 0.0012651 | 0.002664 | 0.001110** | −0.000779 | 0.001055 |
| $\lambda_{QVQV}$ | −0.065857 | 0.0095*** | −0.01457 | 0.0117067 | −0.095414 | 0.011989*** | −0.025230 | 0.010638** |
| $\kappa_{DENS}$ | 0.362203 | 0.0236*** | 0.085646 | 0.0232515*** | 0.310573 | 0.022072*** | 0.068347 | 0.020415*** |
| $\kappa_{AGM}$ | −0.047503 | 0.0123*** | 0.0341619 | 0.0112344*** | 0.002379 | 0.011734 | 0.050963 | 0.011255*** |
| $\eta_{Net}$ | 0.34565 | 0.0469*** | 0.270502 | 0.0522881*** | 0.374673 | 0.044781*** | 0.207331 | 0.049414*** |
| $\lambda_{KQKQ}$ | −0.026572 | 0.0062*** | −0.014341 | 0.0075389* | −0.022529 | 0.006035** | −0.010060 | 0.007511 |
| $\lambda = \sigma_u/\sigma_v$ | 2.04182 | 0..253*** | 2.96542 | 0.35394*** | 1.146890 | 0.197689*** | 1.184720 | 0.182204*** |
| $\sigma = (\sigma_u^2 + \sigma_v^2)^{1/2}$ | 0.145822 | 0.0084*** | 0.158192 | 0.0082829*** | 0.109170 | 0.009191*** | 0.110817 | 0.010076*** |
| Log-likelihood | 473.629 | | 474.803 | | 546.605 | | 542.795 | |

*Notes*: Number of observations: 534.
***Significant at the level of 1%; **significant at the level of 5%; *significant at the level of 10%.

(iii) has the highest maximum-likelihood function estimate.

The model, which best conforms to these criteria for both aggregate output measures $Y_I$ and $Y_{II}$, is Model II.

The estimates of the logarithmic cost inefficiency of the European railways was obtained according to each model's specification as a function of the maximum ikelihood estimates of parameters and of the share residuals. Table 4 reports the mean values of the logarithm of allocative cost inefficiency estimates together with their SEs, the Wald test for the hypothesis that the set of parameters are jointly zero, and the respective probability values.

The results shown in this table appear to indicate that European railways do generate excess costs as a result of allocative inefficient behaviour. Furthermore, the significant SE of the groups mean and the probabilities values for the Wald test, show, in contrast to other studies such Gathon and Perelman (1992), Bosco (1996) or Parisio (1999), that there is also substantially different behaviour between firms with respect to the use of correct input proportion. The mean increase in variable costs due to allocative inefficiency is around 20% with output expressed as output revenue ($Y_I$), with the lowest mean value of 1.9% for the VR/RHK firm and the highest value of 67% for DB. If output is measured as available output ($Y_{II}$) the mean increase in variable costs due to allocative inefficiency is around 27% with the lowest mean firm value of 3.5% obtained for SJ/BV and the highest value of 93% for PKP. For both models with output set $Y_I$ and output set $Y_{II}$,

**Table 4. Mean values of (log) allocative cost inefficiency**

| | Model II | | | | | | | |
|---|---|---|---|---|---|---|---|---|
| | Output $Y_I$ | | | | Output $Y_{II}$ | | | |
| Firms | Estimate | SD | $\chi^2$ | $p$-value | Estimate | SD | $\chi^2$ | $p$-value |
| BR | 0.3939 | 0.0782 | 25.38 | 0.00 | 0.4308 | 0.2137 | 4.06 | 0.04 |
| CD | 0.0278 | 0.0093 | 8.83 | 0.00 | 0.1828 | 0.0181 | 102.20 | 0.00 |
| CFF | 0.2246 | 0.0282 | 63.30 | 0.00 | 0.1502 | 0.1052 | 2.04 | 0.15 |
| CFL | 0.0374 | 0.0383 | 0.95 | 0.33 | 0.1105 | 0.1433 | 0.59 | 0.44 |
| CH | 0.1035 | 0.1311 | 0.62 | 0.43 | 0.1508 | 0.0593 | 6.46 | 0.01 |
| CIE | 0.1313 | 0.0416 | 9.96 | 0.00 | 0.1311 | 0.1623 | 0.65 | 0.42 |
| CP | 0.1903 | 0.0703 | 7.32 | 0.01 | 0.3114 | 0.1709 | 3.32 | 0.07 |
| CP/REFER | 0.0415 | 0.0029 | 201.71 | 0.00 | 0.0427 | 0.0077 | 30.87 | 0.00 |
| DB | 0.5145 | 0.0379 | 183.87 | 0.00 | 0.5109 | 0.0753 | 46.00 | 0.00 |
| DBAG | 0.4246 | 0.0446 | 90.74 | 0.00 | 0.3286 | 0.0182 | 325.22 | 0.00 |
| DSB | 0.0950 | 0.0462 | 4.22 | 0.04 | 0.0959 | 0.0227 | 17.83 | 0.00 |
| EVR | 0.2428 | 0.0461 | 27.75 | 0.00 | 0.1522 | 0.0228 | 44.40 | 0.00 |
| FS | 0.4879 | 0.1532 | 10.14 | 0.00 | 0.6001 | 0.2479 | 5.86 | 0.02 |
| MAV | 0.0607 | 0.0192 | 10.04 | 0.00 | 0.3263 | 0.0119 | 753.15 | 0.00 |
| NS | 0.1807 | 0.0415 | 19.00 | 0.00 | 0.0876 | 0.0448 | 3.82 | 0.05 |
| NSBV/NV | 0.1186 | 0.0020 | 3684.20 | 0.00 | 0.0568 | 0.0031 | 341.92 | 0.00 |
| NSB | 0.0411 | 0.0278 | 2.18 | 0.14 | 0.0572 | 0.0485 | 1.39 | 0.24 |
| OBB | 0.0837 | 0.0557 | 2.26 | 0.13 | 0.1721 | 0.0397 | 18.83 | 0.00 |
| PKP | 0.2954 | 0.0967 | 9.33 | 0.00 | 0.6567 | 0.0288 | 520.95 | 0.00 |
| RENFE | 0.1876 | 0.0591 | 10.09 | 0.00 | 0.1932 | 0.1536 | 1.58 | 0.21 |
| SJ | 0.1064 | 0.0611 | 3.03 | 0.08 | 0.1169 | 0.1502 | 0.61 | 0.44 |
| SJBV | 0.0291 | 0.0158 | 3.40 | 0.07 | 0.0347 | 0.0122 | 8.07 | 0.00 |
| SNCB | 0.1822 | 0.0555 | 10.79 | 0.00 | 0.2585 | 0.0759 | 11.60 | 0.00 |
| SNCF | 0.3896 | 0.0362 | 115.94 | 0.00 | 0.2746 | 0.0788 | 12.16 | 0.00 |
| SNCF/RFF | 0.3955 | 0.0111 | 1280.28 | 0.00 | 0.2563 | 0.0049 | 2683.52 | 0.00 |
| SZ | 0.1168 | 0.0855 | 1.87 | 0.17 | 0.0445 | 0.0818 | 0.30 | 0.59 |
| TCDD | 0.1374 | 0.1082 | 1.61 | 0.20 | 0.5966 | 0.1641 | 13.21 | 0.00 |
| VR | 0.0796 | 0.0292 | 7.44 | 0.01 | 0.1433 | 0.1463 | 0.96 | 0.33 |
| VR/RHK | 0.0184 | 0.0056 | 10.62 | 0.00 | 0.0655 | 0.0065 | 101.51 | 0.00 |
| ZSR | 0.0441 | 0.0944 | 0.22 | 0.64 | 0.1899 | 0.1873 | 1.03 | 0.31 |
| Mean | 0.1894 | 0.1582 | 1.43 | 0.23 | 0.2418 | 0.2152 | 1.26 | 0.26 |

most of the mean firm values are significant at a probability level of 5%. Thus, our results support the view that European railways bear additional cost because they use inputs in the wrong proportions.

Figures 1 and 2 show, for each firm, in successive 5-year periods (1972–1975, 1976–1980, 1981–1985, 1986–1990, 1991–1995, 1996–1999) the estimated mean percentage cost increase due to allocative inefficiency.

When output is represented by train-kilometres- (Fig. 2), then with the exception of TCDD, all firms have decreased their allocative inefficiency during the sample period. However, if the demand effect is taken into account (Fig. 1), then for FS, SNCF, RENFE, NSB and CP, we find that allocative inefficiency has often increased over the same period. In fact, over the sample period, under the pressure of large budget deficit, we know that all firms, with the exception of NS, have implemented internal management policy changes to reduce staff. This could explain the fall in allocative inefficiency shown in Fig. 2. The most likely reason that this fall is not shown in Fig. 1 is that when we use a demand-based measure of output, we also capture effects that are outside the control of management and organization restructuring and these have important impacts on 'global' allocative inefficiency. In fact, this interpretation is consistent with the point of view of those who believe that the social benefits, which railway transport provides are not compatible with objectives based exclusively on inefficiency reductions.

Table 5 reports the mean values of the estimates of technical inefficiency together with their SEs, the Wald test for the hypothesis that the set of parameters are jointly zero and the respective probability values. The estimated cost of technical inefficiency appears to be substantially lower than that associated with allocative inefficiency. From Table 5, the mean increase in variable costs due to technical inefficiency is ≈3.6% (in both output set

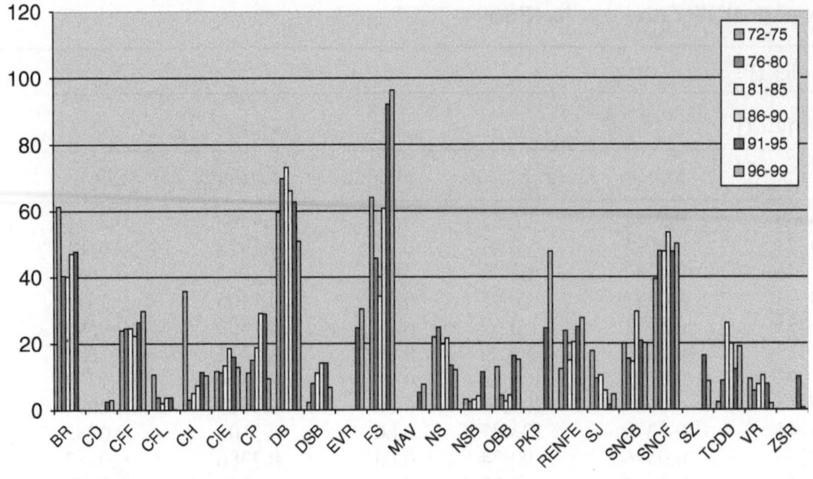


**Fig. 1. Mean cost increase due to allocative efficiency (%): output $Y_I$**

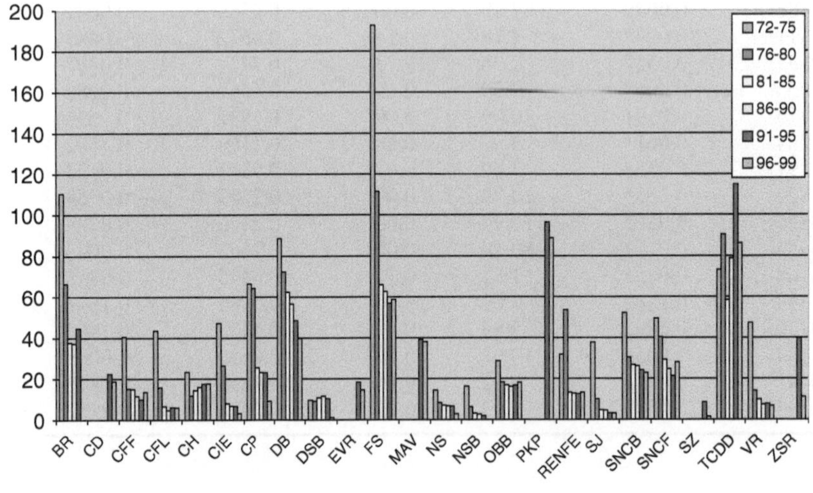


**Fig. 2. Mean cost increase due to allocative efficiency (%): output $Y_{II}$**

alternatives). The lowest mean values are 1.9% (CP/REFER) for output set $Y_I$ and 2.3% (NS BV/NV) with output measured by $Y_{II}$. The highest mean values are of 7.8% (SZ) and 8.3% (VR/RHK), respectively for output sets $Y_I$ and $Y_{II}$. For both models, most of the mean firm values are significant at a probability level of 5%.

Figure 3 and 4 show, for each firm, in successive 5-year periods (1972–1975, 1976–1980, 1981–1985, 1986–1990, 1991–1995, 1996–1999) the estimated mean percentage cost increase due to technical inefficiency.

The graphs show that there is a significant variability in the technical efficiency levels of firms over time. Furthermore, the table shows that there is no clear trends in the behaviour of firms: some show continuously decreasing technical efficiency values (e.g. RENFE, PKP and SNCB), others continuously increasing (e.g. VR, SZ, SNCF, SJ and CFF), while some show more erratic variation over time (e.g. TDCC, DB and NSB). Thus, we have mixed evidence across our sample of firms but despite this there are also some clear finding. First, the results do show that there are firms which, regardless of the output considered, perform well: these are VR and ÖBB. Second, we find that CD performs well if market demand is taken into account but not so well when only internal management is taken into account. Finally, we observe that the most poorly performing firms tend to be those that have separated infrastructure from operational services and which actually show higher technical inefficiency after the separation has taken place. The best example of this effect is VR and VR/RHK, which performed very well until the separation, after which it became the least efficient railway in the sample.

**Table 5. Mean values of (log) technical cost inefficiency**

| | Model II | | | | | | | |
|---|---|---|---|---|---|---|---|---|
| | Output $Y_I$ | | | | Output $Y_{II}$ | | | |
| Firms | Estimate | SD | $\chi^2$ | $p$-value | Estimate | SD | $\chi^2$ | $p$-value |
| BR | 0.0297 | 0.0065 | 21.23 | 0.00 | 0.0344 | 0.0083 | 17.12 | 0.00 |
| CD | 0.0193 | 0.0009 | 420.10 | 0.00 | 0.0326 | 0.0112 | 8.46 | 0.00 |
| CFF | 0.0357 | 0.0076 | 22.06 | 0.00 | 0.0358 | 0.0073 | 23.86 | 0.00 |
| CFL | 0.0340 | 0.0113 | 9.04 | 0.00 | 0.0338 | 0.0085 | 15.89 | 0.00 |
| CH | 0.0377 | 0.0118 | 10.16 | 0.00 | 0.0373 | 0.0133 | 7.86 | 0.01 |
| CIE | 0.0428 | 0.0151 | 8.03 | 0.00 | 0.0393 | 0.0155 | 6.41 | 0.01 |
| CP | 0.0289 | 0.0132 | 4.79 | 0.03 | 0.0330 | 0.0109 | 9.10 | 0.00 |
| CP/REFER | 0.0190 | 0.0036 | 27.51 | 0.00 | 0.0299 | 0.0051 | 33.88 | 0.00 |
| DB | 0.0337 | 0.0124 | 7.45 | 0.01 | 0.0450 | 0.0189 | 5.70 | 0.02 |
| DB AG | 0.0343 | 0.0100 | 11.88 | 0.00 | 0.0406 | 0.0135 | 9.03 | 0.00 |
| DSB | 0.0317 | 0.0077 | 17.01 | 0.00 | 0.0287 | 0.0060 | 22.84 | 0.00 |
| EVR | 0.0233 | 0.0210 | 1.23 | 0.27 | 0.0237 | 0.0041 | 32.75 | 0.00 |
| FS | 0.0345 | 0.0126 | 7.48 | 0.01 | 0.0308 | 0.0129 | 5.68 | 0.02 |
| MAV | 0.0241 | 0.0062 | 15.15 | 0.00 | 0.0366 | 0.0084 | 19.15 | 0.00 |
| NS | 0.0381 | 0.0073 | 27.54 | 0.00 | 0.0445 | 0.0102 | 19.07 | 0.00 |
| NSBV/NV | 0.0551 | 0.0012 | 2258.93 | 0.00 | 0.0229 | 0.0014 | 275.27 | 0.00 |
| NSB | 0.0294 | 0.0086 | 11.60 | 0.00 | 0.0451 | 0.0226 | 3.99 | 0.05 |
| OBB | 0.0243 | 0.0040 | 36.08 | 0.00 | 0.0262 | 0.0069 | 14.32 | 0.00 |
| PKP | 0.0410 | 0.0232 | 3.13 | 0.08 | 0.0598 | 0.0475 | 1.58 | 0.21 |
| RENFE | 0.0374 | 0.0198 | 3.56 | 0.06 | 0.0319 | 0.0102 | 9.81 | 0.00 |
| SJ | 0.0411 | 0.0082 | 25.34 | 0.00 | 0.0333 | 0.0067 | 24.53 | 0.00 |
| SJBV | 0.0454 | 0.0095 | 22.90 | 0.00 | 0.0452 | 0.0109 | 17.18 | 0.00 |
| SNCB | 0.0353 | 0.0138 | 6.52 | 0.01 | 0.0304 | 0.0092 | 10.93 | 0.00 |
| SNCF | 0.0365 | 0.0089 | 16.78 | 0.00 | 0.0314 | 0.0121 | 6.70 | 0.01 |
| SNCF/RFF | 0.0549 | 0.0077 | 50.43 | 0.00 | 0.0313 | 0.0031 | 103.89 | 0.00 |
| SZ | 0.0747 | 0.0266 | 7.87 | 0.01 | 0.0504 | 0.0131 | 14.90 | 0.00 |
| TCDD | 0.0501 | 0.0323 | 2.41 | 0.12 | 0.0403 | 0.0194 | 4.33 | 0.04 |
| VR | 0.0300 | 0.0116 | 6.67 | 0.01 | 0.0248 | 0.0098 | 6.39 | 0.01 |
| VR/RHK | 0.0683 | 0.0050 | 183.24 | 0.00 | 0.0825 | 0.0041 | 404.06 | 0.00 |
| ZSR | 0.0320 | 0.0073 | 19.17 | 0.00 | 0.0260 | 0.0031 | 71.66 | 0.00 |
| Mean | 0.0358 | 0.0163 | 4.82 | 0.03 | 0.0356 | 0.0157 | 5.15 | 0.02 |

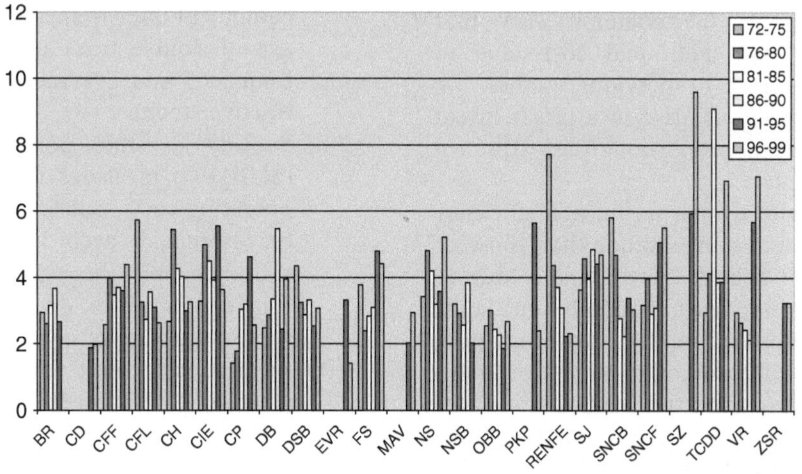


**Fig. 3. Mean cost increase due to technical efficiency (%): output $Y_I$**

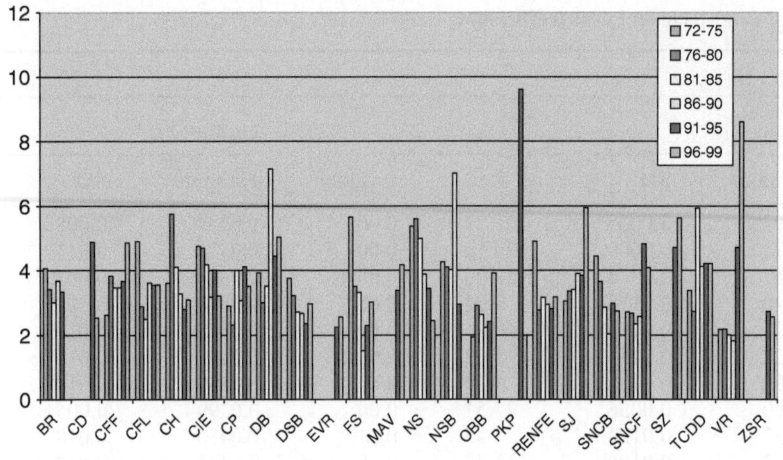


**Fig. 4. Mean cost increase due to technical efficiency (%): output $Y_{II}$**

Table 6 shows a comparison of our results with those of analogous studies using similar data, by providing a ranking of the technical inefficiency values obtained for each railway. Correlations among ranking results are generally low, with the exception of our Model II ($Y_{II}$) and those of Parisio (1999), which gives a rank correlation score of 0.70. In fact it is very difficult to undertake a comparison of results across studies due to the different modelling techniques applied, not least, the fact that in some studies estimates are derived using a production-function framework, which does not take into account allocative inefficiencies.

In fact, the main difference between our results and those of previous studies relates to the relative magnitude of the estimates of technical and allocative efficiency. We find a much greater role for allocative inefficiency in generating cost increases than technical inefficiency. Thus, while our results do support the common view that European railways bear additional costs due to inefficiencies, in contrast to previous studies, we find that these inefficiencies arise to a larger extent because of wrong input proportions than equiproportionate input waste.

As mentioned previously, our technical inefficiency results tend to be lower in magnitude than those of previous studies. We believe this is mainly due to differences in models employed, especially since some models are based on production function estimation, which does not take into account allocative inefficiency effects. Of course allocative inefficiency results themselves are also very sensitive to methodology, and this is shown in the Kumbhakar studies of US railways (Kumbhakar 1988a, b, 1989). However, as mentioned above, analyses by Bosco (1996) and Parisio (1999) do generate allocative inefficiency results, which are very similar to our estimates providing some consistent evidence of the magnitude of this component.

### *The determinants of inefficiency*

In order to identify the determinants of inefficiency, we regress the aggregate inefficiency scores on a set of explanatory variables. From the literature, we find a set of such variables that are commonly used.

(i) Capacity utilization – the average passenger load per train (PLOAD) and the average freight load per train (FLOAD) are used as indices of train utilization.
(ii) Quality of services – the index variable for quality of service ($QV_{max}$) characterizes operational improvements either through higher traffic flows or transport infrastructure and equipment improvements (such as the percentage of double track and of electrified lines, frequency and average maximum velocity of tractive stock).
(iii) Subsidy – the policy subsidy variable (SUB_VC) measures the ratio of subsidy to operating costs. Subsidy policy should ideally be examined according to the types of subsidies and the way in which they are provided, however, due to limited information we use the level of aggregate subsidy only.
(iv) Firm capacity and autonomy – the network length (NET) is used here as a proxy for firm capacity and degree of firm autonomy. Firms with higher autonomy are expected to be able to adjust their network length more easily than firms conditioned to conserve lines considered socially desirable but economically unprofitable.

**Tabel 6. Ranking in terms of technical inefficiency in distinct studies**

| Firms | Gathon and Perelman (1992) | Perelman and Pestieau (1988) | Coelli and Perelman (1999) | Coelli and Perelman (2000) | Gathon and Pestieau (1995) | Deprins and Simar (1988) | Parisio (1999) | Present study Model II ($Y_{I}$) | Present study Model II ($Y_{II}$) |
|---|---|---|---|---|---|---|---|---|---|
| BR | 15 | 13 | 5 | 6 | 4 | 16 | 6 | 4 | 11 |
| CFF | 14 | 10 | 2 | 14 | 3 | 3 | 7 | 11 | 12 |
| CFL | 17 | 15 | 10 | 8 | 16 | 14 | | 8 | 10 |
| CH | 12 | 18 | 11 | 17 | 15 | 7 | | 14 | 13 |
| CIE | 16 | 1 | 4 | 2 | 6 | 2 | | 17 | 14 |
| CP | 6 | 6 | 16 | 10 | 7 | 10 | | 2 | 8 |
| DB | 11 | 14 | 8 | 5 | 13 | 13 | 8 | 7 | 17 |
| DSB | 4 | 3 | 15 | 11 | 18 | 9 | | 6 | 3 |
| FS | 19 | 17 | 17 | 7 | 9 | 12 | 1 | 9 | 5 |
| NS | 2 | 2 | 1 | 1 | 1 | 1 | 4 | 15 | 16 |
| NSB | 7 | 4 | 5 | 3 | 17 | 17 | | 3 | 18 |
| OBB | 18 | 11 | 9 | 16 | 14 | 6 | 2 | 1 | 2 |
| RENFE | 13 | 12 | 13 | 13 | 11 | 11 | | 13 | 7 |
| SJ | 5 | 8 | 14 | 16 | 8 | 8 | | 16 | 9 |
| SNCB | 9 | 16 | 12 | 4 | 12 | 18 | 5 | 10 | 4 |
| SNCF | 2 | 7 | 3 | 9 | 5 | 4 | 3 | 12 | 6 |
| KID | 7 | 19 | | | 2 | 15 | | 18 | 15 |
| VR | 1 | 9 | 7 | 2 | 10 | 5 | | 5 | 1 |

**Tabel 7. The determinants of inefficiency: regression results**

| Independent variables | Dependent variable: $\ln C_\tau + \ln C_a$ | | | | | | | |
|---|---|---|---|---|---|---|---|---|
| | Passenger-kilometres and ton-kilometres as outputs | | | | Passenger and freight train-kilometres as output | | | |
| | Coeff. | SE | *t*-ratio | *p*-value | Coeff. | SE | *t*-ratio | *p*-value |
| ONE | −0.47447 | 0.09434 | −5.02951 | 0.0000 | −0.433349 | 0.10222 | −4.23954 | 0.0000 |
| DSEP | −0.051649 | 0.01141 | −4.5255 | 0.0000 | −0.0056051 | 0.0107 | −0.52395 | 0.6003 |
| LSUB VC | −0.006034 | 0.00561 | −1.07553 | 0.2821 | 0.012891 | 0.00598 | 2.15655 | 0.0310 |
| DUMMYHS | 0.0302919 | 0.00969 | 3.12661 | 0.0018 | −0.0198861 | 0.00822 | −2.41993 | 0.0155 |
| DUMMYTT | −0.035558 | 0.00991 | −3.58691 | 0.0003 | 0.0080892 | 0.01238 | 0.65358 | 0.5134 |
| LNET | 0.0640627 | 0.00662 | 9.67078 | 0.0000 | 0.0581334 | 0.00654 | 8.89428 | 0.0000 |
| LQVMAX | 0.0926551 | 0.01269 | 7.3002 | 0.0000 | 0.0638768 | 0.00594 | 10.7495 | 0.0000 |
| LPERCP | 0.164863 | 0.04942 | 3.33619 | 0.0008 | 0.0492973 | 0.0454 | 1.08581 | 0.2776 |
| LSTAFF | 0.0179109 | 0.00936 | 1.91453 | 0.0556 | 0.231891 | 0.01304 | 17.777 | 0.0000 |
| LPLOAD | 0.110184 | 0.018 | 6.12032 | 0.0000 | 0.0481699 | 0.01677 | 2.87233 | 0.0041 |
| LFLOAD | −0.067083 | 0.01209 | −5.55095 | 0.0000 | 0.0073246 | 0.01184 | 0.61873 | 0.5361 |
| Number of observations | | 364 | | | | 364 | | |
| Within group autocorrelation between | | 0.255–0.990 | | | | 0.099–0.990 | | |
| Log-likelihood | | 674.15523 | | | | 571.63423 | | |

(v) Managerial autonomy – in addition to the network length variable, the percentage of passenger train-kilometres in total train-kilometres- (PERCP) is included as an indicator of managerial operational autonomy. Firms with higher autonomy are more able to adjust their supply of passenger services than firms with higher government control.

(vi) Over-employment and union control – the number of employees per train-kilometres (STAFF) is included in an attempt to characterize firms with over-employment. It could also provide a proxy for the power of union forces and government control.

In addition to these variables we also wish to test for the effects of high-speed technology and vertical separation on cost efficiency. Accordingly, we include in the regression high-speed dummy variables (DHS and DTT) and a dummy variable identifying the organizational implementation of vertical separation policy reform (DSEP).

The regression of cost inefficiency, with dependent variable given by the sum of logarithm of the cost of technical inefficiency and the logarithm of the cost of allocative inefficiency, was estimated using a three-step Generalized Least Square (GLS) estimator for Time-Series Cross Section (TSCS) data.[12] To ease the interpretation of results, the independent variables were expressed also in logs. In line with the cost-function estimation, two alternative regression models were run, one in which the dependent variable is derived from Model II of cost-function estimation with the output measured by the revenue output ($Y_{\mathrm{I}}$); and one in which the dependent variable is derived from Model II with output expressed by train-kilometres ($Y_{\mathrm{II}}$). The results are shown in Table 7.

The ratio of subsidy to the total operating expenses has a statistically significant positive coefficient with output given by $Y_{\mathrm{II}}$ but not by $Y_{\mathrm{I}}$. This may indicate that subsidization provides little incentive to the firm to improve productivity or minimize costs. However, if the demand response is taken into account then perhaps any loss of efficiency is balanced by other particular types of subsidies, such as ticket price and conditional subsidies, which yield demand increases and thus nominal efficiency gains.

The vertical separation of infrastructure and operations (DSEP) appears to increase efficiency. However, this increase is only statistically significant in the first model, which is based on revenue output. This policy allows for efficiency cost savings of 5%, mainly through an improved adjustment of inputs used and revenue outputs, but the gains in cost

[12] Since the test hypotheses of no-autocorrelation and homoscedastic regression, as well as the test against cross group correlation, were rejected at the 1% of probability level, the computation was modelled so allowing for groupwise heteroscedasticity, cross group correlation and within group autocorrelation. Since the basic command for TSCD in Limdep programming demand a balanced panel with contiguous group data, all firms without complete data set (28 observations) were excluded from the regression; thus the number of observations in this groupwise regression models were reduced to 364 observations.

efficiency from internal production process are actually less. It is important to emphasize here that results presented earlier in this article showed an increase in cost due to technical inefficiency provoked by vertical separation. So in fact, overall the results shown in Table 7 suggest that the gains in allocative efficiency provided by this structural reform overcome the loss in terms of technical efficiency estimated earlier in the article.

The variables characterizing the potential production capacity of firms, such as NET and $QV_{max}$, have a statistically significant positive coefficient in both models ($Y_I$) and ($Y_{II}$). Regarding the network variable, we might expect excess capacity to arise due to the possible existence of network branches with low demand. For the variable $QV_{max}$, the positive coefficient results indicate that any inherent cost benefits associated with improved quality are not enough to overcome the negative effect on efficiency due to an excess of the capacity of transport capital stock.

Concentrating on the results from the first model (using $Y_I$), the variables PERCP and PLOAD have statistically significant positive coefficients, which indicate substantial increases in cost inefficiency from greater concentration in passenger services. Note also that the coefficient of FLOAD is statistically significant but with a negative value. The most likely explanation for these results is that passenger services, which have more visible social implications than freight services, are less prone to traffic reduction through governmental policies or transport authority regulators than freight service. Consequently, the inefficiencies induced by excess service capacity arise more from passenger services than freight services, which have undergone more significant adjustments over time. However, it should be stressed, by other side, that this negative coefficient may simply indicate that heavily loaded freight railways are closest to the cost frontier.

Regarding staff usage, the positive coefficient is indicative of over-employment, but its contribution to inefficiency costs seems to be of little importance when compared with the other variables just described.

We have concentrated much of our discussion on the first model (using $Y_I$), in which cost inefficiencies can be described as 'global' since they include sources of inefficiency that are beyond managerial control including influences from public policy on the capacity supplied and on the output consumed. In the second model (using $Y_{II}$), any excess capacity, which arises from the operation of low demand network branches does not feature in the measurement of cost inefficiencies. Thus, we would expect the determinants of cost efficiencies to be different from those estimated for the first model, having a more specific association with managerial practices.

In fact, as expected the second model results do show that the variables related to excess capacity, such as NET and $QV_{max}$, have statistically significant coefficients but produce a much lower effect on inefficiency. The most important difference between Models I and II, however, are associated with the variables describing operational behaviour. The percentage of passenger train-kilometres in total train-kilometres as well as the average freight load per train are not statistically significant, and in contrast to the first model, do not make a contribution to cost inefficiency. Even the average passenger load per train, while statistically significant in Model II, makes a contribution to inefficiency that is less than a half as shown in the first model. The average staff per train-kilometre variable has a statistically significant positive coefficient and its elasticity (0.23) indicates a relatively high degree of importance in giving rise to cost inefficiency. Thus, when demand factors are excluded from output measurement, cost inefficiencies are particularly sensitive to over-employment, with factors such as intensive train occupation and heavier concentration in passenger services having a lower impact.

Regarding the effect of high-speed technology, in the first model using $Y_I$ as output, both traditional high-speed and tilting train technology coefficients are statistically significant; however, traditional high-speed technology contributes to an increase in inefficiency costs and tilting train technology to a reduction of inefficiency costs. If at first glance these are surprising results, they are in conformity with what have been said in relation to other variable impacts. Traditional high-speed technology involves a substantially higher investment in capital stock than tilting train technology and also requires new lines. Thus, it is not surprising that in presence of networks with excess capacity, high-speed technology contributes to an increase in cost inefficiency; while tilting train technology, which uses the existent network, contributes to a reduction of cost inefficiency. It is, however, important to emphasize that traditional high-speed technology is not *per se* the cause of cost inefficiency increase, but is due rather to the inherent excess of capacity produced by its introduction. In relation to the introduction of tilting train technology, our estimates indicate that this gives rise to a decrease in cost inefficiencies of around 3.5%.

Considering the second model based on output $Y_{II}$, in which cost inefficiencies are measured taking into account only the available output, the tilting train technology coefficient is not statistically significant.

This means that the type of service supplied by this technology does not differ substantially in its operational characteristics from usual railway-transport services, and thus, it does not have additional impact on cost inefficiencies. In the case of traditional high-speed technology, we find that its introduction allows for a reduction of cost inefficiencies of around 2%. This confirms our hypothesis that if the excess capacity supplied is not taken into account in the measure of inefficiency, then high-speed technology serves to improve efficiency.

To summarize, we find that cost inefficiencies can essentially be explained by the excess of capacity supplied and by the discrepancies resulting from an over-employment of labour with respect to the best practice level. Over-employment is clearly indicated by the high and positive residuals of the labour input cost-share equation. These explanations are further substantiated by the fact that larger firms located in developed countries, where union labour forces tend to be more successful in demanding better salaries and where there are large networks with higher investment in capital stock improvements, also tend to be those that show high levels of allocative inefficiency.

### *A decomposition of TFP growth*

In this final results section we present measures of TFP growth for our railway firms and decompose the sources of TFP into those derived from scale economies, technological progress, gains in efficiency and changes in quality of service and network characteristics. To do so, we first have to estimate economies of scale and technological progress.

We estimate economies of scale from the expression[13]:

$$\mathrm{RTD} = \frac{1 - \sum_k \varepsilon^{VC}_{K_k}}{\sum_j \varepsilon^{VC}_{Y_j}} \qquad (16)$$

where $\varepsilon^{VC}_{Yj}$ is the elasticity of variable costs with respect to output $j$ and $\varepsilon^{VC}_{K}$ is the elasticity of variable cost with respect to quasi-fixed infrastructure capital stock, calculated for the long-run equilibrium values of the quasi-fixed input factor. These optimal levels of the fixed factor could be derived from the long-run envelope function of the short-run total cost functions.[14]

The mean firm values of economies of scale estimates together with their standard errors, the Wald test for the hypothesis that there are constant returns to scale, and respective probability values are shown in Table 8. The results show, as expected and consistent with the majority of previous studies, increasing returns to traffic density for all firms.[15]

To calculate technological progress, we measure the common rate at which all input can be decreased over time with outputs held fixed. We denote this quantity PGX and introduce it directly into the estimation of TFP growth rate. Thus, technical progress is given by:

$$\mathrm{PGX} = -\frac{\partial \ln g^V / \partial t}{1 - \sum_k (\partial \ln g^V / \partial \ln K_k)} \qquad (17)$$

where $K$ denotes the quasi-fixed factors, $g^V$ the variable cost function and $y_j$ the outputs. Following Morrison (1985, 1986), and Oum *et al.* (1991), the values of PGX were calculated using the long-run equilibrium values of quasi-fixed inputs.

Table 9 shows values of PGX estimated from Model II. Results from these specifications are quite similar under either output set (using $Y_{\mathrm{I}}$ or $Y_{\mathrm{II}}$), with sample mean values of 0.0156 and 0.0136, respectively. The Wald test for the hypothesis that the set of firm's PGX estimates are jointly zero is rejected at the 1% probability level for all firms, except for CD and PKP in the model using $Y_{\mathrm{I}}$ as output set. The Wald test for the hypothesis that the sample set's PGX estimates are jointly zero is rejected at 1% of probability level for both models.

Using output measure $Y_{\mathrm{I}}$, we find that Eastern European firms together with TDCC and SNCF/RFF are those that show the worst performances with values less than 1% while the firms with values higher than 2% are CFL, CH, VR and SJ. When train-kilometres are used as output, technical progress (PGX) shows more homogeneous values among firms and only CD, EVR, TCDD and ZSR show

[13] It is usual in transport analysis to express economies of scale in two distinct concepts: economies of network size and economies of density. However, we will present only the estimation relating to economies of density in order to have conformity with the subsequent treatment for estimation of TFP growth.

[14] Having estimated the short-run variable cost function, the short-run disequilibrium total cost function is obtained by adding the parcel of capital input cost ($\mathrm{TC} = g(Y, W_v, Z, K, t) + r \cdot K$) where $r$ is the rental price of the capital stock $K$. By differentiating this equation with respect to capital stock, equilibrium capital stock is obtained when the opportunity cost of capital (the price of capital $r$) equals the firm's shadow value of capital, and consequently, the optimal level of capital stock is that which results from this equality. Examples of this approach to short and long-run costs can be found in Braeutigam *et al.* (1984), Vellturo *et al.* (1992) and Friedlaender *et al.* (1993).

[15] Similar estimation of economies of network size showed, for the European railways which make up the sample, slight increasing returns to scale.

**Table 8. Mean values of returns to scale (economies of density)**

| | Model II | | | | | | | |
|---|---|---|---|---|---|---|---|---|
| | Output $Y_{\mathrm{I}}$ | | | | Output $Y_{\mathrm{II}}$ | | | |
| Firms | Estimate | SD | $\chi^2$ | $p$-value | Estimate | SD | $\chi^2$ | $p$-value |
| BR | 3.3813 | 0.7126 | 11.17 | 0.00 | 1.6674 | 0.0910 | 53.74 | 0.00 |
| CD | 2.2464 | 0.3108 | 75 489.96 | 0.00 | 1.5570 | 0.0468 | 461 408.96 | 0.00 |
| CFF | 4.7381 | 0.8019 | 21.73 | 0.00 | 1.9228 | 0.0881 | 109.84 | 0.00 |
| CFL | 5.5240 | 2.3498 | 3.71 | 0.05 | 2.1652 | 0.2244 | 26.95 | 0.00 |
| CH | 3.0008 | 0.8609 | 5.40 | 0.02 | 1.7303 | 0.1143 | 40.85 | 0.00 |
| CIE | 2.6900 | 0.3679 | 21.10 | 0.00 | 1.8824 | 0.1192 | 54.81 | 0.00 |
| CP | 2.6398 | 0.3571 | 21.09 | 0.00 | 1.7819 | 0.1537 | 25.87 | 0.00 |
| CP/REFER | 2.8468 | 0.1316 | 196.81 | 0.00 | 1.7411 | 0.0024 | 96 261.01 | 0.00 |
| DB | 5.2251 | 0.6415 | 43.37 | 0.00 | 1.8386 | 0.0293 | 817.33 | 0.00 |
| DB AG | 3.3206 | 0.3483 | 44.38 | 0.00 | 1.6344 | 0.0346 | 335.44 | 0.00 |
| DSB | 3.3549 | 0.4541 | 26.89 | 0.00 | 1.7244 | 0.0285 | 645.07 | 0.00 |
| EVR | 1.8700 | 0.0919 | 89.71 | 0.00 | 1.7557 | 0.1217 | 38.54 | 0.00 |
| FS | 3.1251 | 0.9423 | 5.09 | 0.02 | 1.7180 | 0.1006 | 50.93 | 0.00 |
| MAV | 2.3304 | 0.1664 | 63.92 | 0.00 | 1.5301 | 0.0101 | 2774.70 | 0.00 |
| NS | 4.9668 | 1.0954 | 13.11 | 0.00 | 1.7732 | 0.1180 | 42.96 | 0.00 |
| NS BV/NV | 2.5550 | 0.0096 | 26 098.45 | 0.00 | 1.5263 | 0.0322 | 267.26 | 0.00 |
| NSB | 4.0007 | 0.5142 | 34.05 | 0.00 | 1.9088 | 0.0966 | 88.51 | 0.00 |
| OBB | 3.1794 | 0.7321 | 8.86 | 0.00 | 1.7313 | 0.0993 | 54.21 | 0.00 |
| PKP | 2.3953 | 0.3918 | 12.68 | 0.00 | 1.5531 | 0.0382 | 209.35 | 0.00 |
| RENFE | 3.3372 | 0.6604 | 12.53 | 0.00 | 1.8000 | 0.0960 | 69.49 | 0.00 |
| SJ | 5.7732 | 2.1398 | 4.98 | 0.03 | 2.0216 | 0.1608 | 40.38 | 0.00 |
| SJ/BV | 3.3590 | 0.4294 | 30.18 | 0.00 | 1.7991 | 0.0593 | 181.73 | 0.00 |
| SNCB | 3.8575 | 1.0659 | 7.19 | 0.00 | 1.7904 | 0.0665 | 141.31 | 0.00 |
| SNCF | 3.7453 | 0.3355 | 66.96 | 0.00 | 1.7507 | 0.0573 | 171.83 | 0.00 |
| SNCF/RFF | 2.8820 | 0.0742 | 643.82 | 0.00 | 1.6627 | 0.0059 | 12 517.80 | 0.00 |
| SZ | 2.3866 | 0.2572 | 29.08 | 0.00 | 1.7593 | 0.1002 | 57.47 | 0.00 |
| TCDD | 1.6785 | 0.3848 | 3.11 | 0.08 | 1.8502 | 0.1998 | 18.11 | 0.00 |
| VR | 3.9397 | 0.9142 | 10.34 | 0.00 | 1.9684 | 0.1054 | 84.47 | 0.00 |
| VR/RHK | 3.2154 | 0.0538 | 1694.46 | 0.00 | 1.8493 | 0.0249 | 1164.31 | 0.00 |
| ZSR | 2.0895 | 0.1231 | 78.26 | 0.00 | 1.5929 | 0.1002 | 35.00 | 0.00 |
| Mean | 3.5592 | 1.4097 | 3.30 | 0.07 | 1.8074 | 0.1760 | 21.05 | 0.00 |

values below 1%, NS shows the highest mean productivity growth with a value of 1.78%.

Having estimated the movements of the cost function due to technical progress, the movements throughout the cost function due to economies of scale, the firms' efficiencies and the quality of service and network effects on cost function, the next step is to estimate the rate of growth of TFP. To do so we follow the methodology proposed by Bauer (1990a) which gives a *pure* measure of TFP growth defined as:

$$\dot{\mathrm{TFP}} = \left[1 - \frac{1}{RTD}\right] \cdot \dot{y}^c + \dot{\mathrm{TAE}} \cdot \left(\frac{1}{1-\varepsilon_{c,K}}\right) - \sum_m \varepsilon_{c,q_m} \cdot (\partial q_m/\partial t) \cdot \left(\frac{1}{1-\varepsilon_{c,K}}\right) - \mathrm{PGX} \tag{18}$$

where, $\dot{y}^c = \sum_j \left[\varepsilon_{c,y_j} / \sum_j \varepsilon_{c,y_j}\right] \dot{y}_j$, RTD is the index of economies of scale, $\dot{y}_j$ is the annual rate of change of output $j$, $\varepsilon_{c,y_j}$ is the cost elasticity of output $j$, $\dot{\mathrm{TAE}}$ the annual rate of change of cost efficiency, $\varepsilon_{c,K}$ is the capital stock infrastructure cost elasticity, $\varepsilon_{c,q_m}$ is the quality of service and network characteristics cost elasticities,[16] and PGX is the time rate of change of technological progress.

Table 10 shows the annual growth rate of TFP, as well as a decomposition of this growth into the contributions of gains in efficiency (TEA), of economies of scale (ES), of changes in quality of service and network characteristics (QN) and of technological progress (PGX). We can observe that, taking an average of all companies, TFP growth has taken place at an annual rate of 1.84 and 2.59%, respectively for outputs measured as passenger(ton)-

[16] The variables which compose the vector of the service quality and network characteristics ($q_m$) are: the quality of service variable ($qv_{max}$), the network length (NET) and the high-speed technology variables (DHS, DTT, HS220, TT).

**Table 9. Means value of technical progress (PGX)**

| | Model II | | | | | | | |
|---|---|---|---|---|---|---|---|---|
| | Output $Y_I$ | | | | Output $Y_{II}$ | | | |
| Firms | Estimate | SD | $\chi^2$ | $p$-value | Estimate | SD | $\chi^2$ | $p$-value |
| BR | 0.0128 | 0.0024 | 28.93 | 0.00 | 0.0147 | 0.0012 | 140.59 | 0.00 |
| CD | 0.0064 | 0.0036 | 3.14 | 0.08 | 0.0096 | 0.0015 | 43.20 | 0.00 |
| CFF | 0.0179 | 0.0016 | 127.20 | 0.00 | 0.0164 | 0.0009 | 350.11 | 0.00 |
| CFL | 0.0204 | 0.0052 | 15.20 | 0.00 | 0.0161 | 0.0016 | 103.47 | 0.00 |
| CH | 0.0235 | 0.0038 | 37.47 | 0.00 | 0.0123 | 0.0021 | 33.61 | 0.00 |
| CIE | 0.0149 | 0.0022 | 48.25 | 0.00 | 0.0122 | 0.0009 | 174.19 | 0.00 |
| CP | 0.0170 | 0.0022 | 62.33 | 0.00 | 0.0127 | 0.0007 | 313.17 | 0.00 |
| CP/REFER | 0.0146 | 0.0007 | 485.59 | 0.00 | 0.0137 | 0.0002 | 7715.75 | 0.00 |
| DB | 0.0182 | 0.0013 | 193.57 | 0.00 | 0.0158 | 0.0006 | 806.47 | 0.00 |
| DB AG | 0.0120 | 0.0017 | 48.97 | 0.00 | 0.0141 | 0.0006 | 567.45 | 0.00 |
| DSB | 0.0164 | 0.0023 | 49.43 | 0.00 | 0.0146 | 0.0012 | 154.93 | 0.00 |
| EVR | 0.0047 | 0.0010 | 22.80 | 0.00 | 0.0063 | 0.0004 | 255.01 | 0.00 |
| FS | 0.0123 | 0.0038 | 10.45 | 0.00 | 0.0136 | 0.0018 | 56.99 | 0.00 |
| MAV | 0.0090 | 0.0018 | 25.66 | 0.00 | 0.0108 | 0.0009 | 154.78 | 0.00 |
| NS | 0.0192 | 0.0041 | 21.84 | 0.00 | 0.0178 | 0.0013 | 175.85 | 0.00 |
| NS BV/NV | 0.0078 | 0.0001 | 3154.72 | 0.00 | 0.0145 | 0.0003 | 2691.98 | 0.00 |
| NSB | 0.0226 | 0.0029 | 60.43 | 0.00 | 0.0144 | 0.0007 | 380.21 | 0.00 |
| OBB | 0.0123 | 0.0041 | 9.00 | 0.00 | 0.0128 | 0.0018 | 50.95 | 0.00 |
| PKP | 0.0062 | 0.0029 | 4.42 | 0.04 | 0.0104 | 0.0014 | 58.65 | 0.00 |
| RENFE | 0.0158 | 0.0017 | 83.77 | 0.00 | 0.0138 | 0.0013 | 104.80 | 0.00 |
| SJ | 0.0227 | 0.0030 | 55.50 | 0.00 | 0.0156 | 0.0009 | 320.90 | 0.00 |
| SJBV | 0.0140 | 0.0028 | 25.08 | 0.00 | 0.0134 | 0.0011 | 142.25 | 0.00 |
| SNCB | 0.0135 | 0.0030 | 20.44 | 0.00 | 0.0149 | 0.0015 | 96.89 | 0.00 |
| SNCF | 0.0143 | 0.0013 | 121.33 | 0.00 | 0.0141 | 0.0007 | 357.74 | 0.00 |
| SNCF/RFF | 0.0087 | 0.0005 | 342.09 | 0.00 | 0.0126 | 0.0003 | 2534.57 | 0.00 |
| SZ | 0.0100 | 0.0004 | 550.30 | 0.00 | 0.0112 | 0.0002 | 4113.74 | 0.00 |
| TCDD | 0.0093 | 0.0020 | 21.95 | 0.00 | 0.0084 | 0.0012 | 45.29 | 0.00 |
| VR | 0.0210 | 0.0017 | 152.70 | 0.00 | 0.0139 | 0.0011 | 172.14 | 0.00 |
| VR/RHK | 0.0157 | 0.0006 | 710.97 | 0.00 | 0.0131 | 0.0003 | 2593.86 | 0.00 |
| ZSR | 0.0041 | 0.0013 | 9.43 | 0.00 | 0.0090 | 0.0006 | 214.54 | 0.00 |
| Mean | 0.0156 | 0.0055 | 7.94 | 0.00 | 0.0136 | 0.0027 | 26.26 | 0.00 |

kilometres ($Y_I$) and passenger (freight) train-kilometres ($Y_{II}$). These rates were mostly due to technological progress (1.39 and 1.32%, respectively for $Y_I$ and $Y_{II}$), and to a less degree due to gains in efficiency (1.08%) if output is measured in train-kilometres and due to gains from quality of service and network characteristics improvements (0.59%) if output is measured in passenger(ton)-kilometres.

Changes in scale seem to have had little effect on TFP growth (around −0.18% in both output set measures).[17] These results are in conformity with those obtained by Gathon and Pestieau (1995) and Sánchez and Villarroya (2000), who also found that the greater part of the growth in the level of TFP is explained by technological progress and to a much lesser degree by changes in efficiency and scale economies.

Using the output measured by passenger(ton)-kilometres, the companies with the highest levels of total productivity growth rate are DB AG, SZ, SJ and VR, while EVR, CD and TCDD show the lowest performance levels in the sample. If instead, we analyse total productivity growth rate using train-kilometres as output, CIE, SZ, DB, CFF and PKP are those with the highest rate of total productivity growth, and CH and TCDD are those with the lowest levels. Note, that companies such as CD, CIE, EVR, MAV, ZSR and specially PKP appear to have significantly higher performances when output is measured by train-kilometres than passenger(ton)-kilometres.

[17] The average value is negative which means that scale has had a decreasing effect on total productivity growth. However, if instead of the average of mean firm values we calculate the mean value of all observations in the sample we obtain an average positive value of around 0.1%.

**Table 10. A decomposition of TFP growth**

| | Output $Y_I$ | | | | | Output $Y_{II}$ | | | | |
|---|---|---|---|---|---|---|---|---|---|---|
| Firms | TFP | QN | PGX | SE | TAE | TFP | QN | PGX | SE | TAE |
| BR | 0.0104 | 0.0102 | 0.0127 | −0.0083 | −0.0042 | 0.0291 | 0.0052 | 0.0147 | −0.0015 | 0.0109 |
| CD | −0.0241 | 0.0007 | 0.0074 | −0.0309 | −0.0013 | 0.0203 | 0.0001 | 0.0100 | −0.0074 | 0.0176 |
| CFF | 0.0278 | −0.0019 | 0.0181 | 0.0124 | −0.0008 | 0.0417 | 0.0011 | 0.0165 | 0.0046 | 0.0195 |
| CFL | 0.0155 | 0.0041 | 0.0204 | −0.0151 | 0.0062 | 0.0230 | 0.0013 | 0.0162 | 0.0009 | 0.0046 |
| CH | 0.0027 | −0.0279 | 0.0231 | −0.0148 | 0.0224 | −0.0059 | −0.0065 | 0.0125 | −0.0086 | −0.0033 |
| CIE | 0.0163 | 0.0023 | 0.0150 | 0.0005 | −0.0016 | 0.0460 | 0.0012 | 0.0122 | 0.0085 | 0.0241 |
| CP | 0.0291 | 0.0045 | 0.0168 | 0.0197 | −0.0120 | 0.0259 | 0.0029 | 0.0127 | 0.0053 | 0.0051 |
| CP/REFER* | 0.0938 | 0.0841 | 0.0142 | −0.0112 | 0.0068 | 0.0369 | 0.0499 | 0.0136 | −0.0241 | −0.0025 |
| DB | 0.0279 | 0.0184 | 0.0183 | −0.0039 | −0.0049 | 0.0419 | 0.0090 | 0.0158 | 0.0010 | 0.0160 |
| DBAG | 0.0601 | 0.0113 | 0.0114 | 0.0140 | 0.0233 | 0.0145 | 0.0045 | 0.0139 | 0.0049 | −0.0089 |
| DSB | 0.0194 | −0.0006 | 0.0165 | 0.0029 | 0.0007 | 0.0220 | −0.0008 | 0.0147 | 0.0034 | 0.0046 |
| EVR | −0.0541 | −0.0063 | 0.0049 | −0.0521 | −0.0006 | 0.0182 | 0.0007 | 0.0064 | 0.0057 | 0.0054 |
| FS | 0.0175 | 0.0094 | 0.0123 | 0.0069 | −0.0110 | 0.0266 | 0.0049 | 0.0136 | 0.0018 | 0.0063 |
| MAV | −0.0221 | −0.0018 | 0.0096 | −0.0183 | 0.0116 | 0.0104 | −0.0003 | 0.0110 | −0.0061 | 0.0057 |
| NS | 0.0238 | 0.0031 | 0.0193 | 0.0001 | 0.0014 | 0.0289 | 0.0010 | 0.0178 | −0.0026 | 0.0126 |
| NS B.V./NS N.V.* | 0.0467 | 0.0028 | 0.0076 | 0.0380 | −0.0017 | −0.0484 | 0.0017 | 0.0148 | −0.0606 | −0.0042 |
| NSB | 0.0264 | 0.0024 | 0.0224 | 0.0042 | −0.0027 | 0.0251 | 0.0013 | 0.0144 | 0.0013 | 0.0082 |
| ÖBB | 0.0225 | 0.0023 | 0.0121 | 0.0089 | −0.0008 | 0.0265 | 0.0010 | 0.0128 | 0.0070 | 0.0057 |
| PKP | −0.0557 | 0.0062 | 0.0068 | −0.0341 | −0.0345 | 0.0370 | 0.0044 | 0.0107 | −0.0082 | 0.0302 |
| RENFE | 0.0317 | 0.0132 | 0.0158 | 0.0070 | −0.0043 | 0.0311 | 0.0065 | 0.0139 | 0.0039 | 0.0068 |
| SJ | 0.0410 | 0.0038 | 0.0223 | 0.0143 | 0.0005 | 0.0316 | 0.0013 | 0.0155 | 0.0000 | 0.0148 |
| SJ/BV | 0.0266 | 0.0182 | 0.0139 | −0.0055 | 0.0000 | 0.0239 | 0.0102 | 0.0135 | −0.0015 | 0.0018 |
| SNCB | 0.0247 | 0.0085 | 0.0137 | 0.0024 | 0.0002 | 0.0278 | 0.0046 | 0.0150 | 0.0008 | 0.0075 |
| SNCF | 0.0236 | 0.0133 | 0.0144 | 0.0033 | −0.0074 | 0.0263 | 0.0048 | 0.0142 | 0.0018 | 0.0056 |
| SNCF/RFF* | 0.0018 | 0.0030 | 0.0090 | −0.0071 | −0.0031 | 0.0309 | 0.0016 | 0.0128 | 0.0063 | 0.0101 |
| SZ | 0.0465 | −0.0001 | 0.0099 | 0.0093 | 0.0274 | 0.0420 | 0.0000 | 0.0112 | −0.0012 | 0.0320 |
| TCDD | −0.0108 | −0.0072 | 0.0093 | 0.0009 | −0.0138 | 0.0024 | −0.0017 | 0.0084 | 0.0003 | −0.0046 |
| VR | 0.0354 | 0.0019 | 0.0209 | 0.0165 | −0.0040 | 0.0107 | 0.0003 | 0.0140 | −0.0013 | −0.0023 |
| VR/RHK* | 0.0353 | 0.0011 | 0.0158 | 0.0178 | 0.0006 | 0.0272 | 0.0015 | 0.0131 | 0.0136 | −0.0010 |
| ZSR | 0.0131 | −0.0004 | 0.0044 | −0.0346 | 0.0437 | 0.1040 | −0.0001 | 0.0092 | −0.0020 | 0.0969 |
| Average | 0.0184 | 0.0059 | 0.0139 | −0.0019 | 0.0004 | 0.0259 | 0.0037 | 0.0132 | −0.0018 | 0.0108 |

*Note*: *Firms with <3 observations.

Additionally, we can observe that with the enlargement of DB (from DB to DB AG), there was a significant reduction in the productivity growth rates when output set is measured in train-kilometres but, when output passenger(ton)-kilometres is used, a significant increase in total productivity rates is observed. For companies, which have implemented vertical separation of infrastructure management and operations, we also find significant changes in productivity performance.

## V. Conclusions

This article has examined the economic performance of a panel of 27 European railways over the period 1972 to 1999. The cost structure of the railway industry was analysed using a stochastic frontier cost function with associated cost-share equations modelled within the framework of a translog cost system.

Our analysis indicates that European railways experience a significant cost increase due to allocative inefficiency behaviour, with a sample mean increase in variable costs due to allocative inefficiency of around 20%. Regarding technical inefficiency, we find a mean increase in variable costs of around 3.6%. The firms, which show the highest levels of inefficiencies, are those that are large in size and that have invested more in new technology over the last decades. A comparison of our results with those obtained in Parisio (1999), also using a cost frontier approach, shows a high degree of similarity. Further comparisons with other study results are made difficult due to the use of dissimilar methodology and data.

Despite the difficulty in making comparisons of allocative and technical inefficiencies with previous studies, our results are consistent in 'global' terms with those of previous studies in identifying relatively cost efficient (NS, CFF, SJ, SNCF and RENFE) and cost inefficient (TCDD and FS) firms. Perhaps the most important point of departure from the previous European railway literature is our finding that allocative inefficiency plays a much more significant rule in generating cost increases than technical inefficiency. The conclusion is that firms experience greater difficulty in finding correct input proportion than in achieving equiproportionate excess input usage.

Regarding policy options for cost inefficiencies, it seems that the impact of subsidies on efficiency is very dependent on the types of subsidy and the way in which they are provided. The separation of infrastructure and operations can lead to an increase in technical inefficiency, but it also seems to allow for a better adjustment of inputs used and revenue outputs, which in aggregate actually result in efficienct cost savings of around 5%. Inefficiencies related to excess service capacity arise more from passenger service than freight service, revealing the greater difficulties which European railway firms face in making adjustments in passenger output supply. Overall, we observe that inefficiencies can essentially be explained by the excess of capacity supplied and by the discrepancies resulting from an over-employment of labour input.

Our analysis of TFP confirms the results obtained by Gathon and Pestieau (1995) and Sánchez and Villarroya (2000), that it is technological progress, and not variation in efficiency levels, that provides the most convincing explanation for variance in TFP growth. Scale economies do not appear important in explaining the growth of TFP, but our results do confirm embodied technological progress (such as high-speed technology and quality of service improvements) as an important element favouring productivity. Thus, in the present context of increasing public sector de-regulation and liberalization, it may be important to ensure that infrastructure investments and modernization are encouraged in order to avoid decreasing levels of productivity over time.

## References

Bauer, P. W. (1990a) Decomposing TFP growth in the presence of cost inefficiency, nonconstant returns to scale, and technological progress, *The Journal of Productivity Analysis*, **1**, 287–99.

Bauer, P. W. (1990b) Recent developments in the econometric estimation of frontiers, *Journal of Econometrics*, **46**, 29–56.

Bognetti, G. and Fazioli, R. (1999) Liberalization problems and prospects in European railways, *Annals of Public and Cooperative Economics*, **70**, 303–18.

Bosco, B. (1996) Excess-input expenditure estimated by means of an input-distance function: the case of public railways, *Applied Economics*, **28**, 491–7.

Braeutigam, R. R., Daughety, A. F. and Turnquist, M. (1984) A firm specific analysis of economies of density in the US industry, *The Journal of Industry Economics*, **XXXIII**, 3–20.

Brinkhoff, T. (2002) The principal agglomerations of the world. Available at http://www.citypopulation.de (accessed August 2002).

Brown, B. W. and Walker, M. B. (1995) Stochastic specification in random production models of cost-minimizing firms, *Journal of Econometrics*, **66**, 175–205.

Coelli, T. and Perelman, S. (1999) A comparison of parametric and non-parametric distance function: with application to European railways, *European Journal of Operational Research*, **117**, 326–39.

Coelli, T. and Perelman, S. (2000) Technical efficiency of European railways: a distance function approach, *Applied Economics*, **32**, 1967–76.

Couto, A. (2005) The impact of high speed technology on demand and productivity in European railways: an econometric analysis, Unpublished PhD dissertation, Faculty of Engineering of the University of Porto.

Deprins, D. and Simar, L. (1988) Estimating technical inefficiencies with correction for environmental conditions – with an application to railway companies, *Annals of Public and Cooperative Economics*, **60**, 81–102.

ECIS (1996) *The State of European Infrastructure*, European Centre for Infrastructure Studies, Rotterdam, pp. 1–275.

ESRI (2002) ArcAtlas: our earth – snow cover. Available at http://www.nationalgeographic.com (accessed March 2002).

Farrell, M. J. (1957) The measurement of productive efficiency, *Journal of the Royal Statistical Society*, **Series A**, 253–81.

Friedlaender, A. F., Berndt, E. R., Chiang, J. S. W., Showalter, M. and Vellturo, C. A. (1993) Rail cost and capital adjustments in a quasi-regulated environment, *Journal of Transport Economics and Policy*, **21**, 131–52.

Gathon, H. J. and Perelman, S. (1992) Measuring technical efficiency in European railways: a panel data approach, *The Journal of Productivity Analysis*, **3**, 135–51.

Gathon, H. J. and Pestieau, P. (1995) Decomposition efficiency into its managerial and its regulatory components: the case of European railways, *European Journal of Operational Research*, **80**, 500–07.

IMF (2001) International Financial Statistics, International Monetary Fund. Available at http://www.imf.org (accessed August 2002).

Jane's World Railways (1995) *World Railways – Railway System*, 36th edn J. Abbott (Ed.), Surrey.

Jowdrow, J. A., Lovell, C. A. K., Materov, I. V. and Schmidt, P. (1982) On the estimation of technical inefficiency in the stochastic frontier production function model, *Journal of Econometrics*, **19**, 233–8.

Klein, L. (1962) *An Introduction to Econometrics*, Englewood Cliffs, Prentice-Hall.

Kumbhakar, S. C. (1988a) Estimation of input-specific technical and allocative inefficiency in stochastic frontier models, *Oxford Economic Papers*, **40**, 535–49.

Kumbhakar, S. C. (1988b) On the estimation of technical and allocative inefficiency using stochastic frontier functions; the case of US class 1 railroads, *International Economic Review*, **2**, 727–43.

Kumbhakar, S. C. (1989) Economic performance of US class I railroads: a stochastic frontier approach, *Applied Economics*, **21**, 1433–46.

Kumbhakar, S. (1991) The measurement and decomposition of cost-inefficiency: the translog cost system, *Oxford Economic Papers*, **43**, 667–83.

Maps.com (1999) World elevation. Available at http://www.maps.com (accessed December 2001).

Morrison, C. J. (1985) Primal and dual capacity utilisation: an application to productivity measurement in the US automobile industry, *Journal of Business and Economic Statistic*, **3**, 312–24.

Morrison, C. J. (1986) Productivity measurement with non-static expectations and varying capacity utilization, *Journal of Econometrics*, **33**, 51–74.

OECD (2002) OECD Financial Statistics. Available at www.oecd.org/dataoecd, http://lysander.sourceoecd.org/ (accessed September 2002).

OECD-Statistics (2001a) Measuring capital – OECD manual: measurement of capital stocks, consumption of fixed capital and capital services, pp. 1–132. Available at http://lysander.sourceoecd.org/ (accessed April 2002).

OECD-Statistics (2001b) Measuring capital – OECD manual: measurement of capital stocks, consumption of fixed capital and capital services, pp. 1–132. Available at http://lysander.sourceoecd.org/ (accessed April 2002).

OECD-Statistics (2001c) Measuring productivity – OECD manual: measurement of aggregate and industrial-level productivity growth, pp. 1–154. Available at http://lysander.sourceoecd.org/ (accessed April 2002).

Oum, T. H., Tretheway, M. W. and Zhang, Y. (1991) A note on capacity utilization and measurement of scale economies, *Journal of Business and Economic Statistic*, **9**, 119–23.

Oum, T. H. and Zhang, Y. (1991) Utilisation of quasi-fixed inputs and estimation of cost functions – an application to airline costs, *Journal of Transport Economics and Policy*, **25**, 121–38.

Parisio, L. (1999) A comparative analysis of European railroad efficiency: a cost frontier approach, *Applied Economics*, **31**, 815–23.

Perelman, S. and Pestieau, P. (1988) Technical performance in public enterprises – a comparison study of railways and postal services, *European Economic Review*, **32**, 432–41.

Preston, J. (1994) Does size matter? A case study of Western European railways, UTSG Conference, Institute for Transport Studies, University of Leeds.

Sánchez, P. C. and Villarroya, J. M. (2000) Efficiency, technical change and productivity in the European rail sector: a stochastic frontier approach, *International Journal of Transport Economics*, **XXVII**, 55–76.

Schmidt, P. and Sickles, R. C. (1984) Production frontier and panel data, *Journal of Business and Economic Statistics*, **2**, 367–74.

Uden, M. V. (2001) The European railway stock lists, the european railway server. Available at http://www.railfaneurope.net/list_frameset.html (accessed December 2001).

UIC (1972–1999) *International Railway Statistics*, International Union of Railways, Paris.

Vellturo, C. A., Berndt, E. R., Frielaender, A. F., Chiang, J. S. W. and Showalter, M. H. (1992) Deregulation, mergers, and cost savings in Class I US railroads, 1974–1986, *Journal of Economics and Management Strategy*, **1**, 339–69.

World Bank (2002) World Development Indicators. Available at http://www.worldbank.org/ (accessed August 2002).

## Appendix: Railway Firms

| | |
|---|---|
| BR | British Railways |
| CFF | Swiss Federal Railways |
| CFL | Luxembourg National Railway Company |
| CIE | Irish Transport Company |
| CP | Portuguese Railway Company |
| DB | German Federal Railway |
| CH | Hellenic Railway Organisation – Greece |
| DSB | Danish State Railways |
| FS | Italian State Railways |
| NS | Netherlands Railways |
| NSB | Norwegian State Railways |
| ÖBB | Austrian Federal Railways |
| RENFE | Spanish National Railway System |
| SJ | Swedish State Railway |
| SNCB | Belgian National Railway Company |
| SNCF | French National Railway Company |
| VR | Finish State Railways |
| TCDD | Turkish Republic State Railways |
| BC | Belarus Railways |
| BDZ | Bulgarian State Railways |
| CD | Czech Republic Railways |
| CFR | Railways of Romania |
| EVR | Estonian Railways |
| MAV | Hungary State Railways |
| PKP | Polish State Railways |
| SZ | Slovenian Railways |
| ZSR | Slovak Republic Railways |

# Preventing competition because of 'solidarity': rhetoric and reality of airport investments in Spain

Germá Bel and Xavier Fageda

From a public interest perspective, there could be a justification for constraining market mechanisms with the aim of progressive redistribution. However, some policies might be based on selfish motivations of government agents. In this article, we empirically contrast if the infrastructure policy is based only on public interest motivations or if it is also based on the private motivations of policy makers. In this way, Spain infrastructure policy provides a useful policymaking field to test hypothesis about the behaviour of policy makers. We find some evidence regarding the strength of political motivations in explaining such behaviour. In fact, results from our analysis show that political motivations can eventually play a more relevant role than social welfare maximization.

## I. Introduction

Traditionally, airports have been seen as monopolistic infrastructures that hold tight control over flights with origins and destinations in their hinterlands. Consequently, neither economic analysis nor infrastructure policy used to consider competition as one of the relevant features of airports. Nowadays there exists a clear trend towards corporatization of airports. Like privatization, corporatization has been seen as a way to reform airports whose ownership and management have remained public. Within this context, competition has been seen as a powerful tool to stimulate efficiency.

Competition among airports at the international level is now a standard feature in all developed countries. Moreover, within each country airports compete to grow and win an increasing part of the business. Spain, alone among developed countries with more than one large airport, defies this pattern. Despite having a large population and several large airports, Spain air travel remains organized as a totally integrated network: airports are exclusively owned and managed by a State Owned Enterprise, Air Navigation Agency (AENA). Thus, competition among airports does not exist. The market has no role in issues such as pricing or resource allocation. Some of the more relevant features of airport management, such as investment decisions or prices policy, are decided on bureaucratic basis and approved by the Spanish Parliament together with the National Budget.[1]

Why is the Spanish system such an exception? No matter the political affiliation of the ruling party, politicians in charge and bureaucrats have regularly claimed that inter-territorial solidarity is the main

[1] Another relevant feature of airport management, slots' assignment to airlines, is decided by a commission made of 'AENA' top managers and direct representatives of the Ministry of Transport (Ministerio de Fomento).

rationale for their choice. Their story goes as follows: less developed areas in Spain must have airports for regional development. However, such areas cannot sustain airports costs. In this way, it is said that centralized management and allocation of funds would allow the surplus from the largest and most profitable airports to pay for the deficits incurred by the smallest and least profitable airports. In short, rich airports would be paying for keeping poor airports working. Is this what is actually happening?

As far as social welfare maximization is concerned, there could be a potential justification for constraining market mechanisms with the aim of progressive redistribution.[2] This brings us to a traditional conundrum of public policy; the trade-off between efficiency and equity. However, if we accept that the behaviour of public agents is aimed to their own interest, some policies designed to prevent competition might actually be based on selfish motivations, while justified on the grounds of progressive redistribution.

Through our analysis we will empirically contrast two competing explanations for the persistence of the unusual model in Spain. On the one hand, there does exist the public interest explanation. From the point of view of the 'general interest', market mechanisms would generate a less socially desirable level of airport operating facilities, and public intervention is needed to correct this 'market failure'. This would be consistent with the standard explanation by politicians and bureaucrats we have summarized above. However, our results show that choices of governments have been motivated by neither a progressive redistribution criterion nor the claim of supporting smaller airports.

On the other hand, we explore a public choice approach. Within that framework, the agents of governments are rational utility maximizers: politicians trying to maximize success in elections while bureaucrats, in this case AENA top managers, seek to maximize their own budget. As long as each group pursues its own-interests they will tend to resist institutional arrangements that might constrain their behaviour and enhance opportunities for efficient performance. Within our specific framework, introducing market mechanisms in the provision of public services would limit increases in the discretionary budgets in the control of bureaucrats (Niskanen, 1971). Our results provide evidence that governments distribute investment in airports so that they can increase their electoral support.

The idea of this work is related with the recent literature on regional allocation of public investments. Some recent works in this literature focus the attention on the traditional trade-off between equity and efficiency in public policies (Yamano and Ohkawara, 2000; de la Fuente, 2005). Our article is more closely related to the literature that analyses not just the efficiency-equity issue but also the role of political factors in explaining the regional allocation of public investment in infrastructure.[3] Kemmerling and Stephan (2002) show that, along with the equity objective, political support from citizens for the incumbent party in the central government is crucial in explaining the distribution of investment grants across cities. Castells and Solé (2005) find that political considerations promote differences in the attractiveness of regions to the central government in such a way that a deviation from the efficiency-equity rule can arise.

Certainly, the efficiency-equity trade-off relationship in infrastructure policies is a basic and relevant story. But it is not the sole story to be found in the regional allocation of public investments in infrastructure. This article adds to the literature by analysing a scenario where infrastructure policy may pursue neither efficiency nor equity.

Indeed, airport management in Spain is embodied with specific features that allow us to test a hypothesis about the behaviour of government agents. Since one of the main consequences of integrated airport management is that decisions about investment are centralized in the national government, we want to disentangle the following questions: Is the allocation of investments in Spanish airports effectively based on redistributive purposes? Which factors explain actual allocations? Is airport policy in Spain consistent with publicly announced objectives?

To advance our research we organize the article as follows. First, we briefly review the main features of the Spanish system of airport management and

[2] One could ask whether alternative systems of grants and subsidies could work better to make up the deficits of the nonprofitable airports. In every other country, no matter its system of management and funding, these kinds of tools are used so that unprofitable airports can operate. We do not go with detail into this, since this departs from the central questions in our article.

[3] Another similar strand of literature but less related to our work is that focussed on the political motivations with regard to grant allocations between different government levels. Empirical applications of this issue can be found, for example, in Worthington and Dollery (1998), Case (2001), Costa *et al.* (2003) and Johansson (2003).

finance and analyse it within the framework of international models. Then we proceed with our empirical analysis. Initially, we focus on economic factors, and subsequently, political factors. Finally, we summarize our main results and draw out their main implications.

## II. Airport management in Spain: the exception to the rule

High quality airport facilities foster intercity agglomeration economies and influence the location decision of firms, especially those in knowledge intensive sectors (Button *et al.*, 1999; Brueckner, 2003).[4] Hence, the link between the quality of airport facilities and urban economic growth could provide a rationale for guaranteeing airport facilities in less developed regions. In a similar way, scale economies could provide a motivation to support small airports. Indeed, high fixed costs associated with airport operations may help in explaining the existence of a positive relationship (although not necessarily a linear one) between air traffic and airport profitability – and so the amount of self-finance available for investments (European Commission, 2002). Thus, airports that generate a low volume of traffic may not be profitable

Managing airports as an integrated national network arises as a, though by no means the only, possible strategy of regional policy. In fact, as shown in Table 1, European airports that belong to large national airport networks are usually managed on individual basis. This is the case for Germany, France, Italy and the United Kingdom (and other large Anglo-Saxon countries such as the USA, Canada and Australia). Autonomy is also the case for the Netherlands, Ireland, Denmark, Belgium and Austria. Indeed, in all these countries grants and subsidies to small airports and/or airports located in poor regions are often available from more than one government level.

Where a national network is run in a centralized way, it has just one large airport. Such a situation exists in Sweden, Portugal, Finland and most of the new accession countries. Spanish is unique, because it is the only European country with several large cities and airports in which all airports are managed by a single national agency.

Indeed, the Spanish airports and AENA owns and manages more than 40 commercial airports in Spain. Air Navigation Agency is a public entity belonging to the Ministry in charge of transportation issues, and it enjoys an autonomous legal and economic status. Investment decisions are centralized and are financed through the surplus of the entire airport system.[5] In this way, there is a system of nontransparent, cross-subsidization across Spanish airports. Importantly, politicians have justified centralized management on the grounds that it supports territorial cohesion. The possibility of competition between airports or the benefits of a differentiated commercial policy is not recognized.

Where airports are managed on market criteria, the amount of investment in each airport should be strongly associated with the revenues obtained from local operations. Such revenues are fundamentally determined by the amount of traffic at the airport. On the contrary, when a territorial cohesion criterion is in place, less-developed regions should receive more resources for investment than their share of traffic would justify. Furthermore, scale economies should justify an investment allocation outcome in which large (profitable) airports cross-subsidize small (unprofitable) airports.

Some facts about the investment behaviour of AENA cast doubts about political claims concerning the integrated airport network as a guarantee of the territorial cohesion criterion.

The first year of activity of AENA was 1992 (in the previous period, the Ministry in charge of transportation issues was the unique responsible for airport management). Table 2 shows the relationship between investment and passenger traffic for the Spanish airport network in the period 1992 to 2004, and the corresponding relative position of

[4] In a more general context, a great number of studies have analysed the impact of public capital stock on private sector productivity [e.g. Aschauer's (1989), Duffy-Deno and Ebberts (1991), Garcia-Milà and McGuire (1992), Holtz-Eakin (1994), Flores de Frutos *et al.* (1998), Miller and Tsoukis (2001), Milbourne *et al.* (2003)]. In general terms, such impact is considered to be relevant although there is no agreement on the precise elasticities estimated.

[5] Investment decisions are taken as follows: The Budget proposed by the Spanish Government to the Parliament displays in an annex the investments that AENA intends to implement during the fiscal year. The Spanish Parliament can either approve or reject this proposal, which cannot be modified. It is worth mentioning that there is no allocation of funds from the budget, since all AENA investment is financed with aeronautical fees and commercial revenues.

**Table 1. Major airports and air traffic of passengers in EU-25 countries**

| Country | Number of top 50 EU airports. 2002 | Total passengers ($10^3$). 2003 | National passengers ($10^3$).2003 | International passengers ($10^3$).2003 | Airport management | Airport ownership |
|---|---|---|---|---|---|---|
| United Kingdom | 8 | 177 946 | 24 416 | 153 530 | Individual | private, regional gov. |
| Germany | 8 | 121 136 | 21 193 | 99 943 | Individual | private, regional gov. and national gov. |
| Spain | 9 | 120 248 | 31 324 | 88 925 | **Centralized** | national government |
| France | 6 | 96 296 | 26 712 | 69 584 | Individual | national gov. (Paris), chambers of commerce (rest) |
| Italy | 6 | 73 912 | 24 477 | 49 436 | Individual | private, regional gov. |
| Netherlands | 1 | 41 168 | 154 | 41 014 | Individual | regional gov, national government |
| Greece | 1 | 28 237 | 5030 | 23 207 | Individual | private (Athens), national go. (others) |
| Sweden | 1 | 20 441 | 6875 | 13 567 | **Centralized** | national government |
| Ireland | 1 | 20 010 | 812 | 19 197 | Individual | national government |
| Denmark | 1 | 19 575 | 1606 | 17 969 | Individual | private, national government |
| Portugal | 2 | 17 739 | 2853 | 14 886 | **Centralized** | national government |
| Austria | 1 | 15 799 | 548 | 15 251 | Individual | private, national gov. |
| Belgium | 1 | 15 087 | 2 | 15 085 | Individual | private, regional gov. |
| Finland | 1 | 10 516 | 2701 | 7816 | **Centralized** | national government |
| Czech Republic | 1 | 7761 | 161 | 7600 | Individual | national gov. (Prague)/regional gov. (others) |
| Poland | | 7067 | Na | Na | **Centralized** | national government |
| Cyprus | 1 | 6077 | 1 | 6076 | **Centralized** | national government |
| Hungary | 1 | 5010 | 0 | 5010 | **Individual** | private |
| Malta | – | 2648 | 44 | 2604 | **Individual** | private |
| Luxembourg | – | 1449 | 0 | 1449 | **Centralized** | national government |
| Slovenia | – | 920 | Na | Na | Individual | private, national gov. |
| Lithuania | – | 722 | 1 | 721 | **Centralized** | national government |
| Latvia | – | 712 | 0 | 712 | **Centralized** | national government |
| Estonia | – | 710 | 15 | 695 | **Centralized** | national government |
| Slovakia | – | 626 | 32 | 594 | **Centralized** | national government |

*Source*: Eurostat, European Commission (2002, 2006) and airports web pages.

each region in terms of economic development. We present the results aggregated on a regional basis because the regional level is the one for which most of the variables needed for further analysis are available (individual information for each airport is available upon request). Column (3) shows the relationship for every Spanish region between share of total investment and share of total passengers.

In the period 1992 to 2004, the richest Spanish region with the largest airport, Madrid, accumulated almost 60% of total investment but only 22% of total traffic. The ratio (investment share)/(traffic share) is certainly high: 2.60. Overall, airports in the less developed Spanish regions (Extremadura, Andalusia, Galicia, Murcia and Asturias) received a share of investment lower than their share of air traffic generated. Thus, the allocation of airport investments in Spain does not seem to follow the territorial cohesion criterion regularly used by politicians to justify centralized management. Furthermore, several lightly populated regions with low levels of air traffic have an investment/traffic ratio smaller than one. In short, we must go look further to determine whether airport investments decisions have been effectively aimed to other objectives.

## III. Empirical analysis: determinants of the regional allocation of airport investments

In order to obtain an equation that explains the allocation of airport investments across regions, we consider that policy makers of the central government maximize an objective function. Such objective function could be aimed to social purposes and/or political interests since both aspects could affect the utility of those agents.

To this regard, we follow the approach of Bernham and Craig (1987). The objective function of the central government is defined over

**Table 2. Spanish airport and regional data, 1992-2004. Mean annual values over the period**

| Region* | (1) Share of total investment (Spain = 817 114 $10^3$ constant euros) | (2) Share of total traffic (Spain = 120 291 150 passengers) | (3) Ratio investment-traffic (1/2) | (4) Share of total population (Spain = 38 617 092 inhabitants) | (5) Share of total GDP (Spain = 557 063 815 $10^3$ constant euros) | (6) Relative wealth index (5/4) |
|---|---|---|---|---|---|---|
| Madrid (1) | 57.81% | 22.36% | **2.60** | 13.61% | 17.72% | **1.30** |
| Catalonia (3) | 14.60% | 14.78% | 0.99 | 16.31% | 19.54% | **1.20** |
| Canary islands (8) | 9.06% | 22.31% | 0.41 | 4.38% | 4.12% | 0.94 |
| Balears islands (3) | 6.62% | 18.98% | 0.35 | 2.14% | 2.56% | **1.20** |
| Andalusia (6) | 3.79% | 9.81% | 0.39 | 18.97% | 14.10% | 0.74 |
| Basque C. (3) | 2.44% | 2.07% | **1.18** | 5.46% | 6.61% | **1.21** |
| Valencian C. (2) | 2.15% | 6.08% | 0.35 | 10.69% | 10.12% | 0.95 |
| Galicia (3) | 1.33% | 1.90% | 0.70 | 7.13% | 5.69% | 0.80 |
| Asturias (1) | 0.54% | 0.55% | 0.98 | 2.82% | 2.42% | 0.86 |
| Castille & Leon (3) | 0.38% | 0.21% | **1.82** | 6.51% | 6.05% | 0.93 |
| Aragon (1) | 0.36% | 0.20% | **1.82** | 3.11% | 3.34% | **1.07** |
| Cantabria (1) | 0.20% | 0.19% | **1.04** | 1.39% | 1.33% | 0.95 |
| Navarra (1) | 0.15% | 0.22% | 0.69 | 1.41% | 1.76% | **1.25** |
| Murcia (1) | 0.15% | 0.19% | 0.80 | 2.51% | 2.97% | 0.85 |
| Extremadura (1) | 0.01% | 0.03% | 0.54 | 2.79% | 1.84% | 0.66 |

*Source*: Own elaboration on information obtained from the web page of the Ministerio de Fomento (Spanish ministry of transports), the Spanish statistics Institute (INE) and the web page of IVIE-FBBVA.
*Note*: * In parenthesis, we indicate the number of airports of the region that provide commercial traffic.

infrastructure outcomes in region $i$ ($i = 1, \ldots, I$) from a given country at period $t$ ($t = 1, \ldots, T$) and can be expressed through the following form:

$$W_t = \sum_i O_{it} \quad (1)$$

where $O_{it}$ is a vector of infrastructure outcomes.[6] This expression implies that the central government maximizes infrastructure outcomes. The first derivative with respect to $O_{it}$ is assumed to be positive ($\partial W_t / \partial O_{it} > 0$).

The central government's maximization problem is subject to a resource constraint. This implies that total investments cannot be higher than the total resources available for that purpose:

$$\sum_i INV_{it} = R_t \quad (2)$$

where $R_t$ are total resources available at period $t$ and $INV_{it}$ are airport investments across regions.

Infrastructure outcomes across regions depend on investments made on them, as well as on specific factors such as the intensity of use. Additionally, infrastructure outcomes will also depend on the objectives of the central government since it is needed to consider not only the aggregate effect of infrastructure policies but also its impact on different regions, for example on regions with different income levels.

In this way, the allocation of investments in infrastructures across regions should depend on a vector of regional characteristics at period $t$, $Z_{it}$. Additionally, each element of the vector of regional characteristics may be weighted by a parameter, $\alpha_Z$, such that unequal concern of the central government about different variables (Z), which values may be different – or not – from one region to another, can arise.

Hence we can derive a general specification of the investment equation that is going to be tested in our empirical analysis:

$$\frac{INV_{it}}{R_t} = \sum_i \alpha_Z Z_{it} \quad (3)$$

where $Z_{it} = GDP_{it}$, $PAX_{it}$, $NAC_{it}$, $INCUM_{it}$, $CORRE_{it}$ (See definitions below).

Given the value of $R_t$, $\alpha_Z > 0$ implies that $\partial INV_{it} / \partial Z_{it} > 0$, while $\alpha_{Z'} < 0$ implies that $\partial INV_{it} / \partial Z'_{it} < 0$. In this context, we must consider the elements of the vector of regional characteristics.

Gross Domestic Product per capita (*GDP*) and air traffic (*PAX*), which in the empirical analysis refers to the percentage of passengers carried in the

[6] For simplicity, henceforth the vector of infrastructure outcomes is defined as a variable.

airports from a region with respect to the total traffic in the national network, are included in this vector. Indeed, where territorial cohesion criteria influence the airport investment decisions of the central government, regions with low product per capita should receive more investment than regions with high product per capita. Furthermore, where airport investments are aimed to support small airports those investments in a region should increase less than proportionally to the traffic generated for the airports of that region.

In addition to this, the central government could try to maximize the surpluses of domestic rather than international passengers, since the latter are not incorporated in its objective function. Thus, the proportion of national traffic with respect to the total traffic (*NAC*) should be included in the vector of regional characteristics.

Finally, the political clout of each region, due to the popularity of the central government's incumbent party in the corresponding region (*INCUM*) or due to the correspondence between the incumbent party in the central and regional governments (*CORRE*), may play a central role in the allocation choice of public resources of the central government as we will see below. It is worth noting that in the empirical analysis *INCUM* refers to the percentage of votes in the last general elections for the incumbent party in the central government in the corresponding regions of the sample, while *CORRE* is a dummy variable that takes value 1 when there is a correspondence between the incumbent party in the central government and the incumbent party in the regional government.

Hence Equation (3) can be expressed as follows:

$$\frac{INV_{it}}{R_t} = \mu + \alpha_{GDP}GDP + \alpha_{PAX}PAX + \alpha_{NAC}NAC + \alpha_{INCUM}INCUM + \alpha_{CORRE}CORRE + \varepsilon_{it} \quad (4)$$

where $\varepsilon_{it}$ is a random error term. From our analysis the following hypotheses can be established, which we test in further sections:

**Hypothesis I**: Consistently with claims of progressive redistribution, regions with low product per capita should receive more investment than regions with high product per capita. According to this hypothesis, $\alpha_{GDP}$ in Equation (4) should take a value lower than 0.

**Hypothesis II**: If investments are aimed to support small airports, those investments in a region should increase less than proportionally to the traffic generated for the airports of that region. According to this hypothesis, $\alpha_{PAX}$ in Equation (4) should take a value lower than 1.

**Hypothesis III**: Government looks after cross-subsidies from international passengers to national travellers. Consistently with this, investments should be higher in regions with higher ratios domestic traffic/total traffic. According to this hypothesis, $\alpha_{NAC}$ in Equation (4) should take a value greater than 0.

**Hypothesis IV**: Investment allocations are used to enhance political support. Consistently with this, investments should be higher in regions where the ruling party has strong electoral support and/or the regional government is held by the same party holding national government. According to this hypothesis, $\alpha_{INCUM}$ and $\alpha_{CORRE}$ in Equation (4) should take a value greater than 0.

Hypothesis I, II are consistent with an objective function of policy-makers of the central government that fits a social welfare function, while hypothesis IV is consistent with a welfare function of policy-makers that fits with a political rent-seeking behaviour. Hypothesis III is consistent with an objective function of policy-makers that fits both with a social welfare function and a political rent-seeking behaviour.

### *Economic factors*

It is of central interest in our empirical analysis to examine any type of cross-subsidization that can take place between the regional networks of the Spanish airport system. Hence Equation (3) can be expressed for the empirical analysis in the following way:

$$\frac{INV_{it}}{R_t} = \mu + \alpha_{GDP}GDP_{\text{it}} + \alpha_{PAX}PAX_{\text{it}} + \alpha_{NAC}NAC_{\text{it}} + \varepsilon_{it} \quad (5)$$

where $INV_{\text{it}}/R_t$ refers to the percentage of investment made in airports from region $i$ with respect to the total investment in the national airport network. The explanatory variables are defined as follows:

1. $GDP_{it}$: Gross Domestic Product per capita of region $i$.
2. $PAX_{it}$: Percentage of annual passengers carried in the airports from region $i$ with respect to the total annual traffic in the national airport network.
3. $NAC_{\text{it}}$: Percentage of national passengers carried in the airports from region $i$ with respect to the total annual traffic in the regional airport network.

The error term ($\varepsilon_{it}$) is assumed to be independent and identically distributed over regions and time, with mean 0 and variance $\sigma^2{}_{\varepsilon}$. However, we test (and correct if pertinent) these assumptions in the empirical analysis.

In order to estimate this model, we have constructed a panel data for the period 1992 to 2004 for the 15 Spanish regions with airports. This period captures the first year of activity of the current airport management system and it is long enough to smoothen out distortions from single projects in a particular period. To this regard, as Fig 1 shows, the huge amount of investments made in the last 6 years in comparison to the previous years allows claiming that initial conditions should not play a relevant role.[7]

Data on the territorial allocation of investment have been obtained from the Ministry of Transport; data for Gross Domestic Product per capita have been obtained from the Spanish Statistics Institute. Finally, data of airport traffic have been obtained from AENA. Table A-1 in Appendix shows the description and summary statistics of the variables used for estimating our investment equation.[8]

Table 3 shows the results of our estimates of the investment equation, while Table 4 indicates the elasticities than can be inferred from them. Column 1 presents the results of the estimates when using the Feasible Generalized Least Squares estimator (FGLS). The tests about the validity of the error term assumptions indicate the existence of heteroskedasticity and cross-sectional correlation. A problem of serial autocorrelation does not seem to take place. Column 2 displays the results of the estimates when using the FGLS estimator with the error term corrected for heteroskedasticity and cross-sectional correlation. In this setting, Betz and Katz (1995) show that FGLS estimator involves an underestimation of standard errors. In column 3, we present the results of the estimates when using the Ordinary Least Squares (OLS) estimator with Panel Corrected Standard Errors (PCSE). This latter estimator corrects both for heteroskedasticity and cross-sectional correlation in the error-term and for underestimation of standard errors.

As could be expected, the three estimators provide similar values of the estimated coefficients but different standard errors. Correction for heteroskedasticity and cross-sectional correlation using the

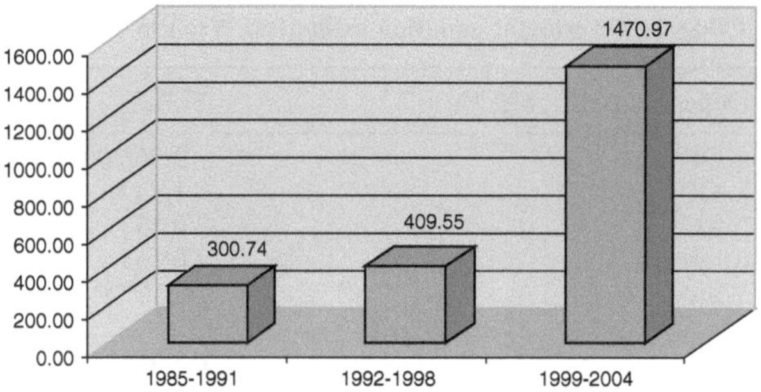


**Fig. 1. Total investments in the Spanish airport network, 1985–2004. Mean annual values over the period (millions of euros 2004)**
*Source*: Own elaboration on information obtained from Ministerio de Fomento. Data in the period 1985 to 1993 is available at the web page of IVIE-FBBVA, while data in the period 1994 to 2004 is available at the web page of Ministerio de Fomento.

FGLS estimator reduces the standard errors (see columns 1 and 2 of Table 3). The estimation with the PCSE estimator is more efficient than that using FGLS without correcting for heteroskedasticity and cross-sectional correlation (see columns 1 and 3 of Table 3) but tends to increase the standard errors obtained with the FGLS estimator with robust standard errors (see columns 2 and 3 of Table 3). In any case, statistical significance of all explanatory variables is not affected for the calculation of the standard errors.

All variables are significant and the overall explanatory power of the equation estimated is reasonably high, regardless of the econometric technique used. Our results show clear evidence that progressive redistribution is not relevant to the airport investment choice of the central government. Indeed, the percentage of total investments in a region seems to increase when product per capita of that region also increases, which is not consistent with hypothesis I above.

In addition to this, we do not find evidence that airport investments are motivated by a scale economies argument (in order to support regions with the smallest airports) because the percentage of total investments increases more than proportionally to the output generated for each regional airport network. Indeed, 10 percentage points increase in the share of

[7] The allocation of investments across regions in the period 1985 to 2004 is similar to that obtained in the period 1992 to 2004. Data for traffic is not available before 1992 so that the empirical analysis is restricted to the period 1992 to 2004.

[8] There is a possible simultaneity bias for the *GDP* variable as long as airport investment can be a determinant of economic growth. However, our units of measurement are flows rather than stocks so that annual investments in airports have a very low weight on the total stock of infrastructure, which must be one of the main determinants of economic growth. In addition, it is worth taking into account that airport effects on economic growth are particularly strong at a microeconomic level (greater market access, travel time reductions, attraction of high-tech firms and so on). Additionally, we argue that the *PAX* variable should not be endogenous either. Indeed, air traffic in a year can be dependent on airport capacity as a stock but not on the contemporaneous annual investments in the airport, which influences only partially that stock for the following years.

**Table 3. Investment equation estimates. $N = 195$**

| Dependent variable: INV | FGLS (1) | | FGLS[1] (2) | | PCSE[2] (3) | |
|---|---|---|---|---|---|---|
| GDP | 3.96e-06 | (1.56e-06)** | 3.93e-06 | (4.03e-08)*** | 3.96e-06 | (8.58e-07)*** |
| PAX | 1.349 | (0.10)*** | 1.342 | (0.01)*** | 1.349 | (0.06)*** |
| NAC | 0.130 | (0.03)*** | 0.128 | (0.002)*** | 0.130 | (0.01)*** |
| Intercept | −0.163 | (0.03)*** | −0.161 | (0.003)*** | −0.163 | (0.02)*** |
| Wald1 | 257.77*** | | 69 350.32*** | | 1373.81*** | |
| $R^2$ | – | | – | | 0.57 | |
| BP | 453.986*** | | – | | – | |
| Wald2 | 1.15e+05*** | | – | | – | |
| $D_p$ | 1.18 | | – | | – | |

*Notes*: [1] SEs robust to heteroskedasticity and contemporaneous correlation.
[2] OLS with PCSE (Standard errors robust to heteroskedasticity and contemporaneous correlation).
SEs in parenthesis
***, ** and * significance at 1, 5 and 10%, respectively.
Wald1 = Wald test ($\chi^2$) of joint significance; BP = Breusch–Pagan LM test of cross-sectional correlation; Wald2 = Wald test for group wise heteroskedasticity; $D_p$ = Bhargava *et al.* (1982) test for serial autocorrelation (modified Durbin-Watson test).

**Table 4. Estimated elasticities (evaluated at sample means)**

| Dependent variable: INV | FGLS (1) | FGLS[1] (2) | PCSE[2] (3) |
|---|---|---|---|
| GDP | 0.80 (0.32)** | 0.79 (0.01)*** | 0.80 (0.19)** |
| PAX | 1.35 (0.16)*** | 1.34 (0.02)*** | 1.35 (0.09)*** |
| NAC | 1.31 (0.33)*** | 1.29 (0.03)*** | 1.31 (0.20)*** |

*Notes*: [1] SEs robust to heteroskedasticity and contemporaneous correlation.
[2] OLS with PCSE (Standard errors robust to heteroskedasticity and contemporaneous correlation).
SEs in parenthesis.
***, ** and * significance at 1, 5 and 10%, respectively.

the total traffic of the airport network implies about 13 percentage points increase in the share of the total investments made in the airport network. Holding the other factors constant, the percentage of total investments is higher in regional airport networks with a higher proportion of national traffic. These results are consistent with our hypothesis III above but not with our hypothesis II.

Table A-2 in Appendix provides additional evidence of the results obtained in our estimates of the investment equation. In this way, Table A-2 presents airport financial data for the last two years in which this information is available, 1997 and 1998.[9] From the data, it can be observed that cross-subsidization across Spanish airports does not take place from high-profitability to low-profitability regional networks, as expected if scale economies were controlled. Actually, the most profitable airport has the highest traffic-investment ratio, while many of the nonprofitable airports have traffic-investment rates lower than one. In fact, data from this table, along with the results of the investment equation estimates, allow us to infer a type of redistribution not mentioned by Spanish airport authorities. All profitable regional networks with low investment-traffic ratios (Balearic Islands, Canary Islands, Andalusia and C. Valenciana) have a common feature. They all have, at least, one large airport focussed on tourist traffic. This fact seems to confirm that cross-subsidization from international to domestic passengers is taken place in the Spanish airport system.

### Political factors

Since neither progressive redistribution nor scale economies seem to be the real objective of the centralization of the Spanish airport network, further analysis is needed to understand the objectives of Spanish airport authorities. Several studies (Cadot *et al.*, 1999; Kemmerling and Stephan, 2002; Castells

[9] Since the late nineties AENA and the Spanish Government have been extremely reluctant to provide financial information on individual airports. Indeed, one of the consequences of an integrated management is that it makes possible for governments to be less transparent and, thus, less subject to democratic control.

**Table 5. Investment equation estimates. $N = 195$**

| Dependent variable: INV | PCSE[1] (1) | | PCSE[1] (2) | | PCSE[1] (3) | |
|---|---|---|---|---|---|---|
| GDP | 3.65e-06 | (9.44e-07)*** | 3.81e-06 | (8.37e-07)*** | 3.66e-06 | (7.54e-07)** |
| PAX | 1.40 | (0.08)*** | 1.36 | (0.07)*** | 1.44 | (0.08)*** |
| NAC | 0.14 | (0.01)*** | 0.13 | (0.02)*** | 0.15 | (0.01)*** |
| INCUM | 0.13 | (0.05)** | – | | – | |
| SWING | – | | 0.0002 | (0.0004) | – | |
| CORRE | – | | – | | 0.06 | (0.01)*** |
| Intercept | −0.22 | (0.04)*** | −0.16 | (0.02)*** | −0.21 | (0.03)*** |
| Wald | 1231.96*** | | 1291.71*** | | 1373.81*** | |
| $R^2$ | 0.58 | | 0.57 | | 0.62 | |

*Notes*: [1] OLS with PCSE (SEs robust to heteroskedasticity and contemporaneous correlation).
SEs in parenthesis.
***, ** and * significance at 1, 5 and 10%, respectively.

and Solé, 2005) show that political motivations based on the self-interest of the public decision-makers can play a crucial role in the allocation of the stock of infrastructure across regions.

Where election systems are based on proportional rules, as is the case in Spain, politicians are motivated to maximize the number of votes their party obtains in highly populated electoral districts.[10] Following Grossman (1994), the incumbent party in the central government may allocate public resources in order to buy the support of voters and political agents across regions. *Ceteris paribus*, more resources will be invested in those regions that have the most - and most valuable - political capital to offer. Such political capital will be greater where the support for the incumbent party in the central government is also greater, and it will be even more valuable where a correspondence exists between the incumbent party in the central government and the incumbent party in the regional government.

Alternatively, some studies argue that the central government could invest more in the regions where the closeness in elections between the two main parties is higher (Dalhberg and Johansson, 2002; Johansson, 2003). Under this hypothesis, the incumbent party tries to obtain higher rates of returns – in terms of votes - from its investments.

In order to capture these political factors, we add to Equation (5) the following political variables:

1. *INCUM:* Percentage of votes in the last general elections for the incumbent party in the central government in the corresponding regions of the sample.
2. *SWING:* The difference in the percentage of votes between the two main parties in the general elections across regions.
3. *CORRE:* Dummy variable that takes value 1 when there is a correspondence between the incumbent party in the central government and the incumbent party in the regional government.

Data for the political variables have been obtained from the website of the Ministry of Domestic Affairs (Ministerio del Interior). It is expected a positive sign in the coefficient of variables *INCUM* and *CORRE*, as specified in our hypothesis IV above, while it is expected a negative sign in the coefficient of the variable *SWING*.

The political variables are estimated separately in order to avoid multicollineality. Tables 5 and 6 show the results of our estimates of Equation (5) with the addition of the political variables. In columns 1 and 2, we show the results when the political variables added are *INCUM* and *SWING*, respectively. In column 3, we show results when the political variable added is *CORRE*. Regarding the econometric techniques used, we follow the same procedure to section on 'Economic factors'. As in the previous estimation without political variables, the tests about the validity of the error term assumptions indicate the existence of heteroskedasticity and cross-sectional correlation but not a problem of serial autocorrelation. In order to clarify the exposition, we just present the results when using the OLS Estimator with PCSE. As in the previous estimation without political variables, the values of the coefficients and its statistical significance are similar to those obtained when using the FGLS estimator.

[10] Where election systems are based on majority rule, as it happens in the USA and UK, for instance, politicians try to maximize the probability of winning seats in a unipersonal electoral district.

**Table 6. Estimated elasticities (evaluated at sample means)**

| Dependent variable: *INV* | PCSE[1] (1) | PCSE[1] (2) | PCSE[1] (3) |
|---|---|---|---|
| *GDP* | 0.74 (0.21)*** | 0.77 (0.18)*** | 0.74 (0.15)*** |
| *PAX* | 1.40 (0.13)*** | 1.36 (0.10)*** | 1.44 (0.12)*** |
| *NAC* | 1.44 (0.23)*** | 1.33 (0.20)*** | 1.51 (0.19)*** |
| *INCUM* | 0.82 (0.34)** | – | – |
| *SWING* | – | 0.02 (0.05) | – |
| *CORRE* | – | – | 0.46 (0.13)*** |

*Notes*: [1] OLS with PCSE (SEs robust to heteroskedasticity and contemporaneous correlation).
SEs in parenthesis.
***, ** and * significance at 1, 5 and 10%, respectively.

Results for the economic variables do not change substantially in relation to those obtained in the specification without political variables. The variable capturing the influence of partisan support, *INCUM*, is statistically and economically significant. Indeed, 10 percentage points increase in the percentage of votes of the incumbent party in a region implies about 8 percentage points increase in the share of the total investments made in the airport network. Thus, we find some evidence that partisan support could play an important role in the investment allocation choices of the central government. Indeed, the incumbent party in the central government seems to compensate regions for partisan support in order to assure votes.

Results for the variable that captures the difference in the percentage of votes between the two main parties in the general elections across regions, *SWING*, show that such effect is, in our context, not relevant. We believe this is not surprising in our analysis, since swing voters are of paramount importance within the framework of one-seat elections systems, where one vote gives the majority. This is not the case in Spain, where jurisdictions are multi-seat and seats are assigned by means of a proportional system (with d'Hont correction). Because of this, maximization of absolute number of votes fits better than marginal changes due to swing voters.

The coefficient of the dummy variable capturing the correspondence between the incumbent party in the central government and the incumbent party in the regional government, *CORRE*, is also economically and statistically significant. Indeed, such correspondence implies almost 4 percentage points increase in the share of the total investments made in the airport network. Thus, political affiliation seems to favour better coordination between decision-makers at different territorial levels of government.

Overall, our results suggest that politics matter in the allocation of airport investments across regions. Divergence between the policy announced and the policy effectively implemented could be explained, at least to some extent, by a desire to maximize the contribution of that policy to the re-election chances of the incumbent party.

## IV. Concluding remarks

The Spanish model of airport management and finance is singular among comparable developed countries. Spain is unique among countries with several large cities and important airports, in that its system is strictly centralized and publicly owned. This peculiar institutional setting prevents competition among Spanish airports, and policy makers and bureaucrats in charge of the system rhetorically justify it on grounds of inter-territorial solidarity.

Through our empirical analysis of the determinants of airport investments in Spain across regions, we find that the choices of the central government have been motivated by neither a progressive redistribution criterion nor the demands of supporting smaller airports. Indeed, *ceteris paribus* high-income regions receive relatively more public resources than low-income regions. In addition to this, we find evidence that investment increases more than proportionally to the output generated by the regional airport networks, while our data shows that cross-subsidization from high-profitability airports to low-profitability regional networks does not seem to take place. On the contrary, we find that cross-subsidization arises from international to domestic passengers.

Given that economic factors do not explain the allocation of investments across regions, we pay attention to the influence of political motivations. We find some evidence that the incumbent party in the central government could try to maximize support from regional citizens. Indeed, more public resources seem to be invested in those regions where the support for the party in central government is greater. In addition to this, more public resources are invested in those regions where the incumbent party in the central government and the incumbent party in the regional government are the same.

Rich and big airports do not pay to keep poor and small airports working. According to our results, solidarity seems to be merely a rhetorical excuse to prevent competition among Spanish airports. In fact, competition would constrain discretionary power of policy-makers and bureaucrats over management and budgets. We are aware that the public choice paradigm for explaining policy-making is too simple and naïve, and policy processes are much more complex than can be explained by the self-interested policy-maker alone. Nevertheless, when analysing why the system of airport management and finance in Spain is different from any other comparable country, we do not find much more than rhetoric about solidarity to prevent competition in order to maximize power and budget.

## Acknowledgements

Our research on infrastructure and competition has received financial support from the ministry of Education & Science SEJ2006-04985/ECON) and from the Fundación Rafael del Pino. Preliminary versions of this article have been presented at Cornell University, Harvard University and the 26th annual meeting of the European Public Choice Society. We are thankful to comments and suggestions from Joan Calzada, John Foote, José A. Gómez-Ibáñez, John Meyer, Antonio Miralles, Albert Solé, and Wu Xun. Usual disclaimer applies.

## References

Aschauer, D. A (1989) Is public expenditure productive?, *Journal of Monetary Economics*, **23**, 177–200.

Bel, G. (2002) Infrastructures i catalunya: alguns problemes escollits, *Revista Econòmica de Catalunya*, **45**, 11–25.

Berhman, J. and Craig, S. G. (1987) The distribution of public services: an exploration of local government preferences, *American Economic Review*, **77**, 37–49.

Betz, N. and Katz, J. N. (1995) What do (and not do) with time-series cross section data, *American Political Science Review*, **89**, 634–47.

Bhargava, A., Franzini, L. and Narendranathan, W. (1982) Serial correlation and fixed effects model, *Review of Economic Studies*, **49**, 533–49.

Brueckner, J. K. (2003) Airline traffic and urban economic development, *Urban Studies*, **40**, 1455–69.

Button, K., Lall, S., Stough, R. and Mark, T. (1999) High-technology employment and hub airports, *Journal of Air Transport Management*, **5**, 53–9.

Cadot, O., Roller, L. H. and Stephan, A. (1999) A political economy model of infrastructure allocation: an empirical assessment, *CEPR Discussion Paper*, **2336**, 1–33.

Case, A. (2001) Election goals and income redistribution: recent evidence from Albania, *European Economic Review*, **45**, 405–23.

Castells, A. and Solé, A. (2005) The regional allocation of infrastructure investment: the role of equity, efficiency and political factors, *European Economic Review*, **49**, 1165–205.

Costa, J., Rodriguez, E. and Lunapla, D. (2003) Political competition and *pork-barrel* politics in the allocation of public investment in Mexico, *Public Choice*, **116**, 185–204.

Dalhberg, M. and Johansson, E. (2002) On the vote-purchasing behavior of incumbent governments, *American Political Science Review*, **96**, 27–40.

de La Fuente, A. (2004) Second-best redistribution through public investment: a characterization, an empirical test and an application to the case of Spain, *Regional Science and Urban Economics*, **34**, 489–503.

Duffy-Deno, K. T. and Eberts, R. W. (1991) Public infrastructure and regional economic development: a simultaneous equation approach, *Journal of Urban Economics*, **30**, 329–43.

European Commission (2002) *Study on Competition between Airports and the Application of State Aid Rules*, Final report, Volumes I and II. European Commission, Brussels.

European Commission (2006) *Study on the Functioning of the Internal Market*. European Commission, Brussels.

Flores de Frutos, R., Gracia-Diez, M. and Perez-Amaral, T. (1998) Public capital stock and economic growth: an analysis of the Spanish economy, *Applied Economics*, **30**, 985–94.

Garcia-Mila, T. and McGuire, T. J. (1992) The contribution of publicly provided inputs to states' economies, *Regional Science and Urban Economics*, **22**, 229–41.

Grossman, P. (1994) A political theory of intergovernmental grants, *Public Choice*, **78**, 295–303.

Holtz-Eakin, D. (1994) Public-sector capital and the productivity puzzle, *Review of Economics and Statistics*, **76**, 12–21.

Johansson, E. (2003) Intergovernmental grants as a tactical instrument: empirical evidence from Swedish municipalities, *Journal of Public Economics*, **87**, 883–915.

Kemmerling, A. and Stephan, A. (2002) The contribution of local public infrastructure to private productivity and its political economy: evidence from a panel of large German cities, *Public Choice*, **113**, 403–24.

Milbourne, R., Otto, G. and Voss, G. (2003) Public investment and economic growth, *Applied Economics*, **35**, 527–40.

Miller, N. J and Tsoukis, C. (2001) On the optimality of public capital for long run economic growth: evidence from panel data, *Applied Economics*, **33**, 1117–29.
Niskanen, W. A. (1971) *Bureaucracy and Representative Government*, Aldine-Atherton, Chicago.
RVyT (1999), data in *Revista Viajes y Turismo*. **0**, 34.
Worthington, A. C. and Dollery, B. E. (1998) The political determination of inter-governmental grants in Australia, *Public Choice*, **94**, 299–315.
Yamano, N. and Ohkawara, T. (2000) The regional allocation of public investment: efficiency or equity?, *Journal of Regional Science*, **40**, 205–29.

## Appendix

**Table A1. Description of the variables and summary statistics (number of observations: 195)**

| Variable | Description | Mean | SD | Minimum value | Maximum value |
|---|---|---|---|---|---|
| *INV* | Total investment in airports of the region ($10^3$ euros) | 54 181.31 | 184 457.3 | 10.22 | 1 552 165 |
| *INV* | The share of investment of each region over total investment | 0.07 | 0.130 | 0 | 0.707 |
| *GDP* | Gross Domestic Product per capita in each region (euros) | 13 368 | 4054 | 6,408 | 23 889 |
| *PAX* | Total output (number of annual passengers carried in airports of the region) | 8 001 865 | 1.05e+07 | 15 547 | 3.81e+07 |
| *PAX* | The share of output of each region over total traffic | 0.07 | 0.08 | 0 | 0.26 |
| *NAC* | Percentage of national passengers over total traffic in airports of each region | 0.66 | 0.27 | 0.08 | 1 |
| *INCUM* | Percentage of votes in the general elections for the incumbent party in each region | 0.41 | 0.10 | 0.18 | 0.58 |
| *SWING* | The difference in the percentage of votes between the two main parties in the general elections across regions | 0.08 | 0.12 | −0.21 | 0.32 |
| *CORRE* | Correspondence between incumbent party in the central and regional government in each region | 0.52 | 0.50 | 0 | 1 |

**Table A2. Spanish airports operating profits. Millions of euros**

| Region | Operating results (Yearly average 1997–1998) | Share of the Total surplus generated by regions with surplus | Share of the net surplus of the network | Ratio investment-traffic |
|---|---|---|---|---|
| Madrid (1) | 89.7 | 39.3% | 45.7% | **2.60** |
| Canary Islands (8) | 40.7 | 17.8% | 20.8% | 0.41 |
| Catalonia (3) | 40.2 | 17.6% | 20.5% | 0.99 |
| Balears Islands (3) | 41.8 | 18.3% | 21.3% | 0.35 |
| Valencian C. (2) | 10.8 | 4.7% | 5.5% | 0.35 |
| Andalusia (6) | 5.1 | 2.2% | 2.6% | 0.39 |
| Surplus in system | **228.3** | **100.0%** | | |
| Extremadura (1) | −0.6 | | −0.3% | 0.54 |
| Castile & Leon (3) | −1.8 | | −0.9% | **1.82** |
| Murcia (1) | −2.0 | | −1.0% | 0.80 |
| Navarra (1) | −2.1 | | −1,1% | 0.69 |
| Asturias (1) | −2.6 | | −1.3% | 0.98 |
| Cantabria (1) | −2.8 | | −1.4% | **1.04** |
| Aragon (1) | −2.9 | | −1.5% | **1.82** |
| Galicia (3) | −6.9 | | −3.5% | 0.70 |
| Basque C.(3) | −7.6 | | −3.9% | **1.18** |
| Losses in system | −32.2 | | | |
| Network surplus | **196.1** | | **100.0%** | |

*Note 1*: 1998 is the last year for which financial data on operating results for individual airports has been made available by AENA. See footnote 11 above.
*Note 2*: Numbers in parenthesis indicate the number of commercial airports in each region.
*Source*: Own elaboration on AENA information (published in Bel, 2002 and RvyT, 1999).

# The market for used cars: new evidence of the lemons phenomenon

Winand Emons and George Sheldon

The lemons model assumes that owners of used cars have an information advantage over potential buyers with respect to the quality of their vehicles. Owners of bad cars try to sell them to ill-informed buyers while owners of good cars hold on to theirs. Consequently, the quality of traded automobiles tends to be sub-average. In contrast to previous empirical work, the following article investigates the behaviour of both buyers and sellers, testing for adverse selection by sellers and for quality uncertainty among buyers with a sample consisting of all 1985 cars registered in the Swiss canton of Basle City over the period 1985 to 1991. Our data supports both adverse selection and buyer uncertainty, suggesting that a lemons problem exists.

## I. Introduction

In Akerlof's (1970) 'lemons' model, buyers cannot distinguish between the qualities of used cars. Consequently, cars of different qualities sell at a common price that reflects the buyers' estimate of average quality. Sellers, on the other hand, know the quality of their vehicles, yet due to the nonobservability of car quality to buyers, can only sell their vehicles at the common price reflecting average quality. Hence, owners of automobiles of above-average quality hold on to their cars, while owners of 'lemons' attempt to sell theirs to ill-informed buyers. The average quality of traded cars is thus lower than that of the population of cars: good used cars are driven out of the market by bad ones. In the limit, this adverse selection phenomenon can even lead to market breakdown.

Empirical tests of the lemons model customarily concentrate on adverse selection. In this approach, the quality of traded goods is often compared with that of the population of goods from which they stem.[1] Examples include Bond (1982, 1984), who compares the maintenance frequency of pickup trucks purchased new and used; Lehn (1984), who finds evidence that free agents who switch teams spend more time on the disabled list than those retained by their clubs; or Greenwald and Glasspiegel (1983), who discover that

[1] Another common test for adverse selection is to investigate the prices of goods prone to adverse selection. If adverse selection holds then goods subject to negative selection should sell at a discount. This approach has been employed by, among others, Genesove (1993), who compares the prices of used cars sold in the wholesale used car market by used car dealers and by new-car dealers, respectively; Chezum and Wimmer (1997), who compare the auction prices of horses sold by breeders who also race horses with those sold by breeders who do not; and Gibbons and Katz (1991), who compare the subsequent wages of workers displaced by plant closings with those of workers laid off. All studies find evidence of adverse selection.

the quality of slaves brought to market in pre-Civil War New Orleans was 20–40% below average. These findings are inconclusive, however, as buyers may be fully informed and nevertheless purchase low-quality goods because they are more willing than sellers to accept the associated risks and costs of owning them. Thus, adverse selection alone does not necessarily imply information asymmetry.

The following study attempts to correct this shortcoming by testing both for the adverse selection by sellers and for the quality uncertainty among buyers. We show that cars put on the market represent a negative selection from the population of registered cars and that the buyers of used cars suffer from quality uncertainty. Taken together, the two results point to the presence of information asymmetry.

We apply our test of the lemons model on a sample consisting of all 1985 cars registered in the Swiss canton of Basle City over the period 1985 to 1991. Our test of adverse selection is based on the results of vehicle safety-inspection records. Cars in Basle are subject to mandatory safety inspections at fixed time intervals. Under certain conditions, however, vehicles that are sold are required to be inspected ahead of schedule, thus enabling us to discriminate between the quality of sold and the quality of nonsold cars. Our results indicate that the probability of a vehicle having a defect increases if the used car was sold privately, supporting the presence of adverse selection. Interestingly, we find that the opposite holds true for used cars sold by dealers. This result conforms with Akerlof's (1970) conjecture that institutions such as warranties and reputation may develop to offset the effects of asymmetric information.[2]

Our test of quality uncertainty, on the other hand, rests on the following simple idea. The lemons model assumes that buyers of used cars are incompletely informed about the true quality of the vehicles they purchase. With time, however, owners should discover the actual condition of their purchased vehicles. Accordingly, those individuals who bought lemons should become increasingly aware of their mistakes and attempt to unload their cars on other buyers. As a consequence, the probability of a recently acquired car being resold should, after perhaps initially increasing, decline as ever less is left to be learned about the vehicle. We demonstrate this result with a simple model of quality uncertainty and then test the model's prediction by investigating the shape of the hazard function of car ownership. If car buyers suffer from quality uncertainty at the time of purchase, the hazard function should decline with the duration of ownership, reflecting the decreasing likelihood of buyers discovering any further defects that would lead them to resell their vehicles.

Of course, in an Akerlof-type of equilibrium buyers expect to purchase low-quality goods on average. But they still do not know whether the purchased goods is above or below this expected low average. Thus, buyers may be disappointed and try to resell the purchased item. With perfect and symmetric information, on the other hand, sellers may simply prefer better quality than buyers at going prices, also leading to an equilibrium in which goods traded are below average. However in this case, no buyer is disappointed and moved to resell purchased goods.

Our hazard function approach has been implemented before in labour market studies that test for the quality uncertainty that underlies job-matching models of labour turn-over (Jovanovic, 1979).[3] However, the following study appears to be the first attempt to employ this methodology to the lemons model.[4] Using the ownership biographies of all 1985 cars registered in Basle in the sample period, we show that the estimated hazard function of car ownership does indeed decline with the duration of ownership as quality uncertainty implies. In addition, we find that

[2] In the US, all states have 'lemon' laws, though they differ as to what they require dealers to do with returned vehicles. It is still possible to sell a car identified in one state as a lemon without warning in another state (see http://www.autopedia.com./html/HotLinks_Lemon.html). In the EU, consumers enjoy less protection. A new directive which took effect in 2002 forces dealers to fix defects within 2 years in a new car or 1 year in a used car (see http://europa.eu.int/scadplus/leg/en/lvb/-l32022.htm). Vaillant (2004) presents evidence that screening devices can also provide an effective protection against adverse selection.

[3] Job-matching models assume that an employee and an employer are not perfectly informed as to whether they meet each other's expectations when entering into an employment contract. In the course of time, however, 'mismatches' are discovered and get sorted out by job separations. Hence, the hazard function of job tenure should, after perhaps initially rising, thereafter decrease. Borland and Lye (1996) Chapman and Southwick (1991), Hautsch *et al.* (2001), Lancaster *et al.* (1987), Ohtake and Ohkusa (1994) and Sheldon (1992) find empirical support for this conjecture.

[4] Engers *et al.* (2005) have subsequently used duration data on car ownership in Virginia to test for the lemons problem. Their model predicts a positive relationship between the length of the initial spell of car ownership and all subsequent ones if the lemons problem holds. Instead, they discover a negative relationship. However, their finding may simply result from the finite lives of cars. If a car has a fixed life of, say, roughly 10 years then the second spell of ownership can last only as long as the remaining life left in the car. For example, if the first owner sells after 2 years, the second owner can drive the vehicle for another 8 years; if the first owner sells after 8 years, the second owner can use the car for only another 2 years.

higher quality cars are less likely to be resold shortly after purchase.

The remainder of this article is organized as follows. Section II describes the data of our study in more detail. Section III explains our method of testing for adverse selection and gives the results. Section IV develops our model of buyer uncertainty and presents our empirical findings. The last section summarizes and concludes.

## II. Data

Our study is based on two separate data sets. The first one consists of protocols from state vehicle safety inspections, and the other of registration records drawn from the databank of the Department of Motor Vehicles in the canton of Basle City. All data pertain to cars manufactured in 1985 and registered in Basle at some time during the sample period from 1985 to 1991. We concentrate on a single vintage to avoid possible cohort effects.

The vehicle safety inspection protocols constitute form sheets filled out by the state inspector on the day the car was initially presented for inspection. The inspection protocols record a vehicle's chassis number (unique to each vehicle), the date on which vehicle was submitted for inspection, vehicle mileage, the detected defects, the make of the car and the grounds for presenting the vehicle.

The protocols distinguish six different reasons for submitting an automobile for inspection: (i) periodic check up, (ii) private or (iii) dealer sale, (iv) ticketing by police for a safety defect, (v) technical alteration or (vi) export out of Switzerland. (i) Periodic inspections occur at fixed intervals: roughly every 4 years in our sample period.[5] Vehicles used for commercial purposes (taxis, rental, driver education), however, have to appear annually. (ii) Privately and (iii) dealer-owned cars sold are subject to inspection if the vehicle is at least 4 years old at the time of sale and has not been inspected in the last year prior to purchase. Inspections occur before the sale of the car. In all cases, the authorities carry out the inspections themselves. The inspection protocols record any deficiency discovered when the car is initially presented. If a car does not pass inspection at its initial presentation, the owner must have the defects repaired and re-submit the vehicle until it passes. In all instances, an inspection is mandatory and not left up to the owner. Since the timing of periodic inspections is not affected by the actions of owners, vehicles brought in for a periodic inspection represent a random sample of the population of registered cars.

We use the protocol data to investigate whether cars put up for sale are more or less likely to display a defect than a randomly chosen vehicle (Section III). The unit of observation is an inspection protocol.

Our second sample consists of registration records that document all vehicle registrations, de-registrations and re-registrations of 1985 cars that occurred in Basle in the sample period 1985–1991. From these records we construct 3806 spells of vehicle ownership, 2645 of which refer to cars bought new and 1161 to automobiles purchased used.[6] An ownership spell begins with the registration of a car by the current owner and ends with the final de-registration of the vehicle by the same individual. An ended spell is considered complete when a new owner re-registers the same car, which implies that a sale has occurred.[7] Otherwise the spell is considered to be incomplete, or right-censored.

The spells record the chassis number of a vehicle, its make, its fuel requirement (diesel or gasoline), the beginning and end date of a spell, the current owner's social security number, the license plate number, the vehicle's current use (private or commercial; taxi, rental or driver education) and whether the spell ended with a sale. We use the ownership spells to analyse the shape of the hazard function, i.e. to investigate how resell probabilities evolve as the length of vehicle ownership increases (Section IV). The unit of observation is an ownership spell.

It is important to note that although both samples pertain to the same cohort of cars, the two samples and their sources are different. The first sample consists of the safety inspections conducted on the cohort of vehicles in Basle City, and the second encompasses their registration records kept in the same canton. Not all cars found in the registration data to have been sold need to have been inspected beforehand, and thus to appear in the inspection data. And not all cars presented for inspection due to a change of ownership need to have been traded between residents of Basle City, and thus to appear in

[5] Although 3-year intervals were mandatory officially during the sample period, most cars were inspected at 4-year intervals due to a lack of personnel.

[6] Used cars purchased, unlike those bought new, also include vehicles that were originally registered outside the canton of Basle City. The registration data pertain solely to periods of ownership in Basle City, however.

[7] The protocol records from the first sample cannot be used to define a sale since not all cars sold are subject to inspection. Furthermore, some cars sold after inspection may have been inspected for reasons not related to a sale.

the registration data as sales. Hence, the possibilities of merging the two data sets are extremely limited.[8] The main information we were able to merge was whether a vehicle that was sold according to the registration data was inspected 3 months prior to sale according to the inspection data.

## III. Test of Adverse Selection

Our test of adverse selection is based on a comparison of the quality of sold and randomly chosen cars, where the definition of car quality rests on the results of the official vehicle safety inspections.[9] We consider cars that passed inspection at their initial presentation to be of higher quality than those that failed. In other words, we view the results of the initial inspection as an indicator of the overall quality of a car and not just of safety and environmental aspects, which the inspections address. This interpretation finds support in our findings below pertaining to the effect of the brand of a car on its passing inspection.

We investigate whether cars put up for sale are more likely to fail their initial inspection than randomly chosen vehicles on the basis of the following probit model:

$$P(y_i = 1|\mathbf{x}_i) = \Phi(\alpha'\mathbf{x}_i) \qquad (1)$$

where $P(y_i = 1|\mathbf{x}_i)$ represents the probability that a car $i$ with observed profile $\mathbf{x}_i$ fails inspection and $\Phi$ denotes the standard normal Cumulative Distribution Function (CDF)

The covariate vector $\mathbf{x}$ contains (i) variables which describe the car and (ii) dummy variables which distinguish between the various grounds for submitting a vehicle for inspection. We measure all descriptive variables in deviations from their respective means and choose vehicles brought in for a periodic inspection as the reference group. Also included in the reference group are seven cars inspected for export and four vehicles for which data on the grounds for inspection were missing. Including these 11 cases should have no effect on the results as they constitute a tiny share of the observations in the reference group (Table 1). The reference group also contains any cars possibly sold after having passed a periodic inspection. Including these cases will not affect our results either as the timing of periodic inspections is exogenously determined by the authorities. The presence of cars possibly sold later among the cars presented for a periodic inspection ensures that the reference group is representative of all qualities. Hence, the coefficients of the dummy variables measure the relative chances of a non-periodically inspected, or self-selected car with average attributes passing inspection compared to that of an identical randomly chosen vehicle.

Our sample comprises 5333 inspections conducted on 4418 cars. Table 1 describes the data contained in the inspection protocols. The brand of car, also included in our analysis, is excluded from the table to conserve space. Our sample contains 45 different makes of car. The first column of the table lists the various possible grounds for submitting a car for inspection. 'Periodic checks' refers to the regular inspections to which cars in Basle are subject at fixed intervals. The table indicates that the large majority (63%) of cars submitted for inspection came in for a periodic check. The second largest group (30%) consisted of cars put up for sale or sold by dealers ('dealer sale').

The next columns give the share of inspected cars with diesel engines and the average mileage of the vehicles at the time of inspection measured in kilometers. The last column in Table 1 pertain to the types of defects for which the safety inspections check. 'Devices' refers to various minor items like windshield wipers and rearview mirrors. As the table indicates, just over 77% of the cars inspected were devoid of defects. The most common faults were linked to lights or the power train (engine and drive shaft). Table 1 also shows that a below-average share (52.7%) of privately sold cars and an above-average share (83.3%) of dealer-sold vehicles had no technical defects, implying that cars offered for sale by private individuals are of lower quality than those vehicle dealers offer.[10] This evidence is merely suggestive, however, as no control is made for the influence of other factors such as mileage, which may vary systematically across categories. The probit estimates presented in Table 2 control for such effects.

The probit estimates show that greater mileage does indeed raise the chances that a car will have a defect. Nonetheless, even after controlling for mileage, privately sold cars still exhibit an above-average propensity of being defective. In every

[8] To illustrate this point, note that according to Table 3, which pertains to the registration data, 28.8% or 46 of the 160 used cars privately sold in Basle City were inspected 3 months prior to sale in Basle City, whereas according to Table 1, which relates to the inspection data, 165 used cars were inspected prior to being put up for private sale.

[9] Emons and von Hagen (1991) use similar safety inspection data to establish weak information efficiency in the German automobile market.

[10] Cars sold constitute vehicles that had to be submitted for inspection because they changed owners, were at least 4 years old at the time of sale and had not been inspected in the last year prior to sale.

**Table 1. Sample mean of vehicle inspections**

| | | | | Type of defect | | | | | | | | |
|---|---|---|---|---|---|---|---|---|---|---|---|---|
| Grounds | Cases | Diesel | Kilometers | Lights | Devices | Frame | Suspension | Steering | Power train | Brakes | Handbrake | None |
| Periodic check | 3363 | 0.050 | 61 020 | 0.132 | 0.077 | 0.051 | 0.047 | 0.026 | 0.115 | 0.023 | 0.007 | 0.751 |
| Private sale | 165 | 0.133 | 66 924 | 0.248 | 0.255 | 0.152 | 0.103 | 0.042 | 0.218 | 0.042 | 0.006 | 0.527 |
| Dealer sale | 1626 | 0.018 | 51 954 | 0.073 | 0.333 | 0.021 | 0.037 | 0.020 | 0.077 | 0.017 | 0.005 | 0.833 |
| Ticketed | 54 | 0.093 | 61 752 | 0.056 | 0.000 | 0.056 | 0.056 | 0.019 | 0.037 | 0.019 | 0.000 | 0.852 |
| Vehicle altered | 114 | 0.123 | 49 727 | 0.053 | 0.070 | 0.079 | 0.079 | 0.018 | 0.026 | 0.009 | 0.000 | 0.789 |
| Export | 7 | 0.143 | 78 896 | 0.000 | 0.000 | 0.000 | 0.000 | 0.000 | 0.143 | 0.000 | 0.000 | 0.857 |
| Unknown | 4 | 0.250 | 80 071 | 0.000 | 0.250 | 0.000 | 0.000 | 0.250 | 0.000 | 0.000 | 0.000 | 0.500 |
| Total | 5333 | 0.045 | 58 242 | 0.115 | 0.068 | 0.046 | 0.046 | 0.024 | 0.104 | 0.021 | 0.006 | 0.771 |

**Table 2. Probit estimates of the probability of a vehicle defect**

| Explanatory variable | Type of defect | | | | | | | | | | | | | | | | | |
|---|---|---|---|---|---|---|---|---|---|---|---|---|---|---|---|---|---|---|
| | Lights | | Devices | | Frame | | Suspension | | Steering | | Power train | | Brakes | | Handbrake | | None | |
| Constant | −1.163*** | (0.029) | −1.473*** | (0.033) | −1.690*** | (0.039) | −1.729*** | (0.040) | −2.036*** | (0.051) | −1.294*** | (0.031) | −2.127*** | (0.057) | −2.601*** | (0.090) | 0.715*** | (0.024) |
| Private sale | 0.404*** | (0.112) | 0.743*** | (0.113) | 0.577*** | (0.127) | 0.404*** | (0.141) | 0.171 | (0.187) | 0.391*** | (0.117) | 0.275 | (0.188) | −0.052 | (0.380) | −0.563*** | (0.102) |
| Dealer sale | −0.342*** | (0.057) | −0.407*** | (0.071) | −0.408*** | (0.083) | −0.109 | (0.072) | −0.094 | (0.091) | −0.189*** | (0.057) | −0.099 | (0.096) | −0.115 | (0.154) | 0.270*** | (0.046) |
| Ticketed | −0.566** | (0.290) | – | | −0.028 | (0.289) | −0.014 | (0.294) | −0.251 | (0.437) | −0.637*** | (0.325) | −0.242 | (0.438) | – | | 0.484** | (0.219) |
| Vehicle altered | −0.460** | (0.198) | −0.010 | (0.184) | 0.270 | (0.179) | 0.307* | (0.180) | −0.192 | (0.306) | −0.671*** | (0.253) | −0.316 | (0.387) | – | | 0.076 | (0.136) |
| Mileage (km × $10^{-5}$) | 0.356*** | (0.052) | 0.243*** | (0.060) | 0.194** | (0.070) | 0.275*** | (0.066) | 0.419*** | (0.071) | 0.470*** | (0.053) | 0.262*** | (0.086) | 0.299*** | (0.116) | −0.463*** | (0.047) |
| Diesel | −0.017 | (0.116) | 0.232* | (0.123) | 0.058 | (0.144) | −0.213 | (0.160) | 0.177 | (0.176) | −0.158 | (0.128) | 0.270 | (0.186) | 0.182 | (0.290) | −0.104 | (0.097) |
| Alfa | 0.128 | (0.160) | −0.202 | (0.185) | −0.112 | (0.211) | 0.370* | (0.199) | 0.420** | (0.197) | 0.065 | (0.152) | 0.509* | (0.290) | 0.529 | (0.352) | 0.016 | (0.136) |
| Audi | −0.217 | (0.161) | −0.383** | (0.184) | −0.836*** | (0.293) | −0.143 | (0.223) | −0.450 | (0.292) | −0.410*** | (0.160) | 0.582** | (0.265) | 0.597*** | (0.316) | 0.473*** | (0.138) |
| BMW | −0.182 | (0.166) | −0.423** | (0.191) | −0.222 | (0.212) | −0.014 | (0.220) | 0.069 | (0.219) | −0.346** | (0.164) | 0.141 | (0.338) | – | | 0.383*** | (0.142) |
| Citroën | −0.102 | (0.162) | −0.425** | (0.192) | 0.176 | (0.188) | −0.006 | (0.219) | 0.225 | (0.204) | −0.111 | (0.153) | 0.408 | (0.293) | 0.928*** | (0.287) | 0.234* | (0.136) |
| Fiat | 0.160 | (0.150) | −0.049 | (0.166) | 0.197 | (0.180) | 0.546*** | (0.185) | 0.196 | (0.197) | 0.328** | (0.138) | 1.050*** | (0.236) | 0.168 | (0.407) | −0.233* | (0.128) |
| Ford | −0.353** | (0.161) | −0.389** | (0.177) | −0.266 | (0.201) | 0.031 | (0.203) | −0.164 | (0.228) | −0.253* | (0.148) | 0.087 | (0.323) | 0.162 | (0.398) | 0.341*** | (0.132) |
| Honda | −0.715*** | (0.185) | −0.580*** | (0.194) | −0.351* | (0.214) | −0.122 | (0.217) | −0.473* | (0.292) | −0.943 | (0.196) | – | | 0.184 | (0.402) | 0.774*** | (0.143) |
| Lancia | 0.442* | (0.252) | −0.006 | (0.306) | −0.352 | (0.457) | −0.134 | (0.457) | 0.776** | (0.306) | 0.161 | (0.263) | – | | – | | −0.041 | (0.238) |
| Mazda | −0.599*** | (0.202) | −0.920*** | (0.268) | −0.553** | (0.274) | −0.012 | (0.237) | – | | −0.962*** | (0.238) | 0.590** | (0.291) | – | | 0.743*** | (0.163) |
| Mercedes | −0.260 | (0.165) | −0.584*** | (0.189) | −0.489** | (0.221) | 0.058 | (0.210) | −0.179 | (0.232) | −0.612*** | (0.171) | −0.460 | (0.425) | 0.104 | (0.403) | 0.485*** | (0.140) |
| Mitsubishi | −0.343** | (0.178) | −0.628*** | (0.215) | −0.250 | (0.222) | −0.394 | (0.274) | −0.067 | (0.248) | −0.787*** | (0.206) | 0.500* | (0.290) | 0.679** | (0.324) | 0.489*** | (0.147) |
| Nissan | −0.487*** | (0.193) | −0.439** | (0.207) | −0.259 | (0.232) | −0.500* | (0.312) | −0.265 | (0.300) | −0.657*** | (0.200) | 0.293 | (0.337) | – | | 0.640*** | (0.158) |
| Opel | −0.344*** | (0.141) | −0.403*** | (0.154) | −0.207 | (0.170) | −0.150 | (0.186) | −0.096 | (0.181) | −0.163 | (0.128) | 0.365 | (0.244) | 0.346 | (0.292) | 0.341*** | (0.117) |
| Peugeot | −0.159 | (0.161) | −0.204 | (0.176) | −0.216 | (0.207) | 0.157 | (0.204) | −0.087 | (0.231) | −0.093 | (0.150) | 0.571** | (0.269) | 0.594** | (0.319) | 0.237* | (0.135) |
| Porsche | −0.373 | (0.326) | −0.412 | (0.367) | – | | – | | – | | – | | – | | – | | 0.776*** | (0.294) |
| Renault | 0.161 | (0.147) | −0.112 | (0.164) | 0.119 | (0.179) | 0.207 | (0.192) | 0.159 | (0.192) | −0.178 | (0.144) | 0.850*** | (0.239) | 0.131 | (0.402) | −0.017 | (0.126) |
| Saab | −0.106 | (0.295) | −0.449 | (0.371) | −0.410 | (0.462) | −0.156 | (0.459) | – | | −0.235 | (0.301) | | | – | | 0.443* | (0.267) |
| Seat | 0.269 | (0.318) | −0.566 | (0.494) | 0.206 | (0.400) | – | | – | | 0.256 | (0.318) | 1.455*** | (0.391) | – | | 0.027 | (0.298) |
| Subaru | 0.129 | (0.220) | −0.040 | (0.247) | 0.467** | (0.243) | −0.083 | (0.344) | −0.185 | (0.426) | −0.127 | (0.230) | 1.022*** | (0.320) | – | | −0.062 | (0.191) |
| Suzuki | −0.010 | (0.208) | 0.047 | (0.220) | −0.237 | (0.298) | −0.013 | (0.297) | 0.041 | (0.323) | −0.253 | (0.217) | 1.020*** | (0.296) | 0.606 | (0.446) | 0.108 | (0.176) |
| Toyota | −0.404*** | (0.152) | −0.483*** | (0.169) | −0.471** | (0.201) | 0.176 | (0.183) | 0.072 | (0.185) | −0.701*** | (0.156) | 0.224 | (0.276) | 0.032 | (0.399) | 0.541*** | (0.125) |
| Volvo | −0.118 | (0.163) | −0.441** | (0.194) | −0.495** | (0.244) | −0.126 | (0.227) | −0.229 | (0.245) | −0.436*** | (0.164) | 0.261 | (0.309) | 0.143 | (0.422) | 0.398*** | (0.141) |
| VW | −0.301** | (0.138) | −0.370*** | (0.151) | −0.083 | (0.164) | 0.181 | (0.172) | −0.388** | (0.197) | −0.236* | (0.126) | 0.505** | (0.230) | −0.158 | (0.384) | 0.346*** | (0.114) |
| Sample size | 5333 | | 5333 | | 5333 | | 5333 | | 5333 | | 5333 | | 5333 | | 5333 | | 5333 | |
| $\ln L_\theta$ | −1900.40 | | −1323.22 | | −990.95 | | −997.02 | | −611.24 | | −1778.71 | | −547.33 | | −200.71 | | −2871.62 | |
| $\ln L^*$ | −1790.83 | | −1240.03 | | −926.34 | | −956.57 | | −571.84 | | −1645.16 | | −506.14 | | −185.72 | | −2694.48 | |
| $-2(\ln L_\theta - \ln L^*)$ | 219.15*** | | 166.37*** | | 129.22*** | | 80.90*** | | 78.79*** | | 267.09*** | | 82.38*** | | 29.97* | | 354.26*** | |
| LRI$(1-(\ln L^*/\ln L_\theta))$ | 0.058 | | 0.063 | | 0.065 | | 0.041 | | 0.064 | | 0.075 | | 0.075 | | 0.075 | | 0.062 | |

*Notes*: *, ** and *** denote statistical significance at the 10, 5 and 1% levels, respectively.
Estimated SEs appear in parentheses.

category, save one ('handbrake'), a privately sold car that went through a safety inspection was more likely to have a defect than a randomly chosen car with the same characteristics. The chances overall are 27% higher according to the results appearing in the final column ('None') of Table 2. Dealer-sold cars, on the other hand, have a 10% lower chance of exhibiting a defect, possibly because dealers have a reputation to lose if they choose to sell lemons. This would conform with Akerlof's (1970) conjecture that institutions may develop to offset the effects of asymmetric information.

The estimated coefficients of the brand dummies suggest that passing the initial safety inspection is an overall sign of higher vehicle quality. This can be seen in the fact that German (Audi, BMW, Mercedes, Porsche) and Japanese (Honda, Mazda, Mitsubishi, Nissan, Toyota) cars, which German data (Emons and von Hagen, 1991) from the sample period show to be more solid, have a greater chance of passing inspection initially than mileage-equivalent Italian (Alfa, Fiat, Lancia) or French (Citroën, Peugeot, Renault) vehicles, which the same data find to be less dependable. Section IV provides further evidence of the existence of these quality differences among car brands.

It is of course possible that whether a car passes an inspection initially depends not only on the basic quality of a vehicle but also on the decision of car owners to have their vehicles checked and repaired before submitting them for inspection. For example, the lower likelihood of cars ticketed by the police for safety reasons ('ticketed') of failing inspection undoubtedly arises from the fact that owners of cars with a ticketed defect have them repaired before presenting them for inspection since the defect is clearly specified and there is no chance that the authorities will miss detecting the problem. Car dealers are another case in point. If one assumes that having a car checked and repaired in advance and submitting it for inspection are both costly undertakings and that dealers have a cost advantage with respect to prior check-ups and repairs, then one should expect dealers to check their vehicles before submitting them for inspection and thus to achieve higher success rates.[11] This argument cannot explain why vehicles presented by private persons due to a sale do worse than those in for a periodic inspection, however, as no obvious cost differential exists between these two groups of nondealers.[12] It therefore seems that the greater defect rate of privately sold cars *vis-à-vis* observably identical randomly chosen vehicles arises from lower quality. Furthermore, since the probit estimates indicate that the higher failure rates are not merely due to chance, it would appear that private sellers are generally aware of the sub-average quality of their cars.

How well buyers are informed is a different matter, however. Generally speaking, little information is available to buyers of a used car in Switzerland. The only certain source of information is the vehicle registration, which merely identifies the current owner. Thus, a buyer cannot base his quality expectations on the number of previous owners as he can, say, in Germany where a document listing all the previous holders remains with the vehicle. Nor can the buyer know with certainty how long the seller has owned his or her car as the vehicle registration gives only the date of the most recent registration, not when the present owner took possession of the vehicle. In addition, the buyer knows from the vehicle registration when the vehicle last passed inspection, but not why the car was presented for inspection or whether the car passed inspection initially or had to be re-submitted after having the detected defects repaired. In short, the buyer does not have access to the inspection protocols which served as our database in this section.

Instead of theorizing about what used car buyers might know or not know prior to purchase, we examine the resell behaviour of buyers in the first months after purchase.

## IV. Test of Quality Uncertainty

Our test of quality uncertainty among car buyers is based on the shape of the hazard function $h(t)$ in the *initial* periods of car ownership. Roughly speaking, a hazard function gives the probability of an event (car resale) occurring at time $t$, given that it has not occurred up to this point.[13] If car buyers suffer from quality uncertainty, the first months of ownership will

[11] Another cause of the higher success rate of dealer-submitted cars could be that inspectors trust dealers more, and hence inspect their cars less thoroughly.

[12] Experience shows that garages tend to make more repairs than necessary if told to fix everything that might not pass inspection. Therefore, it is a sensible strategy for private persons to present their cars for inspection first and then to have any detected defects repaired. The duplication of inspection costs with this strategy is less than the costs of superfluous repairs arising from the 'fix everything' strategy. This explains why private individuals customarily do not have their cars checked by a garage before submitting them for inspection.

[13] Strictly speaking, the probability $p(t)$ of selling one's car in a given interval $t$ to $t+dt$, given that one has not done so by time $t$, equals $h(t)\cdot dt$, where $dt$ represents a small increase in time. In the following, we also term $p(t)$ the hazard rate.

consist of a learning process in which buyers discover the hidden characteristics of their newly purchased vehicles. Assuming that at least some buyers react to any dissatisfaction with their purchases by reselling their vehicles, we should observe that the probability of a newly purchased car being resold generally decreases with the duration of ownership (negative duration dependence), reflecting the decline in the discovery of new hidden negative attributes of the vehicle.

If buyers instead do not suffer from quality uncertainty, then any observed resales should result from subsequent shocks in buyers' tastes or constraints,[14] which do not imply any particular pattern of duration dependence for the hazard function in the short-run. In fact, if these shocks follow a Poisson process, the hazard function of resell will be horizontal (Lancaster, 1990, p. 86). Depreciation or aging, which in principal could also serve as a motive for reselling (*albeit* hardly over the short term considered here), do not imply a falling hazard rate either. In fact, if the optimal age for a heterogenous population of car owners to trade in their cars happened to be normally distributed, the hazard function would be monotonically increasing.[15]

### *Theoretical model*

The intuition behind our reasoning can be captured by the following simple model.[16] We develop the model in two steps: we first view the hazard function of a single spell of car ownership and then focus on the aggregate hazard function of a group of cars of a given average observable quality $\bar{\lambda}$. Our empirical model applies to the aggregate hazard function.

**Single-spell hazard function.** To start, suppose owners take the expected number of defects $\lambda$ a vehicle will suffer per period as an indicator of its quality. The consumer does not know $\lambda$ at the time of purchase but discovers its value by driving the vehicle. Let $\bar{\lambda}$ be the consumer's belief about the average value of $\lambda$ for *traded* cars of a given observable quality.[17] $\bar{\lambda}$ equals the actual average expected number of defects of vehicles of this category, so that expectations are unbiased.

Now consider a consumer who has bought a car with an unobserved mean defect rate $\lambda$ from the class of traded vehicles with expected quality $\bar{\lambda}$. We assume that the actual number of defects $x_t$ the car has in period $t\,(t=1,2,\ldots)$ follows a Poisson process with expectation $\lambda$, i.e. $P\{x_t=k\}=(\lambda^k/k!)e^{-\lambda}$ for $k=0, 1, 2, \ldots$. For the sake of simplicity, define defects broadly enough so that $\lambda \geq 9$. Then $x_t$ can be sufficiently well approximated by the normal distribution so that $x_t \sim N(\lambda, \lambda)$.[18]

In each period $t$, the consumer observes $x_t$ and computes as an estimator of $\lambda$ the average number of defects experienced so far $\hat{\lambda}_t = (1/t)\sum_{\tau=1}^{t} x_\tau$. If $\hat{\lambda}_t$ lies with some given statistical significance $\alpha$ above some unreliability threshold $z \geq \bar{\lambda}$, the consumer will be dissatisfied with the quality of the purchased car to such an extent that he or she will resell it. The choice of the level of statistical significance $\alpha$ should depend on the buyer's costs of erring, and the selection of the minimum acceptable quality $z$ on his or her preferences and on the transaction costs of selling a recently purchased car. The threshold $z$ will lie above $\bar{\lambda}$ as the buyer expects to have bought quality $\bar{\lambda}$.

In each period, the consumer tests whether $\hat{\lambda}_t$ is still compatible with the null hypothesis $\lambda \leq z$. To do so, the consumer computes the test statistic $(\hat{\lambda}_t - z)/\sqrt{z/t}$ and sells his vehicles if $(\hat{\lambda}_t - z)/\sqrt{z/t} > \Phi^{-1}(1-\alpha)$.

[14] Other possibilities such as buyer heterogeneity are considered below.

[15] In this case, the hazard function of resell would equal $\phi(t)/[1-\Phi(t)]$, where $\phi$ and $\Phi$ represent the normal density and CDF, respectively. This expression is monotonically increasing in ownership duration $t$.

[16] It is important to stress from the outset that our model does not purport to provide an equilibrium model of the market for used cars. Our model focuses only on the short-run motives for selling vehicles. In the long-run other considerations come into play, such as depreciation, which lead to increased sales in the longer term. Based on this intuition, Porter and Sattler (1999) construct a model in which durable goods deteriorate over time and owners sell to update to their preferred quality. Similarly, Hendel and Lizzeri (1999) model car owners as selling their used vehicles to enjoy the higher quality offered by a new car. They show that despite adverse selection an equilibrium exists in which the average quality of used cars is positive. These models pertain to the long-term motives for reselling cars and predict initially low-resell rates that later increase with the age and mileage of a vehicle. Stolyarov (2002) finds evidence in the US car market consistent with this prediction. See Gilligan (2004) for a further test. To our knowledge, no model currently exists to explain the phenomenon which our article addresses, i.e. the behaviour of buyers when their purchased cars do not meet expectations.

[17] $\bar{\lambda}$ is a conditional mean. It pertains to the average quality of traded cars, which according to the lemons model should be below the mean quality of the population of observably identical cars.

[18] The Poisson assumption implies that quality uncertainty, as measured by the variance, decreases with mean quality: the lower the mean quality of a vehicle (high $\lambda$), the more the number of defects per period will vary about the mean. We find this assumption attractive as it seems reasonable to expect that the number of defects to vary less among, say, new (i.e. higher quality) cars than used (i.e. lower quality) ones, since the reliability of used cars depends on a myriad of additional factors such as care and maintenance which increases defect uncertainty.

For a car with an expected defect rate $\lambda$, $\hat{\lambda}_t \sim N(\lambda, \lambda/t)$. Since the test statistic is a linear transformation of $\hat{\lambda}_t$, we have $(\hat{\lambda}_t - z)/\sqrt{z/t}) \sim N(\lambda - z)/\sqrt{z/t}, \lambda/t)$. Accordingly, the conditional probability that the consumer sells his car in $t$ given he has not done so up to this point, i.e. the *hazard rate*, is

$$p(t, \lambda, z, \alpha) := \text{Prob}\left(\frac{\hat{\lambda}_t - z}{\sqrt{z/t}} > \Phi^{-1}(1-\alpha)\right)$$

$$= 1 - \Phi\left(\frac{\Phi^{-1}(1-\alpha) - [(\lambda - z)/\sqrt{z/t}]}{\sqrt{\lambda/z}}\right)$$

Having derived the hazard function of resell, we now investigate its duration dependence. Here one has to distinguish between three possible drawings of the unobserved quality $\lambda$ *vis-à-vis* $z$: (i) a more than acceptable quality ($\lambda < z$), (ii) a just acceptable quality ($\lambda = z$) and an unacceptable quality ($\lambda > z$).[19] Among the cars in the first category, the hazard rate is decreasing since $\partial p/\partial t < 0$ in this case. Sales of these cars result from Type I errors: although in reality the cars fulfill an owner's minimum quality requirements $z$, they are sold by mistake due to an unusually high number of observed defects $x_t$ in the first periods of ownership. The hazard rate, or the probability of committing a Type I error, declines over time, however, as the precision of the test statistic increases with the length of ownership. In the limit, the hazard rate goes to zero, i.e. $\lim_{t\to\infty} p(t, \lambda, z, \alpha) = 0$.

The hazard rates of cars that are just acceptable ($\lambda = z$), on the other hand, are constant and equal to $\alpha$, the chosen level of statistical significance. Finally, vehicles that do not meet minimum quality requirements ($\lambda > z$) exhibit an increasing hazard rate $\partial p/\partial t > 0$. In this case, the error lies in holding on to unacceptable cars for any length of time, which represents a Type II error. In time, however, the precision of the test statistic again increases so that all unacceptable cars are eventually resold, i.e. $\lim_{t\to\infty} p(t, \lambda, z, \alpha) = 1$.

In short, our model likens the learning process of buyers to the consistency property of sampling statistics: the more the observations, the greater the certainty. The latter is true no matter how good the buyer's statistical abilities happen to be.

The formula for the hazard rate indicates in addition that increasing the mean number of defects $\lambda$, a given car will generate (or, equivalently, increasing the quality uncertainty associated with it) shifts the hazard function of resale upwards since $\partial p/\partial\lambda > 0$. In other words, the hazard functions of cars of unobservably lower quality lie above those of otherwise comparable vehicles. Our model also implies that $\partial^2 p/\partial\lambda\partial t > 0$ so that the hazard functions of cars with a common observed expected quality $\bar{\lambda}$ increasingly diverge as the length of car ownership increases, i.e. they fan out about $\alpha$, the constant hazard rate of just acceptable cars.

### *Aggregate hazard function*

Our results to this point pertain to the hazard function of a single car with unobserved quality $\lambda$ drawn from a set of cars with the observed mean quality $\bar{\lambda}$. Our empirical model, however, applies to the aggregate hazard function of all vehicles with a common observed mean quality $\bar{\lambda}$.[20] The aggregate hazard function is a weighted average of the cars of this mean quality not yet resold at any given time $t$. Since lower quality cars in this group are resold faster ($\partial^2 p/\partial\lambda\partial t > 0$), acceptable cars make up an ever larger share of those vehicles not yet resold as the duration of ownership increases. Therefore, the aggregate hazard function increasingly adopts the shape of the hazard functions of the acceptable cars in the group of cars with observed mean quality $\bar{\lambda}$. In the limit ($t \to \infty$), the aggregate hazard function converges to the hazard function of the vehicle with the highest unobservable quality in the group and, hence, with the lowest hazard function. Consequently, after perhaps initially increasing as a result of the high sell off of unacceptable cars in the first periods of car ownership, the aggregate hazard function will eventually decrease and converge to zero. Figure 1 presents simulations based on $\bar{\lambda} = 13(23)$, $z = 14(24)$, $\alpha = 0.05$, and uniformly distributed $\lambda$ with support [10,16] ([20,26]) to illustrate this point.[21]

[19] Note that by choosing a minimum acceptable quality $z$, the consumer subdivides the class of cars with expected quality $\bar{\lambda}$ into these three categories.
[20] $\bar{\lambda}$ is captured by the regressors.
[21] The value of 13 for $\bar{\lambda}$ was chosen to ensure that a normal distribution provides a good approximation to a Poisson process. It was then increased to 23 to provide enough change to make the differences in the hazard functions, clearly visible in Fig. 1. The values for $z$ were selected such that $\bar{\lambda} < z$, as our decision model assumes, and so that the difference $z - \bar{\lambda}$ remained constant. Otherwise the values are arbitrary. Note that buyer's heterogeneity with respect to the resell threshold $z$ or the significance level $\alpha$ has no effect on this result. The choice of $z$ merely determines the initial share of increasing, decreasing and constant hazard functions in a given observable category of cars at time 0, and the choice of $\alpha$ simply slows or accelerates individual resell hazards, leaving the sorting process that drives our result unaffected.

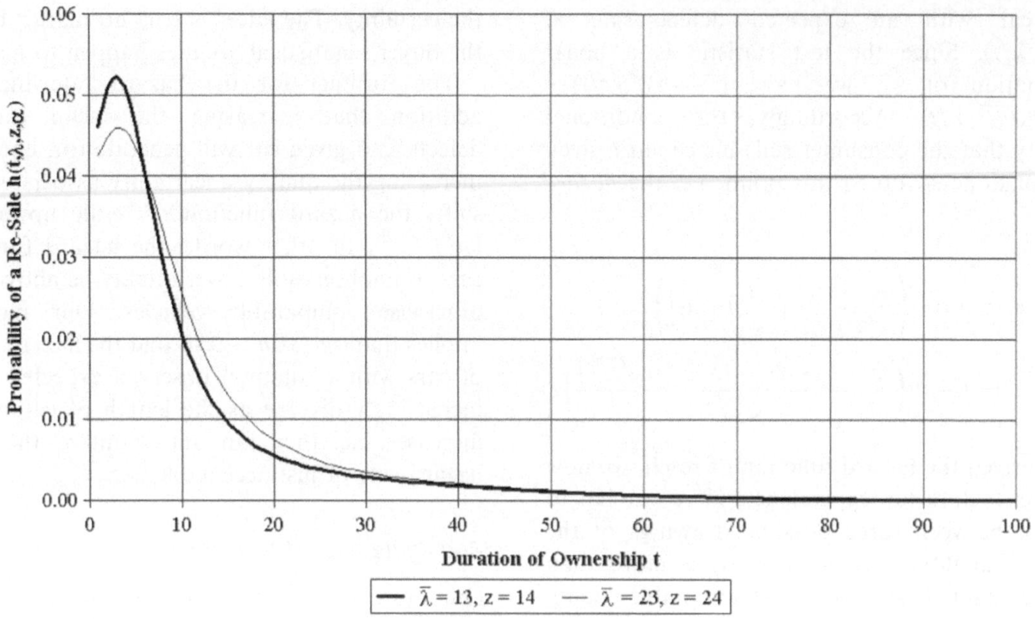


**Fig. 1. Aggregate hazard functions**

The final issue with regard to our model pertains to the effect of an increase in the observed mean quality $\bar{\lambda}$ on the aggregate hazard function. The answer depends on the effect the observed difference has on the car owner's choice of threshold $z$ *vis-à-vis* $\bar{\lambda}$ (i.e. $z-\bar{\lambda}$) and on the distribution of the unobserved quality differences $\lambda$ about $\bar{\lambda}$. To start, let us assume that $z-\bar{\lambda}$ increases and/or that the distribution of the unobserved quality differences about $\bar{\lambda}$ decreases as observed mean quality rises (i.e. $\bar{\lambda}$ falls). In this case, the aggregate hazard function shifts downwards because increasing $z-\bar{\lambda}$ or decreasing the variation of unobserved quality differences about $\bar{\lambda}$ increases the share of acceptable cars ($\lambda<z$) and hence those with decreasing hazard functions. Neither of these two assumptions seems unreasonable. For example, with regard to the first assumption, new cars, which are generally of higher quality than used vehicles, tend to suffer a disproportionately higher loss of value in their first year. This should increase the transaction costs of reselling them and, in turn, raise their relative resell thresholds $z-\bar{\lambda}$. And the second assumption, that the distribution of unobserved vehicle heterogeneity about $\bar{\lambda}$ increases with $\bar{\lambda}$, merely extends the Poisson property of an inverse relationship between mean quality and quality uncertainty.

If one assumes instead that $z-\bar{\lambda}$ and the variation of unobserved quality about $\bar{\lambda}$ remain unchanged when observed mean quality changes (as modelled in Fig. 1), then the aggregate hazard function of cars of higher observed mean quality will start higher and, after perhaps initially increasing, decrease more rapidly than the aggregate hazard function of cars with a lower observed mean quality. To see this, let $z_d<z_p$. Now take an unacceptable car out of each sample, i.e. $\lambda_d>z_d$ and $\lambda_p>z_p$. Furthermore, let $\lambda_d-z_d=\lambda_p-z_p$. We thus compare two cars out of each set, whose expected defect rate exceeds the corresponding threshold by the same amount. Then we have

$$p(t,\lambda_p,z_p,\alpha)<p(t,\lambda_d,z_d,\alpha)$$
$$\Leftrightarrow \Phi^{-1}(1-\alpha)\sqrt{z_p/\lambda_p}-(\lambda_p-z_p)\sqrt{t/\lambda_p}$$
$$>\Phi^{-1}(1-\alpha)\sqrt{z_d/\lambda_d}-(\lambda_d-z_d)\sqrt{t/\lambda_d}$$

which holds as $z_p/\lambda_p>z_d/\lambda_d$ for $\lambda_d>z_d$ and $\lambda_p>z_p$. A similar argument shows that $p(t,\lambda_p,z_p,\alpha)>p(t,\lambda_d,z_d,\alpha)$ for $\lambda_d<z_d$, $\lambda_p<z_p$, and $\lambda_d-z_d=\lambda_p-z_p$. This means that cars of higher observed quality will initially be resold at a higher rate than the others. Yet, eventually the aggregate hazard rate for cars of higher observed quality will, as in the case of our previous assumptions, come to rest below the hazard rate of the others, as Fig. 1 illustrates. Put differently, the probability of a Type I or Type II error is lower for cars of higher observed mean quality under this set of circumstances.

In summary, our model predicts that the aggregate hazard function, after possibly increasing during an initial phase of vehicle testing, declines with the duration of ownership. Furthermore, cars of high-observable quality eventually have lower hazard rates than cars of low-observable quality, if not from the outset.

Note that the quality uncertainty, which our model is intended to test, could also capture uncertainty with regard to car characteristics. For example, a buyer could discover after purchasing a vehicle that it did not have any technical defects but that it nevertheless did not really fit his or her unchanged needs. Characteristic uncertainty is not interesting in the present context as it does not imply asymmetric information. To control for characteristic uncertainty, we also investigate the resell probabilities of cars bought new. Our reasoning is that quality uncertainty should be lower among new cars because of their higher mean quality $\lambda$ and because of possible new-car warranties,[22] whereas characteristics uncertainty should be higher since consumers know far less about the characteristics of a car of a given vintage in the year of its production as they have no track record to fall back on. This is particularly true of newly introduced models. Thus if characteristics uncertainty were to dominate, we would expect the resell probabilities of cars purchased new to lie above those of otherwise identical vehicles bought used.

Regardless of which form of uncertainty dominates, our test nevertheless requires that at least some buyers express any unexpected dissatisfaction by reselling their cars. Since the transaction costs of reselling a newly purchased vehicle may be high, buyers could be poorly informed at the time of purchase and yet not resell vehicles that turn out to be unpleasant surprises. Hence, a perhaps initially rising but lastly falling hazard function is a sufficient,[23] but not a necessary implication of the presence of buyer uncertainty.

### *Empirical methodology*

Our empirical investigation focuses on the shape and locus of the aggregate hazard function of car ownership for vehicles of a given observed mean quality. Observable quality is captured by the covariates of our regression analysis.

Our analysis is based on the ownership biographies of all 1985 cars registered in the canton of Basle City between 1985 and 1991. The car histories were constructed from the records of the Basle City Department of Motor Vehicles. Our observations consist of all spells of nondealer ownership these cars generated in Basle. The social security number of the car owner, included in the registration data, allows us to sort out any cars registered to dealers. We restrict our study to nondealer-owned cars since the resell behaviour of dealers probably does not reflect quality uncertainty. In other words, periods in which a vehicle is registered to a dealer, say, as a demonstration car are not counted as ownership spells and thus excluded from our sample. An ownership spell begins with the purchase of a car and ends with it being resold, where a sale is defined as a situation in which a car with a given chassis number is re-registered to a person with a different social security number. Ownership spells need not end in a sale, however. They could still be in progress at the end of the sample period, or owners could junk their cars or move to another canton before the sample period ends. Spells of this sort are right censored and treated appropriately in the estimation. Spells of ownership begun outside the canton, on the other hand, are left censored and excluded from the sample. In total, our sample consists of 1161 spells of nondealer ownership pertaining to used cars and 2645 spells applying to new cars. We concentrate on the ownership spells of used cars, employing the ownership spells of new vehicles for the purpose of comparison.

We apply both semi-parametric and parametric duration models. Semi-parametric approaches restrict the covariate structure, whereas parametric approaches also constrain the shape of the hazard function. We employ both approaches in the hope of obtaining more robust results.

Our semi-parametric approach is based on grouped durations. The model assumes that the hazard rate, or probability, $p_i(t)$ that an ownership spell $i$ that has lasted to at least time $t-1$ will end in a sale in the interval $[t-1, t)$ can be sufficiently approximated by the following function (see Cameron and Trivedi, 2005, pp. 600–3 for a survey of alternative grouped duration approaches)

$$p_i(t) = \Phi(\alpha_t + \beta'\mathbf{x}_i + \gamma'\mathbf{z}_{it}) \qquad (2)$$

where

$\Phi(\cdot)$ = standard normal cumulative density function,

$\alpha_t$ = interval-specific constant or, alternatively,

$$= \sum_{j=0}^{J} \alpha_j \cdot t^j$$

[22] New-car warranties were fairly uncommon in Europe in 1985. Where they did exist, they never held for longer than a year.
[23] The issue of unobserved heterogeneity, which could call the sufficiency aspect into question, is discussed later in conjunction with Equation 6.

$\mathbf{x}_i =$ vector of constant characteristics describing the vehicle at the time of purchase ($t=0$)
$\mathbf{z}_{it} =$ vector of time-varying characteristics describing the vehicle at ownership time $t$
$t = 1, \ldots, T$.

The $\alpha$ parameters define the underlying or baseline hazard function and provide a basis for testing its shape.

We estimate the parameters of the model with the maximum likelihood procedure. To keep data handling manageable, we group the ownership spell durations, which are measured in days, into 26 (=$T$) equal-length intervals of 90 days, or one quarter. For convenience, we assume that right censoring occurs at the end of an interval. These assumptions lead to the following likelihood function

$$L = \prod_{t=1}^{T} \prod_{i=1}^{I_{t-1}} p_i(t)^{d_{it}} [1 - p_i(t)]^{1-d_{it}} \tag{3}$$

where $I_{t-1}$ represents the number of spells of car ownership still in progress at the beginning of the duration interval $[t-1, t)$ and $d_{it}$ is a dummy variable indicating whether spell $i$ ended in a resale in this interval ($d_{it}=1$) or not ($d_{it}=0$). Note that each spell contributes several observations to (3), the number of observations per spell equalling the number of time intervals the spell enters. Applying (3) necessitates splitting each spell into a corresponding number of sub-spells.

We measure the explanatory variables in (2) as deviations from their respective means[24] so that $\Phi(\alpha_t)$ represents the hazard function of an average spell of ownership in the interval $[t-1, t)$, holding the value of all variables constant. The unknown parameter vectors $\beta$ and $\gamma$ do not vary across spell intervals, i.e. we do not estimate separate probit models for each quarter. This restriction is necessitated by the fact that many of the cars resold in a given time interval are unique with regard to one or more of the right-hand side variables in (3). In this case, specifying interval-specific coefficients would lead to a breakdown of the maximum likelihood estimation procedure (Greene, 2000, p. 832).

Our parametric approach uses nongrouped durations and is based on the following specification:

$$h_i(\tau) = h_0(\tau)\exp(\delta'\mathbf{x}_i) \tag{4}$$

where $\tau$ represents continuous time measured in days and $h_0(\cdot)$ is a baseline hazard function of a given parametric form. In contrast to (2), (4) assumes that the effect of covariates is multiplicatively separable from the baseline hazard function (proportional hazard model). Accordingly, $\delta$ does not contain a constant term. We also exclude time-varying covariates in the parametric approach.

We assume the following Weibull specification for the baseline hazard function $h_0(\tau)$

$$h_0(\tau) = \eta r(\eta\tau)^{r-1} \tag{5}$$

$\eta$ is a location parameter and $r$ a scaling parameter. The hazard function is monotone decreasing for $0<r<1$, constant for $r=1$ and monotone increasing for $r>1$. Estimates of $r$ thus provide an alternative means of testing the shape of the hazard function.

As is well known (e.g. Kiefer, 1988), an aggregate hazard function can decline monotonically although the individual hazard functions making up the aggregate are constant, yet different. For example, car buyers may not suffer from quality uncertainty, but instead differ with respect to their constant propensities to sell their cars (owner heterogeneity). In this case, the hazard function would also display negative duration in the aggregate although no quality uncertainty exists. In contrast to this problem of so-called unobserved spell heterogeneity, our model implies that individual hazard functions are not constant, except in the special case where $\lambda = z$. To test for the presence of unobserved spell heterogeneity, which could bias our results, we follow common practice and condition the baseline survivor function $S_0(\tau)$ of the Weibull model on a random variable $\nu$ intended to capture the unobserved heterogeneity. We choose a very flexible parameterization for $\nu$ by assuming that it has a gamma distribution with mean 1 and variance $\theta$. This leads to the following unconditional baseline hazard function[25]:

$$h_0(\tau) = \eta r(\eta\tau)^{r-1}[S_0(\tau)]^{\theta} \tag{6}$$

As is easily seen, (6) reverts to (5) when unobserved heterogeneity is not present ($\theta=0$).

We also employ maximum likelihood to estimate the parametric model. In contrast to (3), each spell contributes just one observation to the likelihood function.

[24] The means are based on all ownership spells, both those of cars bought new and used.
[25] See Greene (2000, p. 947) for a derivation of (6). Heckman and Singer (1984) note that (6) may over parameterize the survivor function leading to serious errors in inference.

**Table 3. Sample means of ownership spells**

| Variable | Used cars | | New cars | |
|---|---|---|---|---|
| | Resold | Not resold | Resold | Not resold |
| Total number of spells | 160 | 1001 | 465 | 2180 |
| Ownership duration (in quarters) | 3.644 | 5.907 | 16.98 | 22.48 |
| Age at purchase (in quarters) | 18.05 | 19.99 | 0.000 | 0.000 |
| Inspected up to 3 months before purchase | 0.288 | 0.329 | – | – |
| Company owned | 0.000 | 0.000 | 0.002 | 0.002 |
| Commercially used | 0.013 | 0.015 | 0.009 | 0.010 |
| Diesel engine | 0.013 | 0.030 | 0.024 | 0.036 |
| 44 Brands in total | | | | |
| Opel | 0.088 | 0.113 | 0.101 | 0.154 |
| VW | 0.063 | 0.092 | 0.086 | 0.128 |
| Toyota | 0.138 | 0.084 | 0.112 | 0.094 |
| Renault | 0.075 | 0.073 | 0.065 | 0.047 |
| Ford | 0.038 | 0.061 | 0.071 | 0.050 |
| Fiat | 0.069 | 0.058 | 0.067 | 0.039 |
| Honda | 0.044 | 0.040 | 0.043 | 0.053 |
| Audi | 0.038 | 0.043 | 0.054 | 0.048 |
| Citroën | 0.019 | 0.044 | 0.052 | 0.040 |
| BMW | 0.019 | 0.046 | 0.039 | 0.042 |
| Peugeot | 0.031 | 0.040 | 0.034 | 0.042 |
| Alfa | 0.069 | 0.056 | 0.047 | 0.026 |
| Nissan | 0.063 | 0.029 | 0.041 | 0.038 |
| Mitsubishi | 0.063 | 0.036 | 0.043 | 0.033 |
| Mazda | 0.025 | 0.029 | 0.026 | 0.035 |
| Mercedes | 0.031 | 0.036 | 0.019 | 0.032 |
| Volvo | 0.013 | 0.026 | 0.022 | 0.020 |
| Suzuki | 0.050 | 0.021 | 0.013 | 0.013 |
| Subaru | 0.031 | 0.011 | 0.006 | 0.018 |
| Lancia | 0.013 | 0.020 | 0.026 | 0.011 |
| Saab | 0.000 | 0.005 | 0.006 | 0.007 |
| Porsche | 0.006 | 0.005 | 0.004 | 0.005 |
| Seat | 0.000 | 0.003 | 0.004 | 0.005 |
| Other | 0.019 | 0.030 | 0.019 | 0.019 |

*Results*

Table 3 reports the means of the ownership spells in our sample, distinguishing between uncensored ('resold') and right-censored ('not resold') spells. Ownership duration measures the length of time (in quarters) that a vehicle had been held on average at the time the ownership spell ended, either through a sale or right-censoring. The remaining variables constitute the right-hand side variables $(\mathbf{x}, \mathbf{z})$ in our model. With the exception of 'age at purchase', all right-hand side variables represent dummy variables. In the semi-parametric split-spell model, we replace 'age at purchase' with the age of the car at the beginning of each time interval, which results in a time-varying variable ($z$), the sole regressor of this kind in the study.

The inspection variables indicate whether a car was submitted to a safety inspection in the last 3 months prior to purchase, i.e. before the new ownership spell began, implying that any defects discovered were repaired.[26] Our model implies that the improved quality associated with having passed inspection should lead to lower resell hazard rates. Indeed, this is what Table 3 suggests as a smaller share of the used cars resold had been inspected up to 3 months prior to purchase: 28.8% compared to 32.9% for cars not resold.

The dummy variable 'company owned' indicates whether a car was registered to a firm rather than to a person during a particular spell of ownership. As can be seen, no firm purchased a used car in our sample. 'Commercially used' denotes that the

[26] Inspected cars are those inspected for any of the reasons listed in Section II. We do not distinguish between the various reasons for having to present a vehicle for inspection as we assume that passing an inspection places otherwise observably homogeneous vehicles on a common *mean* quality level.

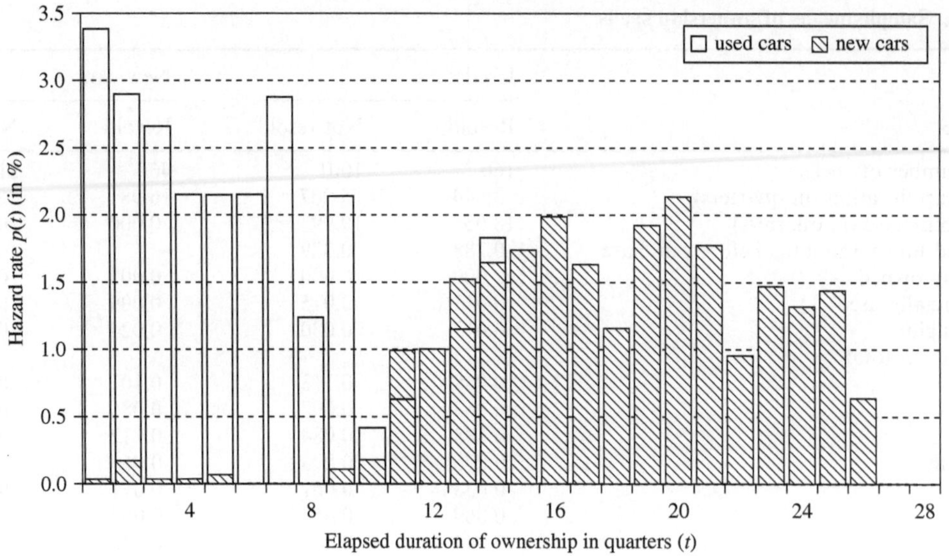


**Fig. 2. Hazard function of new and used car ownership based on semi-parametric estimates controlling for observable heterogeneity**

automobile was being used as a rental car, a taxi or for driver education during the observed spell. The brands listed in Table 3 are those for which dummy variables were created and appear in their order of prominence in our sample.

Table 3 suggests that resold cars (uncensored spells) are held for shorter periods of time prior to resale on average and tend to be somewhat newer, not in commercial use, and gasoline fuelled. Table 3 further indicates that automobiles from Alfa, Fiat, Mitsubishi, Nissan, Renault and Toyota are generally more likely to be traded, whether bought new or used, while German cars (Audi, BMW, Ford, Mercedes, Opel, Porsche, VW) are often more likely to be held back from the market.

We begin the presentation of our regression results with a histogram (Fig. 2) showing the hazard function that the coefficient estimates of the semi-parametric model imply. The hazard rates are based on separate estimates for new and used cars employing interval-specific constants for the baseline hazard instead of a polynomial trend as in Table 4. The regression results underlying Fig. 2 are not presented to conserve space, but all interval-specific constants were statistically significant at the 1% level. Since all covariates were measured in absolute deviations from their respective overall (used and new car combined) sample means, both sets of hazard rates pertain to the same constant average profile of characteristics and can thus be directly compared.[27]

As can be seen, the resell hazard rates for used cars exhibit a roughly declining trend over the 14 quarters of used car ownership that our sample covers. By contrast, the conditional resell probabilities of new cars first increase for two quarters of ownership, then decline over the next six quarters before rising again after about 2 years. Note too that the resell probabilities of new cars lie far below those of used cars in the first quarters of car ownership, implying on the basis of our reasoning presented above that quality uncertainty and not characteristic uncertainty is driving our results.

The evolution of the hazard rates over the first 2 years of car ownership suggests that buyers of both new and used cars suffer from quality uncertainty. The increase in hazard rates thereafter, however, is undoubtedly due to vehicle depreciation and has nothing to do with quality uncertainty. It is nevertheless interesting to note that the resell probability pattern for new and used cars is roughly similar from the 9th to 14th quarter of ownership, suggesting that owners are equally likely to resell new or used cars once differences in quality uncertainty have been eliminated.[28]

[27] The hazard rates are equivalent to life-table estimates where right-censoring is assumed to occur at the end of an interval and the effects of observed heterogeneity have been eliminated. Life-table estimates subdivide the time line into fixed intervals, whereas Kaplan–Meier estimates allow the interval length to vary according to the distribution of spell lengths.

[28] The hazard rates of the cars in our sample purchased new conform roughly to the pattern that Stolyarov (2002) discovered in a study of the US car market. He finds that resell rates, are very low for young cars and peak when vehicles are 4 years old. Thereafter, resell rates stay low for several years and then increase again when the vehicle is about 10 years old.

**Table 4. (Semi-)Parametric estimates of the hazard function of car ownership**

| Explanatory variable | Resale within 5 quarters after purchase | | | | | | | | Resale within 8 quarters after purchase | | | | Resale within 14 quarters after purchase | | | |
|---|---|---|---|---|---|---|---|---|---|---|---|---|---|---|---|---|
| | New cars | | | | Used cars | | | | Used cars | | | | Used cars | | | |
| | Semi-parametric | | Weibull | | Semi-parametric | | Weibull | | Semi-parametric | | Weibull | | Semi-parametric | | Weibull | |
| Constant | −3.540*** | (0.304) | – | | −1.791*** | (0.152) | – | | −1.823*** | (0.142) | – | | −1.776*** | (0.138) | – | |
| $t$ | 1.034* | (0.612) | – | | −0.050* | (0.030) | | | −0.036** | (0.018) | | | −0.038*** | (0.013) | | |
| $t^2$ | −0.714* | (0.389) | – | | – | | – | | – | | – | | – | | – | |
| $t^3$ | 0.117* | (0.065) | – | | – | | – | | – | | – | | – | | – | |
| $\eta \times 10^2$ | – | | 0.002 | (0.007) | – | | 0.018*** | (0.005) | – | | 0.020*** | (0.005) | – | | 0.019*** | (0.008) |
| $r$ | – | | 1.258 | (1.009) | – | | 0.814*** | (0.072) | – | | 0.828*** | (0.064) | – | | 0.800*** | (0.090) |
| $\theta$ | – | | – | | – | | – | | – | | – | | – | | 0.083 | (1.549) |
| Prior inspection | – | | – | | −0.078 | (0.089) | −0.210 | (0.265) | −0.142* | (0.080) | −0.382* | (0.241) | −0.145* | (0.077) | −0.432* | (0.245) |
| Vehicle age | | | | | −0.004 | (0.010) | 0.005 | (0.031) | −0.001 | (0.009) | 0.014 | (0.029) | −0.003 | (0.009) | 0.021 | (0.028) |
| Commercial use | 1.041*** | (0.397) | 2.602 | (4.276) | −0.287 | (0.430) | −0.718* | (1.414) | −0.332 | (0.417) | −0.862 | (1.341) | −0.033 | (0.305) | −0.202 | (1.065) |
| Diesel | – | | – | | −0.428 | (0.407) | −1.146* | (1.367) | −0.492 | (0.394) | −1.366 | (1.309) | −0.214 | (0.291) | −0.652 | (1.073) |
| Alfa | 0.696* | (0.390) | 1.993 | (1.231) | 0.841*** | (0.285) | 2.649*** | (0.978) | 0.397 | (0.265) | 1.186 | (0.811) | 0.440* | (0.258) | 1.410* | (0.833) |
| Audi | – | | – | | 0.614*** | (0.313) | 2.019** | (1.030) | 0.263 | (0.285) | 0.818 | (0.864) | 0.281 | (0.281) | 0.957 | (0.889) |
| BMW | – | | – | | 0.242 | (0.364) | 0.884 | (1.243) | −0.044 | (0.316) | −0.114 | (1.015) | −0.034 | (0.312) | −0.064 | (1.046) |
| Citroën | – | | – | | 0.439 | (0.338) | 1.490 | (1.128) | −0.012 | (0.318) | −0.005 | (0.997) | −0.024 | (0.312) | −0.027 | (1.028) |
| Fiat | – | | – | | 0.650** | (0.295) | 2.097** | (0.999) | 0.404 | (0.262) | 1.172 | (0.809) | 0.398 | (0.258) | 1.268 | (0.836) |
| Ford | – | | – | | 0.431 | (0.318) | 1.488 | (1.089) | 0.068 | (0.287) | 0.259 | (0.909) | 0.146 | (0.276) | 0.552 | (0.911) |
| Honda | – | | – | | 0.699** | (0.305) | 2.250** | (1.003) | 0.311 | (0.278) | 0.944 | (0.842) | 0.300 | (0.273) | 0.990 | (0.866) |
| Lancia | 1.236*** | (0.341) | 3.184 | (2.211) | – | | – | | −0.213 | (0.424) | −0.699 | (1.439) | 0.069 | (0.348) | 0.195 | (1.185) |
| Mazda | – | | – | | 0.551* | (0.344) | 1.775 | (1.154) | 0.226 | (0.308) | 0.671 | (0.956) | 0.231 | (0.303) | 0.738 | (0.981) |
| Mercedes | – | | – | | 0.550 | (0.345) | 1.790 | (1.149) | 0.101 | (0.326) | 0.330 | (1.009) | 0.305 | (0.293) | 0.928 | (0.959) |
| Mitsubishi | – | | – | | 0.726** | (0.306) | 2.300** | (1.025) | 0.515** | (0.269) | 1.456* | (0.827) | 0.517** | (0.264) | 1.578* | (0.861) |
| Nissan | 0.863*** | (0.314) | 2.334** | (1.192) | 1.015*** | (0.295) | 2.997*** | (1.029) | 0.595** | (0.271) | 1.639** | (0.840) | 0.555** | (0.266) | 1.674** | (0.860) |
| Opel | 0.117 | (0.375) | 0.613 | (3.856) | 0.567** | (0.274) | 1.875** | (0.947) | 0.181 | (0.251) | 0.579 | (0.790) | 0.187 | (0.247) | 0.665 | (0.813) |
| Peugeot | – | | – | | 0.551* | (0.324) | 1.828* | (1.070) | 0.093 | (0.304) | 0.333 | (0.942) | 0.191 | (0.287) | 0.657 | (0.936) |
| Porsche | – | | – | | 0.923* | (0.544) | 2.828* | (1.504) | 0.479 | (0.522) | 1.408 | (1.369) | 0.517 | (0.521) | 1.623 | (1.428) |
| Renault | – | | – | | 0.715** | (0.283) | 2.319** | (0.960) | 0.327 | (0.261) | 0.999 | (0.803) | 0.364 | (0.254) | 1.191 | (0.822) |
| Subaru | – | | – | | 1.065*** | (0.354) | 3.138*** | (1.119) | 0.579* | (0.331) | 1.601* | (0.943) | 0.676** | (0.311) | 1.966** | (0.981) |
| Suzuki | – | | – | | 1.124*** | (0.306) | 3.316*** | (0.998) | 0.704** | (0.287) | 1.952** | (0.830) | 0.730*** | (0.284) | 2.165*** | (0.869) |
| Toyota | 0.291 | (0.360) | 0.886 | (0.978) | 0.755*** | (0.271) | 2.350*** | (0.947) | 0.429* | (0.246) | 1.221 | (0.771) | 0.470** | (0.240) | 1.438* | (0.800) |
| Volvo | – | | – | | – | | – | | 0.050 | (0.353) | 0.090 | (1.141) | 0.057 | (0.348) | 0.163 | (1.174) |
| VW | 0.207 | (0.356) | 0.640 | (1.022) | 0.552** | (0.282) | 1.832* | (0.968) | 0.141 | (0.259) | 0.459 | (0.812) | 0.136 | (0.255) | 0.489 | (0.835) |
| (Split) Spells | 13 164 | | 2645 | | 4245 | | 1161 | | 5497 | | 1161 | | 6301 | | 1161 | |
| % Cars resold | 0.004 | | 0.004 | | 0.106 | | 0.106 | | 0.129 | | 0.129 | | 0.138 | | 0.138 | |
| $\ln L_\theta$ | −81.823 | | −73.519 | | −556.78 | | −532.42 | | −688.13 | | −611.23 | | −745.68 | | −645.06 | |
| $\ln L^*$ | −70.285 | | −63.865 | | −536.69 | | −514.65 | | −666.56 | | −592.80 | | −721.35 | | −627.10 | |
| $-2(\ln L_\theta - \ln L^*)$ | 23.075*** | | 19.307** | | 40.191** | | 35.552* | | 43.141** | | 36.850* | | 48.665*** | | 35.906 | |
| LRI $(1-(\ln L^*/\ln L_\theta))$ | 0.141 | | 0.131 | | 0.036 | | 0.033 | | 0.031 | | 0.030 | | 0.033 | | 0.028 | |

*Notes*: *, ** and *** denote statistical significance at the 10, 5 and 1% levels, respectively.
Estimated SEs appear in parentheses.

The hazard rate pattern appearing in Fig. 2 moves us to estimate separate models for three time lengths of car ownership: (i) the first five quarters, where both new and used cars were resold, (ii) the first eight quarters, covering the first 2 years of used car ownership and (iii) the first 14 quarters, in which all resales of used cars in our sample occurred.[29] The results appear in Table 4. We turn first to the results pertaining to the shape of the underlying hazard function and then focus on the results concerning the effect of observable quality differences.

With regard to used cars, our findings are quite clear. Both the semi-parametric and the parametric models point to a monotonically decreasing hazard function, irrespective of the time interval chosen.[30] The estimate of the Weibull parameter $r$ is always significantly less than one, and the estimated coefficient of the trend variable significantly less than zero at high-confidence levels.[31] We also considered higher order polynomial terms, which allow for a nonmonotonic shape, but they proved to be statistically insignificant. The parameter estimates presented in Table 4 imply a decline in the conditional probability of reselling one's car between 30% (semi-parametric model) and 40% (Weibull model) over the first year of car ownership. Based on the predictions of our theoretical model, these results clearly suggest that the buyers of used cars suffer from quality uncertainty.

In the case of new cars, the evidence is less clear. The estimated coefficients of the trend variable in the semi-parametric model imply that the hazard function has a cubic shape, first increasing, then decreasing and then increasing again. However, the data failed to support polynomials of a higher or lower order, which does not speak for the robustness of the result. In contrast, the Weibull model suggests that the hazard function is horizontal, the estimate of the parameter $r$ not differing significantly from one.[32] The lack of clarity is undoubtedly due to the fact that few new cars were resold shortly after purchase: only 10 vehicles or 0.4% of the 2645 new cars in our sample were resold within five quarters after their initial purchase compared to 10.6% of the used cars (Table 4). Hence, the database is probably too narrow to determine the true shape of the short-term hazard function for new cars.

As mentioned before, a declining hazard function could result from constant yet differing hazard functions across owners (owner heterogeneity). Unfortunately, our attempts to control for this unobserved heterogeneity on the basis of model (6) met with limited success. We were only able to obtain an estimate of the heterogeneity parameter $\theta$ for the entire 14 quarters of used car ownership our sample covers, and according to this result unobserved heterogeneity is not a problem. Controlling for unobserved heterogeneity is admittedly a daunting task so that our results can hardly be viewed as final.

We come to the second issue: the effects of observed car quality on the hazard function of car ownership. Our model predicts that higher observable vehicle quality or, equivalently, lower quality uncertainty should lower the hazard function of resell. Our findings support this prediction clearly with respect to new versus used cars (Fig. 2) and to a somewhat lesser extent in regard to inspected and noninspected used cars (Table 4). The qualification pertains to the estimates based on the first 5 months of car ownership, where the sign of the inspection coefficient is correct but not statistically significant. In general, the coefficient estimates imply that a prior inspection lowers resell hazard rates by about 30% over the first year of car ownership.

The estimated coefficients of the brand dummies also point in the direction of the predictions of our model: brands that are more likely to pass inspection (Table 2) and thus to be of better quality also have lower resell hazard rates. This is illustrated in Figs 3 and 4, which cross plot the estimated brand coefficients from the last column in Table 2 with those in the first (Fig. 3) and third columns (Fig. 4) in Table 4. The correlation coefficients ('rho') are not statistically significant, however, so the results are merely indicative.

Overall, our results appear to confirm the predictions of our model: the hazard function of car ownership is clearly decreasing over the short term for used cars, and higher average observable quality (i.e. greater quality certainty) tends to lower resell hazard rates.

Combined with the findings of the previous section, our current results suggest that sellers of used cars

[29] In the parametric model this is achieved by treating all spells of greater length as right-censored, and in the semi-parametric model by dropping split-spells pertaining to longer ownership durations from the sample.

[30] The fact that the Weibull model, which is based on continuous time, and the semi-parametric model, which rests on grouped durations, yield the same results indicates that grouping durations in discrete time intervals does not bias our measurement of duration dependence.

[31] Note that the asterisks in Table 4 pertain to two-tailed tests. The level of significance rises to at least 5% if the null is one-sided as in our model.

[32] The Weibull model is of course unable to capture nonmonotonic duration dependence. However, estimates of a log–logistic model, which allows for a first increasing and then increasing hazard function, also pointed towards a constant hazard rate.

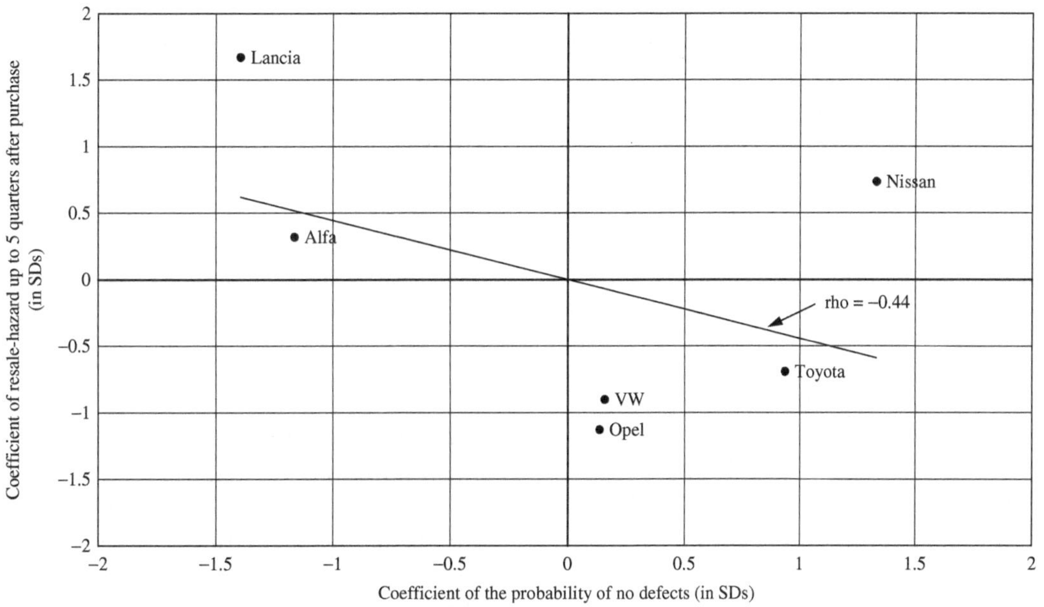


**Fig. 3. Cross plot of the brand coefficients for no defects (Table 2) and resell hazards (Table 4), new cars only**

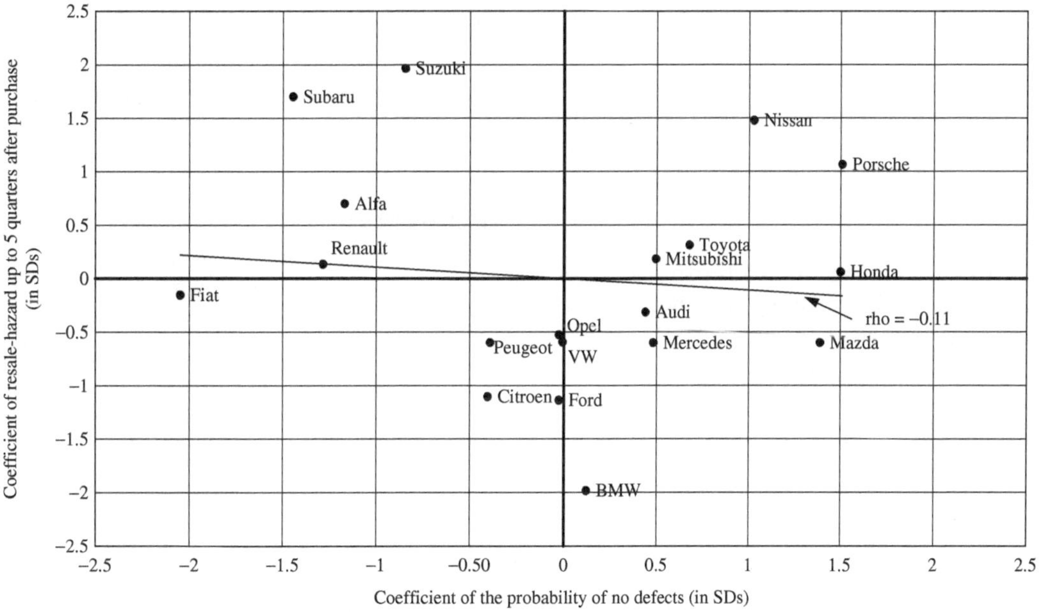


**Fig. 4. Cross plot of the brand coefficients for no defects (Table 2) and resell hazards (Table 4), used cars only**

enjoy an information advantage over buyers. Our reasoning is as follows. In the previous section, we found that the privately sold cars that were required to be inspected because of a change of ownership were more likely to exhibit a defect than a randomly selected vehicle with the same set of observable characteristics. Our test rules out the possibility that the higher defect rate could be due to chance, thus implying that sellers were aware of the sub-average quality of their vehicles. We assume that this result also applies in instances in which the sold used vehicles did not have to be inspected due to a change of ownership or had to be inspected for other reasons. In other words, we assume that the cars inspected due to a sale are representative of all used cars sold. Our data do not permit us to confirm this, however. Secondly, the results in this section clearly suggest that buyers suffer from quality uncertainty: for one, the hazard function of resell appears to decline with the duration of ownership; and, for another, the hazard function shifts downwards when quality uncertainty decreases, as our theoretical model implies. Taken together, these findings imply that buyers of used cars are at an information disadvantage *vis-à-vis* sellers.

Although present, the lemons problem does not appear to be widespread, however. Only 160 or 13.8% (Table 4) of the used cars in our sample were resold after purchase, and of these 123 or roughly 77% were resold within five quarters. Hence, perhaps as few as 10.6% (Table 4) of the used car purchases involved situations in which buyers were at an informational disadvantage. On the other hand, there may have been other dissatisfied purchasers for whom the transaction costs of reselling their cars were too high. Hence, informational asymmetry may be more prevalent than the frequency of resales indicates.

## V. Conclusions

This article has attempted to extend previous empirical work on the lemons model by not only testing for adverse selection among goods sellers choose to trade, as in the previous literature, but also by investigating the presence of quality uncertainty among buyers of these goods. In the latter endeavour, this article broke new ground methodologically by applying hazard function analysis to spells of consumer-goods ownership.

Our results pertaining to adverse selection indicated that cars sold privately are indeed more likely to have a defect than a randomly chosen vehicle. This suggests that owners of poorer quality cars knowingly put them up for sale. At the same time, our estimates relating to the quality uncertainty of purchasers indicate that buyers are not fully aware of what they are purchasing. This is evidenced by our finding that the probability that buyers will resell their vehicles is higher in the first months of ownership than later. This holds true whether a car was bought new or used, or whether it was inspected before purchase or not. However, the higher the mean quality of a car and thus the lower the degree of quality uncertainty, the less likely the vehicle will be quickly resold, further supporting our conjecture that quality uncertainty lies behind buyers' propensity to resell their vehicles shortly after purchase.

Admittedly, some of our observations can be explained using alternative stories. For example, the lower defect rate of dealer-submitted cars may be the result of the cost advantage of dealers in repairing cars. Yet, this argument cannot explain the higher defect rate of cars put up for sale by nondealers in comparison to the defect rate of randomly chosen cars. In addition, the falling hazard rate could also be due to unobserved consumer heterogeneity or car-characteristic uncertainty. However, our findings point in the opposite direction. All other theories we are aware of predict either constant or increasing hazard rates over the short-run. Thus, the lemons model seems to provide the best explanation for our results when viewed in their entirety.

## Acknowledgements

Financial support from the WWZ-Forum at the University of Basle is gratefully acknowledged. We thank the Department of Motor Vehicles of Basle City for supplying us with the data used in this study, as well as Tom Flury and Frank Losert for painstakingly transcribing the vehicle safety inspection records into electronic form. Special thanks are due Kurt Schmidheiny for extensive discussions. We also thank Pedro Pita Barros, Andreas Diekmann, David Genesove, Mark Israel, Erik Lehmann, Tom Gilligan, Klaus Pötzelberger and three anonymous referees for helpful comments.

## References

Akerlof, G. (1970) The market for 'lemons': quality uncertainty and the market mechanism, *Quarterly Journal of Economics*, **84**, 488–500.

Bond, E. W. (1982) A direct test of the 'lemons' model: the market for used pickup trucks, *American Economic Review*, **72**, 836–40.

Bond, E. W. (1984) Test of the 'lemons' model: reply, *American Economic Review*, **74**, 801–4.

Borland, J. and Lye, J. (1996) Matching and mobility in the market for Australian football coaches, *Industrial and Labor Relations Review*, **50**, 143–58.

Cameron, A. and Trivedi, P. (2005) *Microeconometrics: Methods and Applications*, Cambridge University Press, Cambridge.

Chapman, K. and Southwick, L. (1991) Testing the matching hypothesis: the case of major-league baseball, *American Economic Review*, **81**, 1352–60.

Chezum, B. and Wimmer, B. (1997) Roses or lemons: adverse selection in the market for thoroughbred yearlings, *Review of Economics and Statistics*, **79**, 521–6.

Emons, W. and von Hagen, J. (1991) Asset prices and public information: an empirical investigation in the market for automobiles, *European Economic Review*, **35**, 1529–42.

Engers, M., Hartmann, M. and Stern S. (2005) Are lemons really hot potatoes, Working Paper. Available at www.people.virginia.edu/~sns5r/resint/empiostf/hotpotatoes.pdf

Hautsch, N., Lehmann, E., Warning, S. and Frick, B. (2001) Shirking or mismatch? Coach-team separation in German professional soccer, University of Constance Discussion Paper No. 313.

Heckman, J. and Singer, B. (1984) A method for minimizing the impact of distributional assumptions in econometric models for duration data, *Econometrica*, **52**, 271–320.

Hendel, I. and Lizzeri, A. (1999) Adverse selection in durable goods markets, *American Economic Review*, **89**, 1097–115.

Genesove, D. (1993) Adverse selection in the wholesale used car market, *Journal of Political Economy*, **101**, 644–65.

Gibbons, R. and Katz, L. (1991) Layoffs and lemons, *Journal of Labor Economics*, **9**, 351–80.

Gilligan, T. W. (2004) Lemons and leases in the used business aircraft market, *Journal of Political Economy*, **112**, 1157–80.

Greene, W. (2000) *Econometric Analysis*, 4th edn, Prentice Hall, London.

Greenwald, B. and Glasspiegel, R. (1983) Adverse selection in the market for slaves: New Orleans 1830–1860, *Quarterly Journal of Economics*, **98**, 479–99.

Jovanovic, B. (1979) Job matching and the theory of turnover, *Journal of Political Economy*, **87**, 972–90.

Kiefer, N. (1988) Economic duration data and hazard functions, *Journal of Economic Literature*, **26**, 646–79.

Lancaster, T. (1990) *The Econometric Analysis of Transitional Data*, Cambridge University Press, Cambridge.

Lancaster, T., Imbens, G. and Dolton, P. (1987) Job separations and job matching, in *The Practice of Econometrics. Studies on Demand, Forecasting, Money and Income* (Eds) R. Heijmens and H. Neudecker, Kluwer Academic Publishers, Dordrecht, pp. 31–43.

Lehn, K. (1984) Information asymmetries in baseball's free agent market, *Economic Inquiry*, **22**, 37–44.

Ohtake, F. and Ohkusa, Y. (1994) Testing the matching hypothesis: the case of professional baseball in Japan with comparison to the US, *Journal of the Japanese and International Economies*, **8**, 204–19.

Porter, R. and Sattler, P. (1999) Patterns of trade in the market for used durables: theory and evidence, NBER Working Paper No. 7149.

Sheldon, G. (1992) Dauerhaftigkeit der beschäftigung in der Schweiz, in *Mikro- und Makroökonomische Aspekte der Arbeitslosigkeit* (Ed.) W. Franz, BeitrAB 165, Institut für Arbeitsmarkt- und Berufsforschung, Nuremberg, pp. 36–73.

Stolyarov, D. (2002) Turnover of used durables in a stationary equilibrium: are older goods traded more?, *Journal of Political Economy*, **110**, 1390–413.

Vaillant, N. (2004) Discriminating in matchmaking: evidence from the price policy of a French marriage bureau, *Applied Economics*, **36**, 723–9.

# Hedonic prices for cars: an application to the Spanish car market, 1981–2005

Anna Matas and Josep-Lluis Raymond

In this article we provide a comparison of different formulations for hedonic regression analysis in order to construct a quality adjusted price index for the Spanish car market over the period 1981 to 2005. Specifically, we address the issue of instability of coefficients over time, and propose two alternative estimation procedures based, firstly, on a moving sample of observations and, secondly, on a moving average of estimated coefficients in single period equations. The statistical tests applied support the proposed methodologies. On empirical grounds two conclusions can be emphasized. Firstly, our study concludes that, taking quality changes into account, car prices in Spain deflated by consumer price index (CPI) declined by 40% between 1981 and 2005. This result is robust to the alternative estimation procedures employed in the study. Secondly, an analysis of $\sigma$-convergence shows that for quality adjusted prices a clear trend in $\sigma$-convergence emerges between 1986 and 1992, whereas such a trend does not exists for observed prices. This result has to be related to Spain's integration into the European Community (EC).

## I. Introduction

Quality improvements over time for some durable goods pose the long-discussed question of how to construct price indexes taking quality changes into account. As is well-recognized, the hedonic approach offers an adequate methodology to adjust prices for quality changes.

In this article we address the issue of instability of coefficients of the hedonic equations over time, and present two alternative methodologies to deal with this problem. As is known, the hypothesis of parameter stability over time assumed by the traditional pooled regression approach is often rejected by the data. On the other hand, single period regression equations tend to estimate erratic coefficients, due, at least partly, to econometric problems. Our proposal builds on an intermediate solution between the two aforementioned approaches. We propose firstly to estimate the hedonic equation using a moving sample, and secondly, to compute the implicit price for the characteristics from a weighted moving average of the coefficients estimated in the single period regressions. Moreover, statistical tests are provided to test the simplifying assumptions. The proposed methodologies are also compared with the frequently used adjacent year approach. Besides, the study offers a comparison of quality-adjusted price indexes constructed using each of the alternative methodologies.

We have applied the proposed methodology to the Spanish car market over the period 1981 to 2005. The choice of the car market is justified by the large number of quality improvements in the performance and characteristics of cars that has taken place as a result of technological changes. Quality improvements can be observed in different areas, such as comfort, safety, performance, reliability and fuel efficiency. In fact, the seminal articles on hedonic methodology by Court in 1939 and Griliches in 1961 are both applied to the car market.

On empirical grounds, the article presents a decomposition of the variation in observed automobile price into the variation due to changes in the characteristics and a pure or quality-constant price effect. Moreover, the approach makes it possible to compute an index for the various quality dimensions. Finally, the article shows a process of $\sigma$-convergence in quality-adjusted prices related to Spain's integration into the EC.

## II. The Hedonic Methodology

### *Background*

The first empirical research relating price and quality is attributed to the work of Waugh, who in 1928 estimated a price function on vegetables (Berndt, 1991). In 1939, Court estimated a multiple regression equation, which he named hedonic method, which related car prices to the relevant car characteristics, with the final objective of constructing a quality-adjusted price index for the automobile market in the United States. However, it was not until Griliches's work in 1961, also applied to the car market, that the hedonic approach became widespread. Nowadays it is used by some statistical agencies to compute price indexes adjusted by quality, and there has been a renewed interest from empirical and theoretical research. In particular, this method is applied to the computer, automobile and housing markets. A recent and up-to-date review can be found in Triplett (2004). For the car market, see the studies by Ohta and Griliches (1986), Bajic (1993), Arguea *et al.* (1994), Raff and Trajtenberg (1995), Murray and Sarantis (1999), Izquierdo *et al.* (2001), Reis and Santos Silva (2002), van Dalen and Bodie (2004) and Requena-Silvente and Walker (2006).

The underlying hypothesis of the hedonic analysis is that goods can be viewed as a bundle of attributes or characteristics, and the demand for a good is really a demand for the attributes it contains. According to this hypothesis, the price of a good can be expressed as a function of its characteristics, and the relationship between price and characteristics is called the hedonic function. The estimation of a hedonic price equation makes it possible to distinguish between the variation in prices explained by a change in the characteristics and the variation that can be attributed to a pure price effect.

Initially, hedonic regressions were viewed as an *ad hoc* empirical instrument to construct a quality-adjusted price index. Its theoretical basis is found on the consumer theory developed among others by Houthakker (1952) and Lancaster (1966) in the characteristics space. Later, Rosen (1974) expanded the theoretical foundation.[1] In this study, we interpret the hedonic equation as an instrument to approximate the evolution of price indexes, taking into account the variation in product characteristics. Regression coefficients can be interpreted as implicit prices for characteristic.

Despite the large literature devoted to the hedonic price function, some methodological problems have yet to be solved.[2] One of these problems is how to deal with the instability of coefficients over time. In the following section, two possible solutions to this issue are proposed.

[1] Rosen (1974) developed a theoretical framework for hedonic prices as equilibrium prices for supply and demand functions, both defined on the characteristics of products. Under this framework, the characteristic coefficients in the hedonic equation are the result of the interaction between the consumer's marginal valuation and the producer's marginal cost. As has been demonstrated by many authors, only under very restrictive assumptions it is possible to identify estimated coefficients as consumers' preferences or producers' costs. However, this problem does not affect the possibility of computing the hedonic index as an approximation to the exact hedonic index (Feenstra, 1995). Moreover, several publications by Pakes (2003, 2004) have recently revived the interest in the economic rationale of hedonic prices. This author derives the hedonic framework from the industrial organization theory in the context of technological change, differentiated product markets and heterogeneous consumers. Under his approach producers' mark-ups are a function of the characteristics and costs of all goods and of the distribution of consumer attributes, and vary over time and depending on products. Under this approach, the coefficients in the hedonic equation may vary quickly over time and do not necessarily have to take the expected sign. Pakes's formulation has received great attention in hedonic literature. It has however generated some still unresolved controversies (see, for instance, Triplett, 2004, p. 159).

[2] See Diewert (2003) and Triplett (2004, Chapters V and VI).

### *Alternative proposals for estimating hedonic prices*

Given that the coefficients in the hedonic equation can be interpreted as the result of the interaction of the demand and supply curves for characteristics, a shift in any curve might cause a change in the estimated coefficient over time. Thus, in empirical implementation, the stability of the parameters over time has to be tested. The most obvious alternative consists of estimating year-by-year equations and testing equality restrictions among coefficients.

The problem with single year equations is that the estimated coefficients tend to be very erratic due to the reduced number of degrees of freedom along with a high level of multicollinearity among characteristics. In that case, it is not possible to obtain a reliable valuation of individual characteristics or any group of them over time.[3]

The present article proposes two alternative methodologies for improving the way the value of the characteristics is estimated. The first alternative is based on the estimation of the regression equations using a moving sample of the observations, and the second, on a weighted moving average of the estimated coefficients in the single period equations. In each case it is necessary to fix the best order for the averages. With the aim of validating the alternatives, the underlying hypothesis of equality of coefficients is tested for each specification. Additionally, the study shows how the new proposals improve the results obtained in the adjacent period approach, which is the common way to address the problem of coefficients instability.

Finally, our results corroborate the previous finding that instability of individual coefficients is not a problem for the construction of a hedonic price index. The adjusted quality price index is very similar for all alternatives approaches. This result confers robustness on the estimation of the hedonic price index. The five alternatives used in estimating the hedonic equations are set out below.

**Time dummy variable method or pooled equation.** This method assumes constant coefficients and includes time dummy variables. It has been widely used in empirical research in hedonic prices. All the observations are 'pooled' into a single regression equation and the estimated coefficients are common to all periods. The estimated equation can be expressed as:

$$p_{it} = \alpha + \delta_t + \beta' X_{it} + \gamma' Z_{it} + \varepsilon_{it}, \quad t = 1, 2, \ldots, T \quad (1)$$

where $p_{it}$ is the price of car model $i$ in period $t$, $X_{it}$ is the vector of car characteristics, $Z_{it}$ is the vector of car brands and $\delta_t$ annual dummy variables.

The hypothesis of stability of coefficients over time can be tested using a conventional $F$-test.

**Single period equations.** In the unconstrained approach, separate equations are specified for each time period:

$$p_i = \alpha + \beta' X_i + \gamma' Z_i + \varepsilon_i \quad (2)$$

**Adjacent year equations.** This approach combines data from two periods so that the characteristic coefficients are held constant only for two periods. A time dummy variable, $\delta$, is included for the second year. This approach is also targeted to improve the problem of instability of coefficients and, hence, we will devote special attention to the comparison of its results with those of our proposals.[4]

$$p_{it} = \alpha + \delta \cdot D + \beta' X_{it} + \gamma' Z_{it} + \varepsilon_{it}, \quad t = t, t+1$$

where $D$ is a dummy variable that takes value 1 for observations in the second year. The $F$-test is used to test the constraint on equality of coefficients.

**Moving sample of order *h*.** This is the first of the new alternatives suggested in this work. The estimated equation can be expressed as:

$$p_{ih} = \alpha_{\mathrm{ms}h} + \delta_h + \beta'_{\mathrm{ms}h} X_{ih} + \gamma'_{\mathrm{ms}h} Z_{ih} + \varepsilon_{ih}, \quad h = 1, 2, \ldots, H \quad (3)$$

where the sub-index 'ms' denotes that the parameter corresponds to a moving sample of $h$ periods.

The regression equation is estimated for a centred moving sample of order $h$. A different vector of coefficients is estimated for each moving sample and, as in the previous case, an $F$-test allows us to test

[3] Empirical evidence shows that the estimated coefficients in yearly equations are highly volatile. As long as these coefficients approximate implicit prices for characteristics, it seems desirable for both their magnitude and sign to behave according to the expected values. In our view, the volatility in the estimates can be largely explained by econometric problems. The main problems when estimating hedonic equations are multicollinearity and the reduced number of degrees of freedom which result in large variance of some of the estimated coefficients which in turn produce instability in their value. This view has however been recently disputed by Pakes in several provocative articles. In the context defined in footnote 2, this author argues that the coefficients in the hedonic function do not necessarily obey any of the restrictions associated with utility or costs functions (Pakes, 2004). As has been recognized (Berndt and Rappaport, 2003; Triplett, 2004, pp. 236–38), although some of the issues in Pakes's work are still controversial, it has made remarkable contributions to the hedonic theory. The issue we address in this article is the econometric problems that arise when estimating yearly equations with limited sample size.

[4] In this point we acknowledge the suggestion of an anonymous referee.

equality among coefficients and to establish the order of the moving sample.

**Weighted moving average of the coefficients estimated in the single period regressions.** The second new alternative put forward involves computing the implicit price for the product characteristics by constructing a weighted moving average of the coefficients estimated in the single period equations. This approach has the advantage that it makes it possible for the coefficient to take different values over time, while at the same time the erraticity found in annual estimates is smoothed out. Again, the restriction imposed on the coefficients and the order of the moving average can be tested. The basis for this procedure can be stated as follows.

To fix ideas, let the order of the moving average be 3. We have three estimates for $\beta_{i,j}$, where $i$ stands for a product characteristic and $j$ for a year: $\hat{\beta}_{i,-1}, \hat{\beta}_{i,0}, \hat{\beta}_{i,+1}$. Let us assume that these are unbiased estimates. Then, the following estimator can be constructed:[5]

$$\hat{\beta}_i = \lambda_{-1} \cdot \hat{\beta}_{i,-1} + \lambda_0 \cdot \hat{\beta}_{i,0} + \lambda_{+1} \cdot \hat{\beta}_{i,+1} = \lambda_{-1} \cdot \hat{\beta}_{i,-1} + \lambda_0 \cdot \hat{\beta}_{i,0} + (1 - \lambda_{-1} - \lambda_0) \cdot \hat{\beta}_{i,+1} \quad (4)$$

Generally, the estimator can be written as:

$$\hat{\beta}_i = \lambda' \cdot \hat{\theta}_i, \quad \text{where } \hat{\theta}'_i = \left(\hat{\beta}_{i,-1}\hat{\beta}_{i,0}\hat{\beta}_{i,+1}\right) \quad (5)$$

$\lambda' \cdot l = 1$, where $l$ is a unit vector.

It holds:

$$\text{var}(\hat{\beta}_i) = \lambda' \cdot \text{cov}(\hat{\theta}_i) \cdot \lambda \quad (6)$$

By using the Lagrange multiplier method, the expression to minimize is:

$$\Phi = \lambda' \cdot \text{cov}(\hat{\theta}_i) \cdot \lambda + \mu \cdot (1 - \lambda' \cdot l)$$
$$\frac{\partial \Phi}{\partial \lambda} = 2 \cdot \text{cov}(\hat{\theta}_i) \cdot \lambda - \mu \cdot l = 0 \quad (7)$$
$$\lambda = \frac{1}{2} \cdot \text{cov}(\hat{\theta}_i)^{-1} \cdot l \cdot \mu$$

Multiplying by $l'$:

$$l' \cdot \lambda = 1 = \frac{1}{2} \cdot l' \cdot \text{cov}(\hat{\theta}_i)^{-1} \cdot l \cdot \mu$$
$$\Rightarrow \mu = 2 \cdot \left[l' \cdot \text{cov}(\hat{\theta}_i)^{-1} \cdot l\right]^{-1} \quad (8)$$

We have:

$$\lambda = \frac{1}{2} \cdot \text{cov}(\hat{\theta}_i)^{-1} \cdot l \cdot \mu = \text{cov}(\hat{\theta}_i)^{-1} \cdot l \cdot \left[l' \cdot \text{cov}(\hat{\theta}_i)^{-1} \cdot l\right]^{-1}$$
$$= \frac{\text{cov}(\hat{\theta}_i)^{-1} \cdot l}{\left[l' \cdot \text{cov}(\hat{\theta}_i)^{-1} \cdot l\right]} \quad (9)$$

Hence, the estimator of $\lambda$ that minimizes the variance of $\hat{\beta}$ is:

$$\lambda = \frac{\left[\text{cov}(\hat{\theta}_i)\right]^{-1} \cdot l}{l' \cdot \left[\text{cov}(\hat{\theta}'_i)\right]^{-1} \cdot l} \quad (10)$$

If $\text{cov}(\hat{\theta}_i)$ is a diagonal matrix, as can be expected in our case given that we run separate estimates, the weighting for $\text{cov}(\hat{\theta}_i)$ will be:

$$\lambda_i = \frac{1/\text{var}\left(\hat{\beta}_{i,j}\right)}{\sum_j 1/\text{var}\left(\hat{\beta}_{i,j}\right)} \quad (11)$$

Finally, we propose a procedure to determine the number of periods to be included in the moving average. Let us again assume that we have a 3-moving average. To guarantee that the estimated average has sense, we need the following assumption for the underlying population:

$$\beta_{i,-1} = \beta_{i,0} = \beta_{i,+1} = \beta_i$$

If $\hat{\beta}_{i,-1}$ is the estimated price for characteristic $i$ using the sample for year $-1$, $\hat{\beta}_{i,0}$ is the estimated price for characteristic $i$ using the sample for year 0 and $\hat{\beta}_{i,+1}$ is the estimated price for characteristic $i$ using the sample for year $+1$, the following hypotheses must be satisfied:

$$\hat{\beta}_{i,-1} \rightarrow N(\beta_i, \sigma^2_{-1})$$
$$\hat{\beta}_{i,0} \rightarrow N(\beta_i, \sigma^2_0)$$
$$\hat{\beta}_{i,+1} \rightarrow N(\beta_i, \sigma^2_{+1}) \quad (12)$$

Assuming temporal independence in $\hat{\beta}_i$, under the null hypothesis it must be verified that:

$$\left(\frac{\hat{\beta}_{i,-1} - \beta_i}{\sigma_{-1}}\right)^2 + \left(\frac{\hat{\beta}_{i,0} - \beta_i}{\sigma_0}\right)^2 + \left(\frac{\hat{\beta}_{i,+1} - \beta_i}{\sigma_{+1}}\right)^2 \rightarrow \chi^2_3 \quad (13)$$

This distribution is still asymptotically satisfied when the population $\sigma$ is substituted by its estimates. The proposed criterion would be similar for testing higher order moving averages.

Accordingly, the order of the moving average can be tested for each characteristic. The higher the selected order of the moving average, the higher will be the smoothing imposed on the parameters, but at the same time the higher the number of $\beta_t$ lost (a 3-moving average implies losing the $\beta$ for the first and last year in the sample, whereas a 5-moving average implies losing two $\beta$ at the beginning and two $\beta$ at the end), and the lower the adjustment capacity of the underlying price model.

[5] Granger and Newbold (1986) made a similar proposal for combining individual forecasts derived from separate models.

**Table 1. Variable definition for vehicle characteristics**

| | |
|---|---|
| Performance | Displacement (CID, cubic inch displacement)<br>Horsepower/weight |
| Ease of drive | Power assisted steering (dummy variable)<br>Automatic gear (dummy variable) |
| Size | Volume (length × width × height)<br>Minivan (dummy variable) |
| Comfort | Number of doors<br>Air conditioning (dummy variable)<br>Climate control (dummy variable)<br>Electric windows (dummy variable) |
| Fuel efficiency | Fuel consumption (litres per 100 km/horsepower)<br>Diesel (dummy variable) |
| Safety features | Antilock Braking System (ABS) (dummy variable) |

## III. The Data

The data set for our study covers a 24-year period from 1981 to 2005. Over this period we collected data for car models with higher sales figures in Spain, coming to roughly 90% of total registrations. The total number of observations is 1970, with an average of 82 models per year, although the number of models increases for more recent years.[6] In our opinion, the sample gathered is a representative sample of market trends.

The prices and characteristics of the car models were obtained from specialist magazines. The price used thus corresponds to list prices, as is often the case in hedonic analysis. In addition, car prices include value added tax (VAT) and special car tax. Table A.1 in the appendix offers descriptive statistics for the dependent variable.

A relevant issue in hedonic analysis is the selection of the explanatory variables in the model. These variables should reflect the set of characteristics that consumers look for when choosing a new car. In this study, the selection of the variables to be included as regressors was based on the results reported in the literature,[7] taking into account the limitation of our data source. We expect that the characteristics used are a reasonable approximation to the consumer's price determinants. The variables are grouped into six categories and summarized in Table 1.

Dummy variables for car manufacturers were included in order to account for unobservable attributes that are related to characteristics like reliability or other unobserved attributes. Finally, annual dummy variables on imported cars entered the equation to capture the effect of tariffs. It should also be mentioned that we tried a number of other explanatory variables in preliminary analyses that did not prove to be statistically significant.[8]

## IV. Estimation Issues

The first issue to be considered is the functional form for the hedonic regression. Given that economic theory does not restrict the functional form for hedonic functions,[9] we proceeded by choosing the functional form that best fits the data. The starting point was the Box–Cox formulation, transforming the dependent variable and independent variables with a different parameter, which nests the most common functional forms used in hedonic regressions. To select the final specification we computed the likelihood function after taking into account the transformation of the dependent variable in order to guarantee that its value could be compared among the different specifications. Table 2 presents the value of the likelihood function for the Box–Cox and semi-log formulation using the time dummy variable approach.[10] Although

[6] The information on sales volumes was provided by the *Instituto de Estudios de Automocion* (Spanish motor vehicle manufacturers' association). Unfortunately, no data was available for the different model versions. Our choice was to select a middle-range model.

[7] We draw heavily on Raff and Trajtenberg (1995).

[8] For instance, number of gears, maximum speed, number of airbags and central locking.

[9] Rosen (1974) established that the hedonic functional form is an empirical issue. Subsequent studies showed that only under very restrictive assumptions is it possible to restrict the functional form.

[10] It should be noted that the same result was reached by the single year equations approach. Nevertheless, it would be too cumbersome to present all the estimations year-by-year.

**Table 2. Selection of the functional form**

| Functional form | $L^*$-value | Schwarz criterion |
|---|---|---|
| Box–Cox ($\lambda_{l.h.s} = 0.03$) ($\lambda_{r.h.s} = 1.05$) | −26 403.48 | −26 699.33 |
| Semi-log | −26 404.79 | −26 696.84 |

Schwarz criterion has been computed as $L^* - (k/2)\ln(N)$, where $k$ is the number of estimated parameters and $N$ the sample size.

the likelihood function was maximized for a Box–Cox, the semi-log formulation (taking logs of the dependent variable) could not be rejected and it was also the preferred option in terms of the Schwarz criterion. Given these results, and taking into account that the semi-log formulation is simple to estimate and easy to interpret, this was the selected specification.[11]

A second issue to be considered is whether the hedonic regression should be weighted or unweighted.[12] Our preferred option has been not to weight. In fact, as Deaton (1997) remarks, under the standard assumptions of the linear regression model weighting leads to a loss of efficiency. Even if those assumptions are not satisfied, weighting will not generally be the appropriate solution.[13]

Once the functional form had been selected, we proceeded to estimate the hedonic equation according to the five alternatives set out in Section II. All the equations have been estimated in current prices. This decision does not affect the estimated coefficient for the characteristics, it only affects the coefficient of the time dummy variables.

First, the estimation results for the pooled regression model, presented in Table A.2 in the appendix, show a good fit. In addition, the estimated coefficients take the expected sign and are statistically significant. Since some heteroskedasticity was observed, the variance–covariance matrix was computed using the White procedure. However, the SEs were very similar in both formulations; i.e. under the standard approach or using White formulation. It is interesting to test whether disturbance heteroskedasticity is present over time. In order to test this possibility we followed the procedure suggested by Berndt and Rappaport (2003). Thus, we regressed the squared residuals on a constant and a set of annual dummy variables, and computed the $F$-test for joint equality of the residual variances across all years. The null hypothesis of homoskedasticity over time was not rejected ($F = 1.299$, $p$-value $= 0.151$).

The estimated coefficients for the dummy variables can be interpreted as the percentage increase in car price derived from the introduction of a new attribute. For instance, those cars with a climate control system are 13% more expensive, holding the rest of the characteristics constant. Brand effects are computed with respect to Seat, probably the most representative Spanish car manufacturer. The significance of the estimated coefficients shows that there is a brand-quality effect over and above the included car attributes. Mercedes cars appear as the most expensive brand, once the characteristics have been controlled for. In the semi-log formulation, the coefficient for the time dummy variables reveals the variation in the log of the price adjusted by quality change. That is, the antilogarithm of the estimated coefficient for year $t$ can be interpreted as the percentage change in the car price between the base period and period $t$, maintaining quality constant. In our case, the coefficient estimated for year 2005 implies that, holding

[11] The semi-log functional form has been widely used with automobile data; see, for instance, Bajic (1993), Murray and Sarantis (1999), van Dalen and Bodie (2004) and Requena-Silvente and Walker (2006).

[12] A clear distinction should be made between weighting the hedonic regression and weighting the hedonic price index (see, Triplett, 2004, pp. 189–193).

[13] A frequently discussed issue in the literature is whether in order to estimate the hedonic price equations the variables must be weighted or not. In fact, under the usual regression model hypothesis, weighting the observations by the market shares of car models has not a conceptual justification. As it is well known, in this case weighting must lead to a loss of efficiency meanwhile not weighting must lead to a Best Linear Unbiased (BLU) estimation. Also, under these hypotheses, both weighted least squares and unweighted least squares must be consistent. So, if the model specification satisfies the standard hypothesis, it could be expected that weighted and unweighted least squares will lead to similar values for the estimated coefficients. Nonetheless, for the exposed reasons, the not weighted least squares is the preferred alternative. In our case, using a sample for the period 1987 to 2004 for which data on sales by car model are available, the estimated parameters in the weighted and not weighted alternatives are rather similar. Computing a 95% confidence interval for the valuation of the characteristics that results from the two options the two intervals always overlap, and taking as a reference the unweighted estimates, the percentage of overlapping is 47% for the variable displacement, 74% for horsepower/weight, 92% for size, 84% for fuel consumption, 84% for diesel, 54% for minivan, 67% for number of doors, 94% for air conditioned, 87% for climate control, 88% for Antilock Braking System (ABS), 63% for assisted steering, 94% for electric windows and 100% for automatic gear.

**Table 3. Estimation results**

| | Yearly equations | | | | Adjacent year | | | | Third-order sample average | | | | Fifth-order sample average | | | |
|---|---|---|---|---|---|---|---|---|---|---|---|---|---|---|---|---|
| | No. regressors | No. sign. Coeff. (5%) | SE | No. Obs. | No. regressors | No. sign. Coeff. (5%) | SE | No. Obs. | No. regressors | No. sign. Coeff. (5%) | SE | No. Obs. | No. regressors | No. sign. Coeff. (5%) | SE | No. Obs. |
| 1981 | 20 | 10 | 0.05425 | 47 | – | – | – | – | – | – | – | – | – | – | – | – |
| 1982 | 22 | 12 | 0.06895 | 58 | 24 | 15 | 0.05991 | 105 | 28 | 19 | 0.06504 | 168 | – | – | – | – |
| 1983 | 24 | 13 | 0.06757 | 63 | 26 | 16 | 0.06709 | 121 | 28 | 21 | 0.07150 | 189 | 33 | 26 | 0.07241 | 301 |
| 1984 | 24 | 12 | 0.07629 | 68 | 26 | 18 | 0.06927 | 131 | 29 | 22 | 0.06793 | 196 | 35 | 28 | 0.07076 | 318 |
| 1985 | 25 | 13 | 0.06671 | 65 | 27 | 17 | 0.06890 | 133 | 31 | 24 | 0.06831 | 197 | 36 | 29 | 0.06773 | 329 |
| 1986 | 27 | 15 | 0.06162 | 64 | 29 | 20 | 0.06531 | 129 | 32 | 24 | 0.06454 | 198 | 36 | 29 | 0.06829 | 332 |
| 1987 | 28 | 11 | 0.06485 | 69 | 30 | 19 | 0.05843 | 133 | 32 | 23 | 0.06158 | 199 | 37 | 31 | 0.06575 | 331 |
| 1988 | 27 | 13 | 0.07175 | 66 | 30 | 19 | 0.06299 | 135 | 33 | 22 | 0.06223 | 202 | 37 | 28 | 0.06307 | 329 |
| 1989 | 28 | 15 | 0.06490 | 67 | 30 | 19 | 0.06261 | 133 | 32 | 22 | 0.06201 | 196 | 38 | 27 | 0.06240 | 335 |
| 1990 | 27 | 12 | 0.06650 | 63 | 30 | 21 | 0.06084 | 130 | 33 | 22 | 0.06136 | 200 | 39 | 30 | 0.06457 | 337 |
| 1991 | 28 | 15 | 0.05830 | 70 | 29 | 17 | 0.06202 | 133 | 34 | 23 | 0.06051 | 204 | 39 | 29 | 0.06126 | 342 |
| 1992 | 30 | 15 | 0.06581 | 71 | 32 | 19 | 0.05776 | 141 | 34 | 25 | 0.05547 | 212 | 38 | 30 | 0.05884 | 350 |
| 1993 | 29 | 20 | 0.05253 | 71 | 31 | 25 | 0.05640 | 142 | 34 | 27 | 0.05662 | 217 | 40 | 32 | 0.05607 | 364 |
| 1994 | 31 | 18 | 0.05947 | 75 | 32 | 25 | 0.05322 | 146 | 36 | 29 | 0.05269 | 223 | 40 | 32 | 0.06127 | 374 |
| 1995 | 34 | 18 | 0.06007 | 77 | 35 | 25 | 0.05449 | 152 | 37 | 27 | 0.06281 | 232 | 39 | 33 | 0.06598 | 387 |
| 1996 | 35 | 11 | 0.07541 | 80 | 36 | 22 | 0.06693 | 157 | 37 | 27 | 0.07050 | 241 | 42 | 34 | 0.06871 | 409 |
| 1997 | 35 | 14 | 0.08161 | 84 | 36 | 23 | 0.07289 | 164 | 40 | 28 | 0.07061 | 257 | 42 | 34 | 0.06852 | 429 |
| 1998 | 38 | 20 | 0.06002 | 93 | 37 | 26 | 0.06994 | 177 | 40 | 29 | 0.06514 | 272 | 42 | 32 | 0.06881 | 449 |
| 1999 | 38 | 22 | 0.06057 | 95 | 39 | 25 | 0.05609 | 188 | 40 | 26 | 0.06093 | 285 | 43 | 30 | 0.06848 | 472 |
| 2000 | 38 | 15 | 0.07541 | 97 | 39 | 23 | 0.06384 | 192 | 41 | 26 | 0.06728 | 295 | 43 | 31 | 0.06455 | 492 |
| 2001 | 39 | 14 | 0.07738 | 103 | 40 | 21 | 0.07109 | 200 | 41 | 24 | 0.06678 | 304 | 43 | 29 | 0.06488 | 505 |
| 2002 | 39 | 17 | 0.06486 | 104 | 40 | 22 | 0.06656 | 207 | 41 | 22 | 0.06370 | 313 | 43 | 25 | 0.06599 | 523 |
| 2003 | 39 | 20 | 0.06513 | 106 | 40 | 24 | 0.05968 | 210 | 41 | 26 | 0.06256 | 323 | 43 | 26 | 0.06770 | 527 |
| 2004 | 39 | 19 | 0.06846 | 113 | 40 | 22 | 0.06480 | 219 | 41 | 22 | 0.06709 | 320 | – | – | – | – |
| 2005 | 36 | 15 | 0.07580 | 101 | 37 | 20 | 0.07097 | 214 | – | – | – | – | – | – | – | – |

constant the characteristics, nominal car prices have increased by a factor of 2.31 between 1981 and 2005.

The estimated coefficients for the dummy variables on imported cars clearly showed the process of tariff reductions that took place once Spain joined the EC in 1986.[14] The coefficients were no longer significant after 1992, when the tariff reached zero for Europeans cars. In the preliminary estimations, we include a dummy on imported cars for those years after 1992. However, the coefficients were not significant. In the final equation therefore, the dummy for imported cars was limited to the period 1981 to 1992.

The main problem with the time dummy variable method is that it assumes parameter stability over time. With the aim of relaxing this assumption, we proceeded according to the proposals detailed in Section II. We began by estimating the most general model, i.e. the yearly regression equations, followed by the adjacent year approach. We then estimated the hedonic function for a moving sample of order 3 and 5, and finally we calculated the coefficients on car attributes as a moving average of the estimated coefficients in the single year equations. Again the order of the moving average was limited to 3 and 5. Table 3 summarizes the results of yearly, adjacent year and moving sample estimations.[15]

As is usual, the estimated coefficients in the single year regressions varied considerably from one year to another, and their observed behaviour could not be explained either on economic or on technical grounds. The adjacent period approach reduced the instability of coefficients but still the erratic behaviour of the coefficients could be observed. However, the estimations using order 3 and 5 moving samples smoothed out the changes in the estimated coefficients. To illustrate this fact, in Fig. 1 we plotted the estimated coefficients in the adjacent year and order 5 moving sample specifications for two car attributes: engine power (horsepower/weight) and car size.

In order to provide more formal evidence about the advantage of the moving sample approach over

[14] The process of tariff reduction started in 1986 and finished in 1992. Over those years taxes on European cars fell from 65% to zero.

[15] We estimated 93 different equations. Since presentation of all equations would be too cumbersome, the results are summarized in Table 3.

**Table 4. Comparison of coefficients' instability for different estimation approaches**

| | SE of the characteristic elasticity | | | | SE of the AR model for the estimated elasticities | | | | Number of wrong signs for the estimated coeff. | | | |
|---|---|---|---|---|---|---|---|---|---|---|---|---|
| | Yearly equations | Adjacent years | Third order | Fifth order | Yearly equations | Adjacent years | Third order | Fifth order | Yearly equations | Adjacent years | Third order | Fifth order |
| Displacement | 0.1098 | 0.0703 | 0.0555 | 0.0426 | 0.0963 | 0.0673 | 0.0563 | 0.0330 | 1 | 0 | 0 | 0 |
| Horsepower/ weight | 0.1263 | 0.0804 | 0.0633 | 0.0483 | 0.1091 | 0.0858 | 0.0515 | 0.0312 | 1 | 1 | 0 | 0 |
| Volume | 0.1734 | 0.1110 | 0.0877 | 0.0671 | 0.1516 | 0.0990 | 0.0671 | 0.0390 | 0 | 0 | 0 | 0 |
| Fuel consumption | 0.0980 | 0.0612 | 0.0496 | 0.0376 | 0.0925 | 0.0661 | 0.0441 | 0.0235 | 2 | 0 | 0 | 0 |

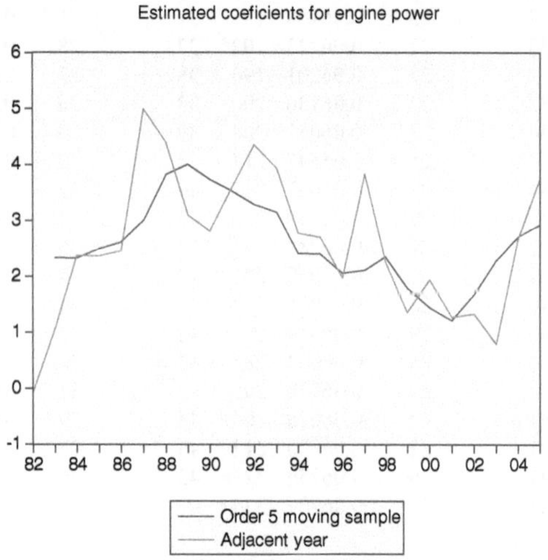


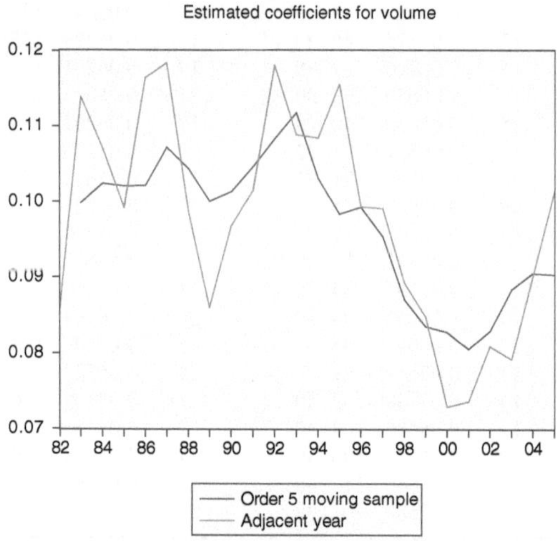


**Fig. 1. Estimated coefficients for two alternative specifications**

the yearly equations and the adjacent year ones we constructed three different criteria: the SE of the estimated elasticities, a measure of the degree of predictability of the coefficients and the number of wrong signs for the estimated coefficients. We construct a measure of predictability by adjusting an autoregressive model to the series formed by the estimated elasticities for the characteristic variables for each year in the sample. The SE of this model is interpreted as an indicator of predictability of the estimated elasticities under the four alternative approaches. These criteria have been computed for the continuous variables in the equation. We report the SE of the elasticities, and not directly the SE of the coefficients, in order to make comparisons between variables meaningful. Table 4 shows the results. It can be observed that the moving sample will always be the selected approach under the three criteria's.

Additionally, we have constructed a normal distribution for the elasticity of the continuous variables estimated according to the adjacent year approach and the order 3 and 5 moving samples. Figure 2 shows how the precision of the estimation increases when we change from year equations to the moving sample.[16]

The validity of the new proposals needs to be tested against the yearly equation model. Thus, the hypotheses regarding the temporal stability of the characteristic coefficients with respect to the single year equations were tested using the *F*-test. The results are presented in Table 5. Comparing the yearly regressions with the pooled model, the hypothesis of parameter stability over time is rejected. In contrast, at a 5% significance level, the hypothesis of equality restrictions both for the adjacent year approach and for the order 3 moving sample was not rejected in any of the cases, whereas that for the order 5 moving

[16] A normal distribution has been generated for each estimated elasticity, the mean being the average of the estimated elasticities for each year in the sample and the SD the average of the estimated SEs. It is interesting to remark that the mean value of the estimated elasticities under the three estimation approaches are very similar but the SDs substantially differ.

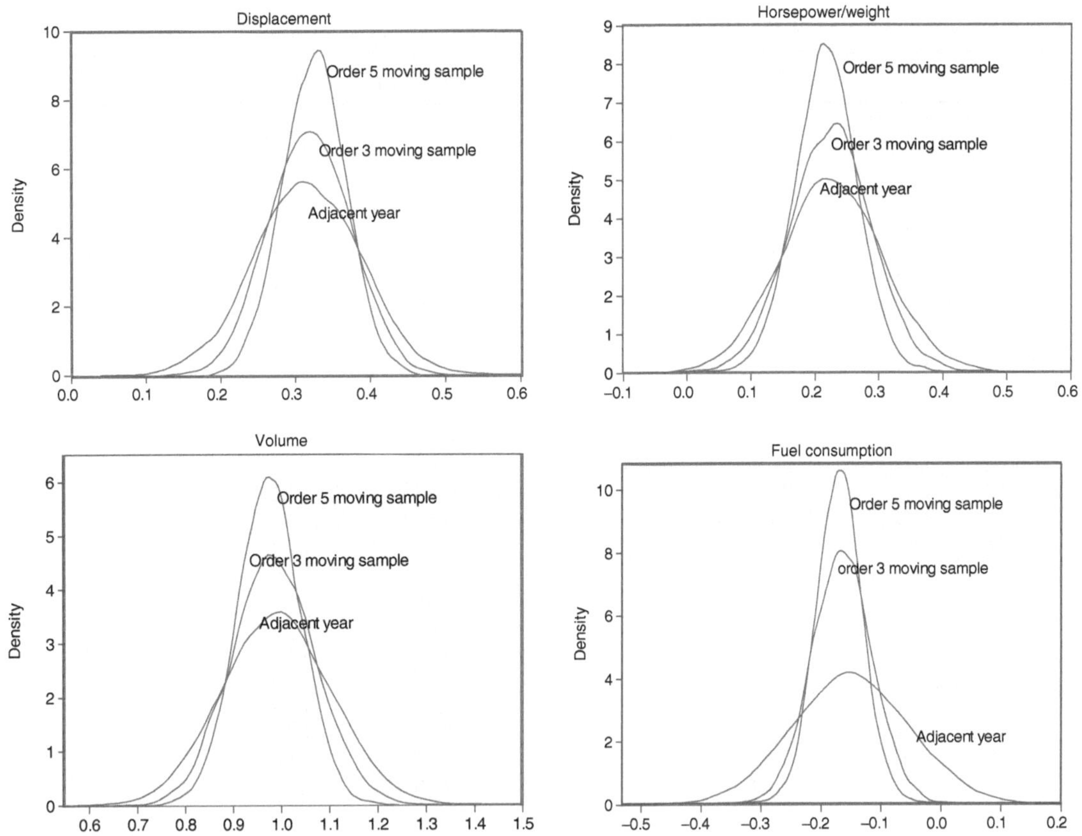


**Fig. 2. Normal density functions for the estimated elasticities**

sample was marginally rejected only in 3 cases out of 21.

The second proposal to correct for erraticity in the estimated coefficients consists of calculating the weighted average of annual coefficients, using the inverse of the variance as weights. As was previously stated, when deciding on the order for the moving average, a trade-off exists between the degree of smoothing and the flexibility of the coefficients in accommodating structural changes over time. Given the time span for our data, we propose to use order 3 and 5 moving averages and test the equality constraints. In this case the test on equality restrictions entails testing equality among coefficients according to the proposal detailed in Section II. For the order 3 moving average, the null hypothesis of stability of the slope coefficients was rejected only in 5 cases out of 745 computed averages, at a significance level of 5%. For the order 5 moving average, the hypothesis was rejected in 12 cases from 667.

At the usual significance levels, the results on equality restrictions support the alternative methodologies suggested in this article. That is, the procedures based either on moving samples or on moving averages of coefficients allow for temporal changes in the estimated coefficients, as demand or supply curves shift over time, while avoiding the situation where the erratic variation in the coefficients, tied to the multicollinearity problem and to the reduced sample size, hinders their economic interpretation.

## V. Results

### *Computation of quality-adjusted prices*

In the previous section we provided support for alternative methodologies to estimate hedonic equations. Now we turn to the essential objective of hedonic equations; i.e. computing quality-adjusted price indexes or hedonic indexes. The question is: does the methodology used make a difference to the price index in our case? To answer this question we computed the rate of change of the price index applying each alternative procedure.

The hedonic regression in period $t$ has the following form:

$$\ln(p_{it}) = \alpha_t + \beta' \cdot X_{it} + \gamma' \cdot Z_{it} + \varepsilon_{it} \tag{14}$$

**Table 5. *F*-test general model (yearly regressions) vs. constrained models**

| | Adjacent year | | Third-order sample average | | Fifth-order sample average | | Pooled equation | |
|---|---|---|---|---|---|---|---|---|
| | *F*-stat. | *F* critical value (5%) | *F*-stat. | *F* critical value (5%) | *F*-stat. | *F* critical value (5%) | *F*-stat. | *F* critical value (5%) |
| 1981–2005 | – | – | – | – | – | – | 1.67 | 1.00 |
| 1982 | 0.50 | 1.75 | 1.02 | 1.50 | – | – | | |
| 1983 | 0.76 | 1.75 | 1.02 | 1.43 | 1.43 | 1.22 | | |
| 1984 | 0.61 | 1.75 | 0.72 | 1.32 | 1.20 | 1.22 | | |
| 1985 | 0.58 | 1.70 | 0.94 | 1.32 | 0.99 | 1.22 | | |
| 1986 | 1.04 | 1.70 | 1.00 | 1.43 | 0.96 | 1.22 | | |
| 1987 | 0.37 | 1.70 | 0.53 | 1.43 | 0.96 | 1.22 | | |
| 1988 | 0.37 | 1.70 | 0.51 | 1.43 | 0.73 | 1.22 | | |
| 1989 | 0.32 | 1.70 | 0.45 | 1.43 | 0.73 | 1.22 | | |
| 1990 | 0.43 | 1.70 | 0.80 | 1.43 | 0.91 | 1.22 | | |
| 1991 | 0.98 | 1.70 | 0.70 | 1.43 | 0.95 | 1.22 | | |
| 1992 | 0.40 | 1.65 | 0.59 | 1.32 | 0.84 | 1.22 | | |
| 1993 | 0.60 | 1.65 | 0.69 | 1.32 | 0.69 | 1.22 | | |
| 1994 | 0.54 | 1.65 | 0.48 | 1.32 | 0.83 | 1.22 | | |
| 1995 | 0.31 | 1.65 | 0.75 | 1.22 | 0.89 | 1.00 | | |
| 1996 | 0.82 | 1.65 | 0.77 | 1.22 | 1.06 | 1.00 | | |
| 1997 | 0.46 | 1.65 | 0.85 | 1.22 | 1.06 | 1.00 | | |
| 1998 | 0.81 | 1.55 | 0.77 | 1.22 | 0.85 | 1.00 | | |
| 1999 | 0.46 | 1.55 | 0.52 | 1.22 | 0.75 | 1.00 | | |
| 2000 | 0.45 | 1.55 | 0.58 | 1.22 | 0.68 | 1.00 | | |
| 2001 | 0.40 | 1.50 | 0.46 | 1.22 | 0.64 | 1.00 | | |
| 2002 | 0.43 | 1.50 | 0.45 | 1.22 | 0.63 | 1.00 | | |
| 2003 | 0.30 | 1.50 | 0.60 | 1.22 | 0.75 | 1.00 | | |
| 2004 | 0.71 | 1.50 | 0.71 | 1.22 | – | – | | |
| 2005 | 0.94 | 1.50 | – | – | – | – | | |

The semi-log formulation makes it possible to define the mean variation of quality-adjusted prices as the difference between the variation in the average observed prices minus the variation that can be attributed to the changes in the mean values of each of the $X$ characteristics and each of the $Z$ brands for different time periods. Thus, the variation in the index for periods $t$ and $t-1$ will be given by:

$$\Delta \ln I_t = (\bar{\ln p}_t - \bar{\ln p}_{t-1}) - \hat{\beta}' \cdot (\bar{X}_t - \bar{X}_{t-1}) - \hat{\gamma}' \cdot (\bar{Z}_t - \bar{Z}_{t-1}) \quad (15)$$

This method of calculating the price index is preferred to the usual time dummy variable coefficient for two reasons. Firstly, the functional form of the hedonic equation does not necessarily determine the functional form of the price index. Secondly, it makes it possible to calculate a weighted price index without introducing weights in the estimation procedure.[17]

In accordance with Equation 15, we computed the price index variation rate for six of the hedonic formulations employed: adjacent year; 3-moving sample; 5-moving sample; 3-moving average of the coefficients of single period estimates, 5-moving average of the coefficients of single period estimates and pooled equation.[18] As can be observed in Fig. 3, our findings are that all indexes are remarkably close across alternative methodologies.[19]

The fact to be stressed is that, although the marginal prices for characteristics differ substantially depending on the methodology employed, the rate of variation of the quality-adjusted price index is very similar for all six alternative formulations. The reason for this apparent paradox is that the

[17] See Triplett (2004, pp. 60–61).

[18] When computing the index for the single year equation between years $t$ and $t-1$, it is necessary to choose the reference year. A common option suggested in the literature (Diewert, 2003) is to use the arithmetic average of the coefficients estimated in $t$ and $t-1$. This procedure offers very similar results to those obtained when estimating according to adjacent year method. In fact, as Triplett (2004, p. 63) argues, one of the earliest empirical regularities found in the hedonic literature is that the adjacent period regression often yields coefficients that are approximately the average of the coefficients estimated from a separate regression in the two periods. This is the reason why the single year approach is not presented.

[19] The moving sample and moving average formulations do not allow the index for the latest years in the sample to be calculated. These values have been forecast by using an Auto-Regressive (AR) model.

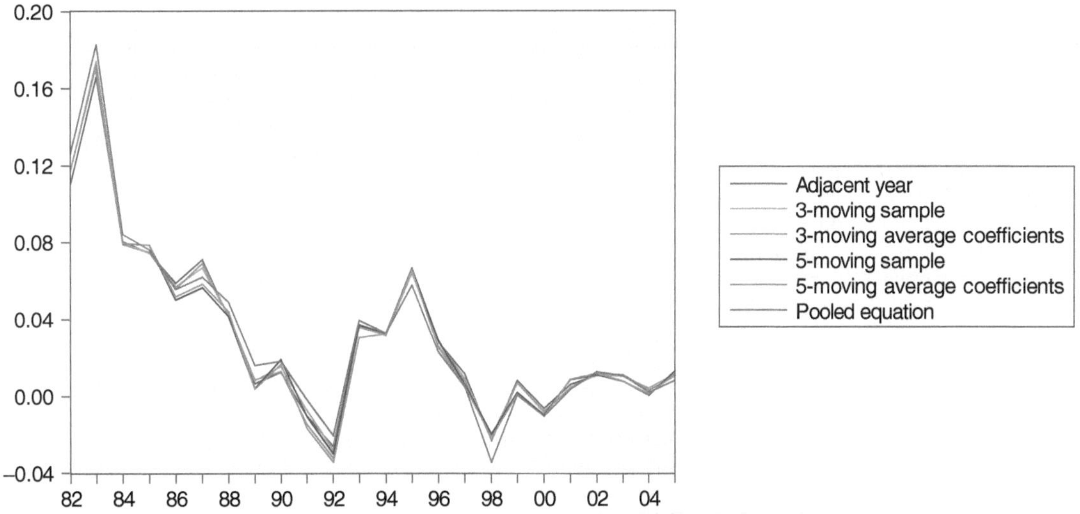


**Fig. 3. Rate of variation of the quality-adjusted price index**

multicollinearity and the reduced degrees of freedom distort the yearly regression coefficients. However, when adding up the contributions of all explanatory variables, the differences cancel out, so that the behaviour of quality-adjusted prices is very similar, irrespectively of the formulation employed to estimate the characteristics.

The previous result can be tested in a more formal way as follows. By comparing the price index for two alternatives, we have:

$$d_{ijt} = \Delta \ln(I_{it}) - \Delta \ln(I_{jt}) \quad (16)$$

where $i$ and $j$ denote different estimation methods. Thus,

$$d_{ijt} \rightarrow N(0, \sigma_{ij}) \quad (17)$$

Consequently,

$$\sum_{t=2}^{T} \left( \frac{d_{ijt}}{\hat{\sigma}_{ij}} \right)^2 \rightarrow \chi^2_{T-1} \quad (18)$$

Table 6 summarizes the statistic computed for all possible pairs of combinations between alternative estimations. In all cases, the null hypothesis could not be rejected at the usual significance level.

To sum up, our contribution to hedonics is a new strategy that can be defined as a compromise solution for estimating the marginal prices for characteristics between two polar alternatives: the time dummy variable model – which assumes that marginal prices for characteristics are constant over time – and single period estimations – that allow estimated coefficients to vary freely year-by-year. In any event, in our study the price indexes based on models with different assumptions about parameter stability are robust to the specified hypothesis.

### *Price indexes behaviour*

Once the methodological issues have been dealt with, this section focuses on the empirical results yielded by the study. The reported results are based on an order 3 moving average equation. Taking into account that equality restriction among the price indexes has not been rejected, the selection of this equation is due to the fact that it provides smoothed coefficients, at the cost of losing only two observations.

First, we present an analysis of the decomposition of the observed prices for cars according to the different components included in the hedonic equation. Specifically, price variation between period $t$ and $t-1$, $(\ln \bar{p}_t - \ln \bar{p}_{t-1})$, can be decomposed into the sum of the following terms:

$$(\ln \bar{p}_t - \ln \bar{p}_{t-1}) = \hat{\beta}' \cdot (\bar{X}_t - \bar{X}_{t-1}) + \hat{\gamma}' \cdot (\bar{Z}_t - \bar{Z}_{t-1}) + \Delta \ln(I_t)\hat{\beta}' \quad (19)$$

where $\hat{\beta}' \cdot (\bar{X}_t - \bar{X}_{t-1})$ is the variation that can be attributed to the characteristics, $\hat{\gamma}' \cdot (\bar{Z}_t - \bar{Z}_{t-1})$ is the variation that can be attributed to the brands, $\Delta \ln(I_t)$ is the hedonic variation computed as in Equation 15.

The hedonic variation in real terms is computed as $\Delta \ln(I_t) - \Delta \ln(\text{CPI})$.

The indexes were computed for each year at the mean value of the explanatory variables. Table 7 provides the results. The first and third columns illustrate the rise of the nominal and real (CPI-deflated) car prices. Thus, according to our

**Table 6. Test of price indexes equality**

| | $\chi^2$-statistic | d.f. | *p*-value |
|---|---|---|---|
| Adjacent year vs. third-order sample average | 23.51 | 23 | 0.431 |
| Adjacent year vs. third-order moving average of the coeff. | 23.34 | 23 | 0.441 |
| Adjacent year vs. fifth-order sample average | 23.37 | 22 | 0.381 |
| Adjacent year vs. fifth-order moving average of the coeff. | 26.76 | 22 | 0.220 |
| Adjacent year vs. pooled equation | 23.33 | 23 | 0.442 |
| Third-order sample average vs. pooled equation | 22.28 | 23 | 0.503 |
| Third-order moving average of coeff. vs. pooled equation | 23.02 | 23 | 0.460 |
| Fifth-order sample average vs. pooled equation | 21.12 | 22 | 0.513 |
| Fifth-order moving average of coeff. vs. pooled equation | 22.70 | 22 | 0.419 |
| Third-order sample average vs. third-order moving average of coeff. | 24.95 | 23 | 0.353 |
| Third-order sample average vs. fifth-order sample average | 22.44 | 22 | 0.434 |
| Third-order sample average vs. fifth-order moving average of coeff. | 26.96 | 22 | 0.213 |
| Third-order moving average of coeff. vs. fifth-order sample average | 20.25 | 22 | 0.567 |
| Third-order moving average of coeff. vs. fifth-order moving average of coeff. | 23.25 | 22 | 0.388 |
| Fifth-order sample average vs. fifth-order moving average of coeff. | 23.53 | 22 | 0.372 |

**Table 7. Decomposition of car price index into different components**

| | Price (nominal) | CPI | Price (real) | Characteristics index | Brand index | Hedonic index | Hedonic index (real) |
|---|---|---|---|---|---|---|---|
| 1981 | 1.000 | 1.000 | 1.000 | 1.000 | 1.000 | 1.000 | 1.000 |
| 1982 | 1.168 | 1.144 | 1.021 | 1.026 | 1.013 | 1.125 | 0.983 |
| 1983 | 1.449 | 1.283 | 1.129 | 1.050 | 1.033 | 1.336 | 1.041 |
| 1984 | 1.621 | 1.428 | 1.135 | 1.076 | 1.043 | 1.446 | 1.012 |
| 1985 | 1.811 | 1.554 | 1.165 | 1.105 | 1.052 | 1.558 | 1.002 |
| 1986 | 1.960 | 1.691 | 1.159 | 1.133 | 1.050 | 1.647 | 0.974 |
| 1987 | 2.156 | 1.780 | 1.212 | 1.171 | 1.043 | 1.765 | 0.992 |
| 1988 | 2.379 | 1.866 | 1.275 | 1.212 | 1.067 | 1.841 | 0.987 |
| 1989 | 2.467 | 1.992 | 1.238 | 1.247 | 1.066 | 1.856 | 0.932 |
| 1990 | 2.603 | 2.126 | 1.224 | 1.282 | 1.080 | 1.880 | 0.884 |
| 1991 | 2.661 | 2.252 | 1.181 | 1.339 | 1.072 | 1.852 | 0.822 |
| 1992 | 2.700 | 2.386 | 1.132 | 1.394 | 1.080 | 1.794 | 0.752 |
| 1993 | 2.818 | 2.495 | 1.129 | 1.404 | 1.079 | 1.859 | 0.745 |
| 1994 | 2.947 | 2.613 | 1.128 | 1.426 | 1.077 | 1.919 | 0.734 |
| 1995 | 3.110 | 2.735 | 1.137 | 1.438 | 1.054 | 2.050 | 0.750 |
| 1996 | 3.246 | 2.832 | 1.146 | 1.475 | 1.046 | 2.104 | 0.743 |
| 1997 | 3.336 | 2.888 | 1.155 | 1.500 | 1.049 | 2.120 | 0.734 |
| 1998 | 3.393 | 2.941 | 1.154 | 1.559 | 1.051 | 2.072 | 0.705 |
| 1999 | 3.532 | 3.009 | 1.174 | 1.602 | 1.057 | 2.086 | 0.693 |
| 2000 | 3.525 | 3.112 | 1.133 | 1.626 | 1.048 | 2.069 | 0.665 |
| 2001 | 3.745 | 3.224 | 1.162 | 1.727 | 1.044 | 2.077 | 0.644 |
| 2002 | 3.939 | 3.323 | 1.185 | 1.793 | 1.046 | 2.101 | 0.632 |
| 2003 | 4.048 | 3.424 | 1.182 | 1.825 | 1.044 | 2.124 | 0.620 |
| 2004 | 4.171 | 3.528 | 1.182 | 1.878 | 1.043 | 2.131 | 0.604 |
| 2005 | 4.351 | 3.614 | 1.204 | 1.934 | 1.045 | 2.153 | 0.596 |

sample, over the period 1981 to 2005, nominal car prices in Spain increased by a factor of 4.4; in real terms the factor falls to 1.2. However, part of the price growth is explained by quality improvements. As can be seen in the fourth column, the quality index, measured by the characteristics included in the equation, increased by a factor of 1.9. The effect of changes in brand composition (fifth column) was almost nil. As a result, it can be seen that the real quality-adjusted price index fell by 40%.

It should be noted that changes in car taxes are included in our hedonic index. The most important changes in taxation were a nine-point increase in the tax rate in 1986 and a five-point reduction in 1992. Our approach gives a lower rate of quality-adjusted price increases compared with the rates used by the Spanish statistical agency.

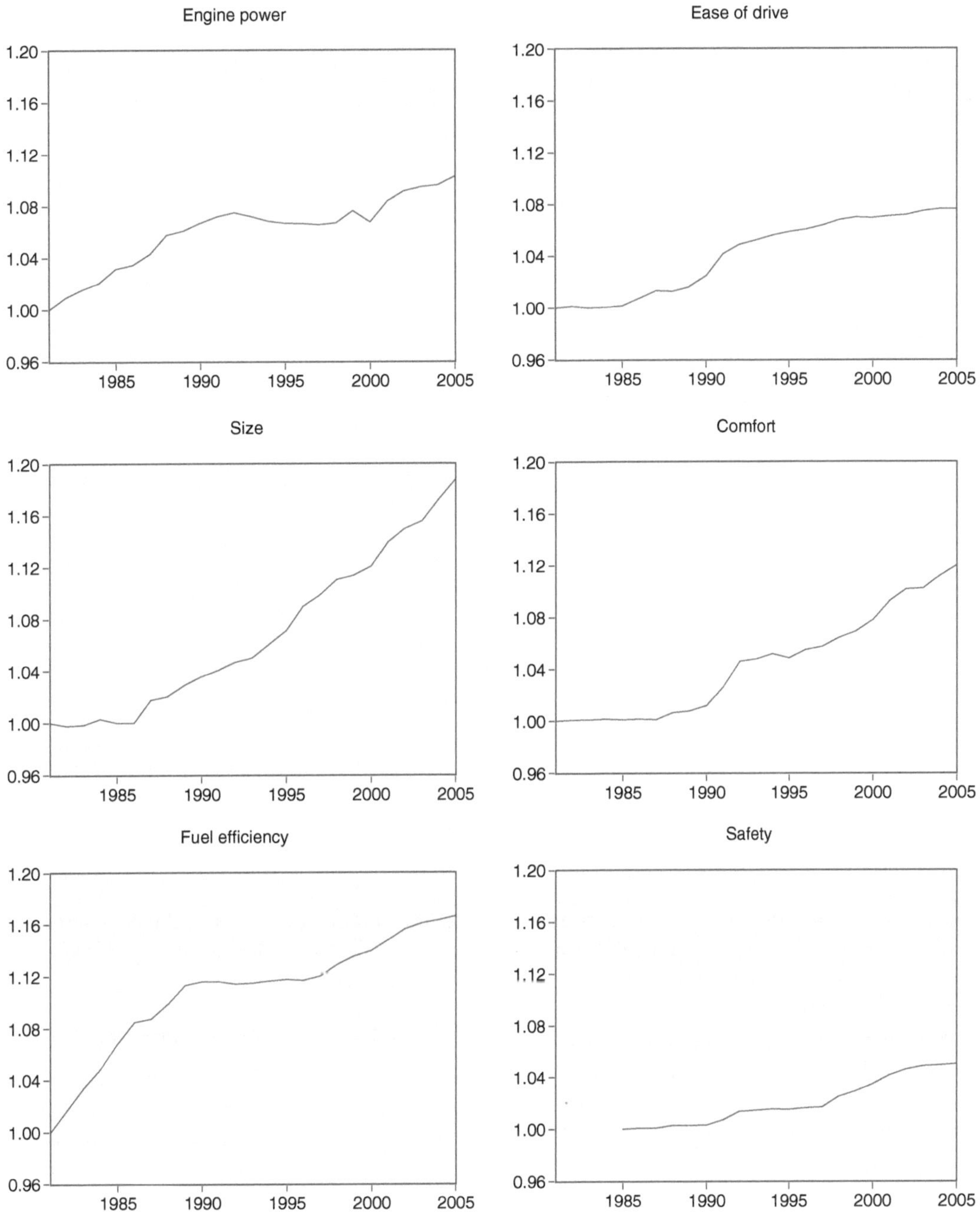


**Fig. 4. Quality indexes (1981 = 1)**

This is a common result when applying hedonic regressions. van Dalen and Bodie (2004) estimated a hedonic model for new passenger cars in the Netherlands over the period 1990 to 1999 that lead to quality corrected price increases between 7.3 and 17.7 percentage points below the official CPI index for new passengers cars, although the latter partially corrects for quality changes. A similar result has been found by Izquierdo *et al.* (2001) in their study of car prices in Spain during the period 1997 to 2000.

### *Quality indexes for groups of characteristics*

Following the same procedure as in price indexes, we have computed quality indexes for the six categories established in Table 1: performance, ease of drive, size, comfort, fuel consumption and safety.

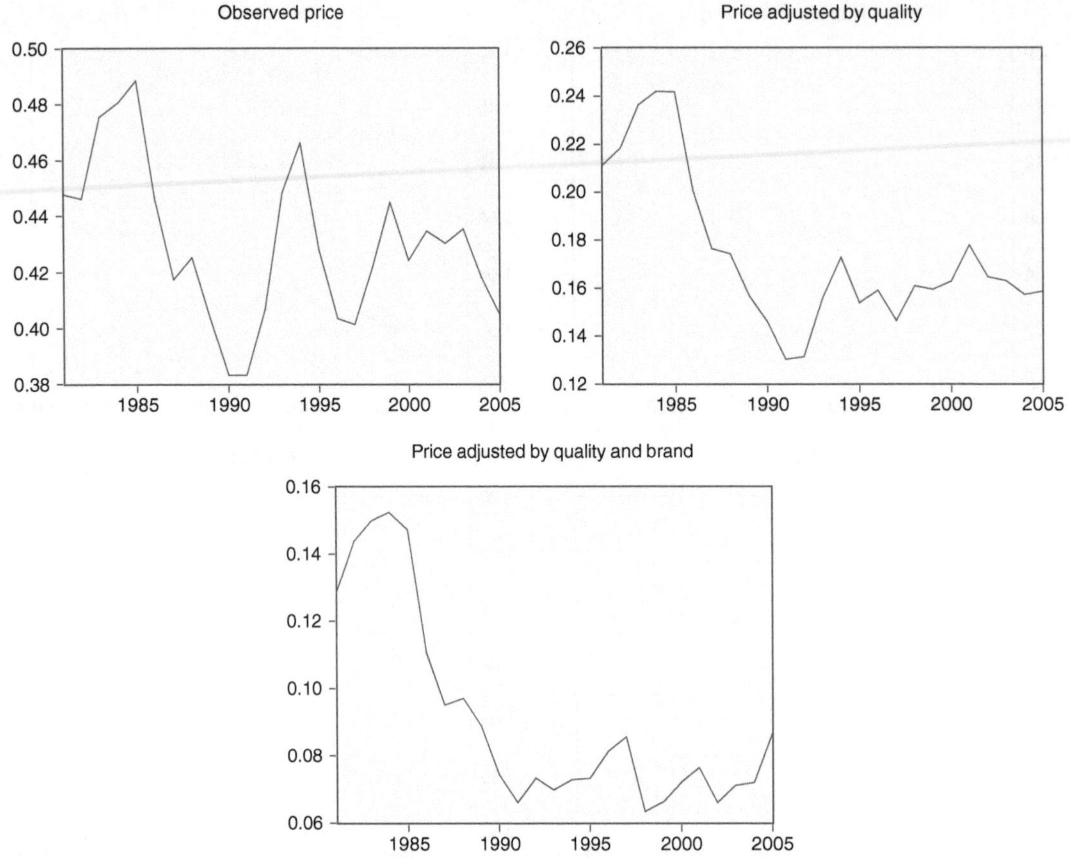


**Fig. 5. Sigma-convergence**

Fig. 4 plots the temporal profile. The variables representing size show the highest contribution to quality improvement of cars. The index takes value 1 in 1981 and it increases up to 1.19 in 2005. The growth of this index has to be related to the small size of Spanish cars in 1981, as well as to the existence of other nonobserved quality attributes that improve with size. Secondly, the increase in fuel consumption has also had a positive effect on quality (1.16 in 2005). The time profile of this variable can be related to the fuel price. Thus, up to 1988 the quality index rose very sharply as a consequence of technical changes introduced by car manufacturers after the energy crises of 1973 and 1979. However, the decline in oil prices in the second half of the 1980s slowed down efficiency gains, which picked up again after 1997. Thirdly, during the 1980s a steep increase in the quality index related to engine power was observed followed by much lower rates thereafter. This result agrees with the findings of previous studies, and can be explained by the improvements in engine efficiency, that allowed far better performance without increasing engine power. Finally, the substantial contribution of those variables representing comfort to the quality of cars should be mentioned. In this case, a certain relationship with Spanish income growth can be observed.

### *Price convergence and economic integration*

Spain joined the EC in 1986. One of the main arguments put forward to favour the process of economic integration is the consequent increase in competition which in turn translates into efficiency gains. Although it is difficult to find situations where this hypothesis can be directly tested, we should expect a convergence in quality-adjusted prices favoured by a higher level of market competition. We address this issue by computing the $\sigma$-convergence for different definitions of car prices. Fig. 5 provides the results.

For observed real prices, no clear pattern emerges. Despite the process of economic integration, price dispersion oscillates without a defined trend. However, when adjusting prices for quality changes, a clear process of convergence can be seen between 1986 and 1992, corresponding to the period of tariff reduction. This result is even clearer when prices are adjusted for both quality and brand changes.

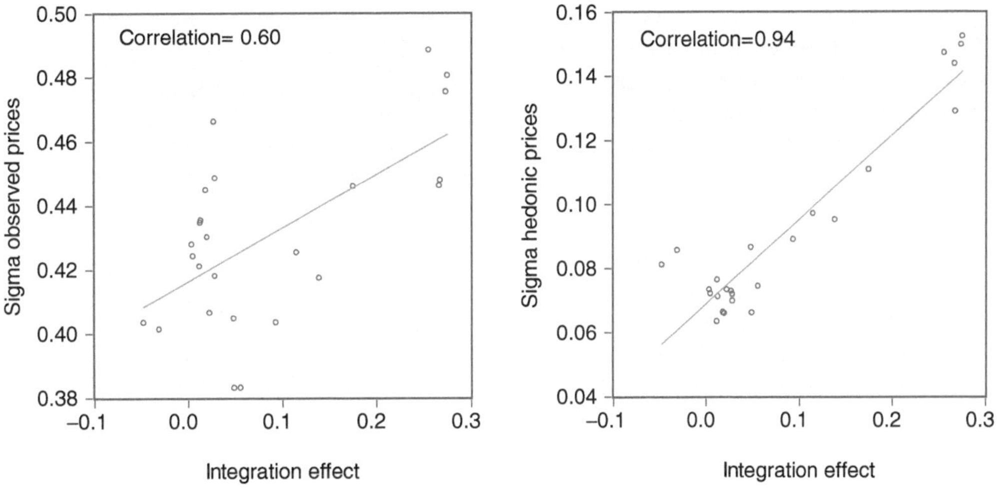


**Fig. 6. Price convergence and economic integration**

Hence, while for observed prices there was no process of convergence, for hedonic prices, which are the relevant ones in terms of measuring the degree of market competition, a clear reduction of price dispersion emerged. The reason lies in the substantial increase in high quality car imports with significant quality improvements with respect to Spanish cars, which resulted in a wider dispersion of observed prices, whereas the dispersion in quality-adjusted prices narrowed.

The effects of economic integration on the level of market competition can also be analysed by re-estimating the pooled regression equation including annual dummy variables on imported cars to capture its impact on prices.[20] The estimated coefficients for these variables can be interpreted as the effect of market integration, and as such can be related to the degree of dispersion in the price variable. A simple scatter diagram illustrates the correlation between the effect of tariff reduction, through the estimated coefficients, and the $\sigma$-convergence. Figure 6 shows a weak relationship between tariff reduction and $\sigma$-convergence for observed car prices, while a strong negative correlation appears when prices are adjusted for quality changes.

## VI. Conclusions

The aim of this article has been to estimate hedonic prices for a manufactured good – the car – that has been subject to significant technical change.

From a methodological point of view, we have addressed one of the limitations of hedonic regressions, the instability of coefficients over time. As long as the estimated coefficients can be interpreted as marginal prices for characteristics, an accurate estimation of them is needed. It is common in the literature to consider two polar assumptions. On the one hand, the pooled regression model assumes constant coefficients over time. In this case, the coefficients usually take the expected sign and are precisely estimated, but parameter equality is very often rejected by the data. On the other hand, unrestricted single year equations are estimated, which frequently generate very erratic and poorly estimated coefficients. The adjacent year is the usual approach to address this problem. Nonetheless, erraticity is still present. Our study proposes two solutions consisting in constructing a moving sample of the observations and a weighted moving average of the coefficients estimated in the single year equations. In both cases, the new alternative makes it possible to allow for annual changes in marginal prices of characteristics without imposing constraints that would be rejected by the data.

In relation to the empirical results, two issues can be emphasized. Firstly, CPI deflated car prices in Spain rose by 20% between 1981 and 2005. However, once quality improvements are taken into account, real car prices fell by 40%. This result is common in the literature that computes hedonic prices for goods subject to rapid technological progress and quality improvements. Additionally, it has to be stressed that the 40% drop is robust to the alternative estimation procedures employed in the study.

Secondly, for observed car prices there is no general trend of $\sigma$-convergence over the sample period; however, once quality improvements are taken into

[20] In the original specification these variables were limited to the period 1981 to 1992.

account, a clear trend in $\sigma$-convergence emerges between 1986 and 1992. This result has to be related to the tariff reduction following Spain's integration in the EC, which led to a more competitive market.

## Acknowledgements

This work has benefited from a research grant from the Spanish Ministerio de Educación y Ciencia (SEJ 2006-14849). The authors thank A.I. Guerra for her support in collecting the data and the *Instituto de Estudios de Automoción* for providing the information on automobile sales and to J. Asensio for his comments.

## References

Arguea, N. M., Hsiao, C. and Taylor, G. A. (1994) Estimating consumer preferences using market data – an application to US automobile demand, *Journal of Applied Econometrics*, **9**, 1–18.

Bajic, V. (1993) Automobiles and implicit markets: an estimate of structural demand model for automobile characteristics, *Applied Economics*, **2**, 541–51.

Berndt, R. E. (1991) *The Practice of Econometrics: Classic and Contemporary*, Addison-Wesley Publishing Company, Reading, MA, pp. 102–49.

Berndt, R. E. and Rappaport, N. J. (2003) Hedonics for personal computers: a re-examination of selected econometric issues, *R&D, Education and productivity, an international conference in memory of Zvi Griliches*, Paris, August 25–27, Draft manuscript: research still in progress.

Dalen, J. van and Bodie, B. (2004) Quality-corrected price indices: the case of the Dutch new passenger car market 1990–1999, *Applied Economics*, **34**, 1169–97.

Deaton, A. (1997) *The Analysis of Households Surveys: A Microeconometric Approach to Development Policy*, The Johns Hopkins University Press, Baltimore.

Diewert, E. (2003) Hedonic regressions: a review of some unresolved issues, *7th Meeting of the Ottawa Group*, Paris, 27–29 May 2003.

Feenstra, R. C. (1995) Exact hedonic price indexes, *The Review of Economics and Statistics*, **77**, 634–53.

Granger, C. W. J. and Newbold, P. (1986) *Forecasting Economic Time Series*, 2nd edn, Academic Press, Orlando, Chapter 10, pp. 227–42.

Houthakker, H. S. (1952) Compensated changes in quantities and qualities consumed, *The Review of Economic Studies*, **19**, 155–64.

Izquierdo, M., Licandro, O. and Maydeu, A. (2001) *Mejoras de calidad e índices de precios del automóvil en España*, Banco de España, Estudios Económicos, Madrid, p. 72.

Lancaster, K. J. (1966) A new approach to consumer theory, *Journal of Political Economy*, **74**, 132–57.

Murray, J. and Sarantis, N. (1999) Price-quality relations and hedonic price indexes for cars in the United Kingdom, *International Journal of the Economics and Business*, **6**, 5–27.

Ohta, M. and Griliches, Z. (1986) Automobile prices and quality: did the gasoline price increase change consumer tastes in the U.S.?, *Journal of Business and Economic Statistics*, **4**, 187–98.

Pakes, A. (2003) A reconsideration of hedonic price indexes with an application to PC's, *American Economic Review*, **93**, 1578–96.

Pakes, A. (2004) *Hedonics and the Consumer Price Index*. Mimeo.

Raff, D. M. G. and Trajtenberg, M. (1995) Quality adjusted prices for the American automobile industry: 1906–1940, Working Paper 5035, NBER, Cambridge, MA.

Reis, H. J. and Santos Silva, J. M. C. (2002) Hedonic prices indexes for new passenger cars in Portugal (1997–2001), Working Paper 10-02, Banco de Portugal, Lisbon.

Requena-Silvente, F. and Walker, J. (2006) Calculating hedonic price indices with unobserved product attributes: an application to the UK car market, *Economica*, on line publication.

Rosen, S. (1974) Hedonic prices and implicit markets: product differentiation in pure competition, *Journal of Political Economy*, **82**, 34–55.

Triplett, J. (2004) Handbook on hedonic indexes and quality adjustments in price indexes: special application to information technology products, STI Working Paper 2004/9, OECD, Paris.

## Appendix

**Table A1. Descriptive statistics**

| | No. observations | Average price (euros) | SD |
|---|---|---|---|
| | | (CPI-deflated) | |
| 1981 | 47 | 16478.5 | 9097.3 |
| 1982 | 58 | 16757.1 | 8802.0 |
| 1983 | 63 | 18807.0 | 10531.9 |
| 1984 | 68 | 18928.6 | 10393.4 |

*(continued)*

**Table A1. Continued**

| | No. observations | Average price (euros) (CPI-deflated) | SD |
|---|---|---|---|
| 1985 | 65 | 19 484.2 | 10 718.7 |
| 1986 | 64 | 19 029.9 | 9919.8 |
| 1987 | 69 | 19 624.6 | 9650.7 |
| 1988 | 66 | 20 664.3 | 9826.0 |
| 1989 | 67 | 19 859.2 | 8811.7 |
| 1990 | 63 | 19 470.4 | 8131.4 |
| 1991 | 70 | 18 784.8 | 7785.2 |
| 1992 | 71 | 18 148.7 | 7860.2 |
| 1993 | 71 | 18 475.3 | 9108.6 |
| 1994 | 75 | 18 625.9 | 9672.9 |
| 1995 | 77 | 18 406.5 | 8382.2 |
| 1996 | 80 | 18 382.7 | 8061.0 |
| 1997 | 84 | 18 507.4 | 8048.0 |
| 1998 | 93 | 18 621.2 | 8348.8 |
| 1999 | 95 | 19 164.8 | 9219.5 |
| 2000 | 97 | 18 319.1 | 8329.8 |
| 2001 | 103 | 18 827.7 | 8432.8 |
| 2002 | 104 | 19 187.1 | 8562.3 |
| 2003 | 106 | 19 176.8 | 8605.0 |
| 2004 | 113 | 19 039.5 | 8225.6 |
| 2005 | 101 | 19 271.6 | 7980.2 |

**Table A2. Estimation results for the pooled equation**

Dependent variable: LOG(Price)
Included observations: 1970
White Heteroskedasticity-consistent
SE and Covariance

| Variable | Coeff. | SE | *t*-stat. | Prob. |
|---|---|---|---|---|
| C | 12.33359 | 0.049774 | 247.7927 | 0.0000 |
| Displacement | 0.000222 | 1.08E-05 | 20.49526 | 0.0000 |
| Horsepower/weight | 2.301612 | 0.247389 | 9.303607 | 0.0000 |
| Volume | 0.091077 | 0.003050 | 29.85688 | 0.0000 |
| Fuel consumption | −2.067027 | 0.183303 | −11.27656 | 0.0000 |
| Diesel | 0.069964 | 0.008492 | 8.238396 | 0.0000 |
| Minivan | 0.039537 | 0.016749 | 2.360549 | 0.0183 |
| No. doors | 0.029148 | 0.005915 | 4.928121 | 0.0000 |
| Air conditioned | 0.053243 | 0.006215 | 8.566656 | 0.0000 |
| Climate control | 0.127339 | 0.007673 | 16.59570 | 0.0000 |
| ABS | 0.046201 | 0.006698 | 6.897887 | 0.0000 |
| Assisted steering | 0.067912 | 0.006651 | 10.21149 | 0.0000 |
| Electric windows | 0.025584 | 0.006178 | 4.141281 | 0.0000 |
| Automatic gear | 0.085218 | 0.017102 | 4.982959 | 0.0000 |
| Alfa Romeo | 0.091467 | 0.017487 | 5.230558 | 0.0000 |
| Audi | 0.258700 | 0.011970 | 21.61241 | 0.0000 |
| Austin | −0.074346 | 0.025075 | −2.964914 | 0.0031 |
| BMW | 0.346397 | 0.010389 | 33.34168 | 0.0000 |
| Chrysler | −0.233620 | 0.021121 | −11.06121 | 0.0000 |
| Citroen | 0.043901 | 0.009586 | 4.579825 | 0.0000 |
| Daewoo | −0.114095 | 0.015723 | −7.256535 | 0.0000 |
| Fiat | 0.008876 | 0.011847 | 0.749286 | 0.4538 |
| Ford | 0.034471 | 0.008564 | 4.024977 | 0.0001 |
| Honda | 0.089910 | 0.018446 | 4.874273 | 0.0000 |
| Hyundai | −0.142778 | 0.011942 | −11.95573 | 0.0000 |
| KIA | −0.267411 | 0.044292 | −6.037499 | 0.0000 |

(*continued*)

**Table A2. Continued**

Dependent variable: LOG(Price)
Included observations: 1970
White Heteroskedasticity-consistent
SE and Covariance

| Variable | Coeff. | SE | *t*-stat. | Prob. |
|---|---|---|---|---|
| Lancia | 0.098621 | 0.012422 | 7.939430 | 0.0000 |
| Mazda | 0.035517 | 0.015353 | 2.313313 | 0.0208 |
| Mercedes | 0.414736 | 0.011592 | 35.77729 | 0.0000 |
| Mitsubishi | 0.054551 | 0.023226 | 2.348656 | 0.0189 |
| Nissan | 0.030624 | 0.011925 | 2.568030 | 0.0103 |
| Opel | 0.082621 | 0.008827 | 9.360237 | 0.0000 |
| Peugeot | 0.057520 | 0.008135 | 7.070261 | 0.0000 |
| Renault | 0.007337 | 0.007427 | 0.987918 | 0.3233 |
| Rover | 0.043062 | 0.015401 | 2.796093 | 0.0052 |
| Saab | 0.197645 | 0.015198 | 13.00467 | 0.0000 |
| Skoda | −0.061187 | 0.020247 | −3.021983 | 0.0025 |
| Talbot | −0.020536 | 0.009720 | −2.112741 | 0.0348 |
| Toyota | 0.045968 | 0.012418 | 3.701838 | 0.0002 |
| Volvo | 0.227725 | 0.013648 | 16.68590 | 0.0000 |
| Volkswagen | 0.118445 | 0.008642 | 13.70599 | 0.0000 |
| Year 1982 | 0.106147 | 0.018453 | 5.752221 | 0.0000 |
| Year 1983 | 0.261728 | 0.017167 | 15.24589 | 0.0000 |
| Year 1984 | 0.339597 | 0.016736 | 20.29105 | 0.0000 |
| Year 1985 | 0.406745 | 0.017252 | 23.57620 | 0.0000 |
| Year 1986 | 0.498870 | 0.017538 | 28.44517 | 0.0000 |
| Year 1987 | 0.567498 | 0.016520 | 34.35153 | 0.0000 |
| Year 1988 | 0.624455 | 0.018241 | 34.23388 | 0.0000 |
| Year 1989 | 0.645247 | 0.018856 | 34.22006 | 0.0000 |
| Year 1990 | 0.679791 | 0.018422 | 36.90009 | 0.0000 |
| Year 1991 | 0.683766 | 0.017354 | 39.40096 | 0.0000 |
| Year 1992 | 0.679761 | 0.019555 | 34.76090 | 0.0000 |
| Year 1993 | 0.731340 | 0.017146 | 42.65282 | 0.0000 |
| Year 1994 | 0.763649 | 0.017163 | 44.49353 | 0.0000 |
| Year 1995 | 0.818267 | 0.017397 | 47.03626 | 0.0000 |
| Year 1996 | 0.840995 | 0.017872 | 47.05540 | 0.0000 |
| Year 1997 | 0.846782 | 0.018356 | 46.13110 | 0.0000 |
| Year 1998 | 0.810593 | 0.017363 | 46.68580 | 0.0000 |
| Year 1999 | 0.809771 | 0.017577 | 46.07055 | 0.0000 |
| Year 2000 | 0.798102 | 0.017887 | 44.61910 | 0.0000 |
| Year 2001 | 0.800529 | 0.018220 | 43.93748 | 0.0000 |
| Year 2002 | 0.813099 | 0.018027 | 45.10523 | 0.0000 |
| Year 2003 | 0.825567 | 0.018300 | 45.11407 | 0.0000 |
| Year 2004 | 0.829190 | 0.018550 | 44.69939 | 0.0000 |
| Year 2005 | 0.837513 | 0.018972 | 44.14556 | 0.0000 |
| Year 1981·import | 0.264849 | 0.042542 | 6.225597 | 0.0000 |
| Year 1982·import | 0.264331 | 0.034747 | 7.607373 | 0.0000 |
| Year 1983·import | 0.271647 | 0.024829 | 10.94067 | 0.0000 |
| Year 1984·import | 0.272940 | 0.024230 | 11.26461 | 0.0000 |
| Year 1985·import | 0.253548 | 0.021787 | 11.63772 | 0.0000 |
| Year 1986·import | 0.173231 | 0.020021 | 8.652421 | 0.0000 |
| Year 1987·import | 0.137589 | 0.017780 | 7.738514 | 0.0000 |
| Year 1988·import | 0.113397 | 0.020192 | 5.615971 | 0.0000 |
| Year 1989·import | 0.091651 | 0.018818 | 4.870388 | 0.0000 |
| Year 1990·import | 0.053550 | 0.017336 | 3.088959 | 0.0020 |
| Year 1991·import | 0.045937 | 0.015027 | 3.056973 | 0.0023 |
| Year 1992·import | 0.019186 | 0.018042 | 1.063358 | 0.2878 |
| *R*-squared | 0.982608 | Mean-dependent var. | | 14.58690 |
| Adjusted *R*-squared | 0.981910 | SD-dependent var. | | 0.561995 |
| SE of regression | 0.075588 | Akaike info criterion | | −2.288733 |
| Sum squared resid. | 10.81578 | Schwarz criterion | | −2.070406 |
| Log likelihood | 2331.402 | *F*-stat. | | 1407.247 |

# The impact of cell phones on motor vehicle fatalities

Peter D. Loeb, William A. Clarke and Richard Anderson

This article develops a set of models for the determinants of automobile fatalities with particular attention devoted to the effects of increased cell phone usage. Cell phones have been associated with both life taking and life-saving properties. However, prior statistical evaluations of the effects of cell phones have led to fragile results. We develop in this article econometric models using time-series data, allowing for polynomial structures of the regressors. The models are evaluated with a set of specification error tests providing reliable estimates of the effects of the various policy and driving-related variables evaluated. The statistical results indicate the effect of cell phones is nonmonotonic depending on the volume of phones in use, first having a net life-taking effect, then a net life-saving effect, followed finally with a net life-taking effect as the volume of phone use increases.

## I. Introduction

The determinants of motor vehicle accidents have been the topic of interest among economists, public policy makers and health professionals for many years. Studies have been conducted on the determinants of motor vehicle accidents in aggregate, as well as by components, i.e. automobiles, trucks, motorcycles, etc. The interest in transportation accidents also led to studies involving railroads, ships and aircraft as well as accidents due to the interaction of two or more modes of transportation. In addition to interest in accidents themselves, there has been an interest in the determinants of the outcomes of these accidents, i.e. injuries, fatalities and property damage.[1] Centering our discussion on motor vehicle accidents, numerous studies have investigated the effect on motor vehicle accidents due to: speed, speed variance, alcohol, speed limits, vehicle miles travelled, measures of income, unemployment rates, technology advances, the age of the fleet, population characteristics, police enforcement, seat belt legislation and the effects of the deregulatory climate which came about in the 1980s, among others. More generally, these potential determinants of accidents and factors reducing accidents may be placed into three categories: those associated with the vehicles themselves, e.g. technology improvements; those due to the roadways, e.g. speed limits; and those relating to drivers, e.g. alcohol consumption, income, seat belt usage, etc. More recently, the question has arisen as to the effect of cell phones on motor vehicle accidents. While it may generally be argued that the probability of a motor vehicle accident increases with the use of cell phones by drivers, it is not necessarily as obvious when considering motor vehicle fatalities. Some analysts claim that fatalities, like accidents

[1] See Loeb *et al.* (1994) for a detailed discussion of the determinants of transportation accidents.

increase when drivers use cell phones, due to an inability of at least some drivers to dial and talk while driving (similar to an inability to chew gum and tie one's shoes).[2] In addition, there is evidence that cell phones reduce the driver's attention span and reaction time which in turn increases the probability of an accident. Further, others have argued that the distraction of using a cell phone is not restricted to the time while on the cell phone itself, but may extend for several minutes after the phone conversation has terminated.[3] On the other hand, the opposite argument has been made that cell phones can reduce fatalities, that is, given an accident, cell phones increase the probability of obtaining help promptly which may result in the saving of lives.[4] In any case, cell phone use by the public at large has increased dramatically since 1985. In 1985, there were approximately 340 200 cell phone subscribers. By the year 2004, this number grew to over 182 140 000 subscribers.[5] It probably would be descriptive to say the growth of cell phone subscribers was explosive rather than exponential over time. In addition, Glassbrenner (2005), in a National Highway Traffic and Safety Administration (NHTSA) study, estimates that in 2005, 10% of all drivers at any moment during daylight hours are using a hand-held or hand-free cell phone. Looking at hand-held phones only, Glassbrenner estimated that driver hand-held use rose from 5% in 2004 to 6% in 2005.[6] As such, we see not only tremendous growth in cell phone subscribers but also an increase in usage of these devices over time by drivers.

The question then arises as to the net impact that cell phones have on motor vehicle fatalities. This study provides some econometric insight into the effect of cell phone use on motor vehicle fatalities. This is accomplished using econometric techniques on an annual time-series dataset covering the period 1975 to 2003. The models developed are subjected to a set of specification error tests to assure that the results are statistically viable.[7]

## II. Background

Between 1975 and 1980 motor vehicle fatalities trended upward (from 44 525 to 51 091) and then trended downward to 42 643 in 2003.[8] The determinants of these fatalities have been the subject of numerous studies in the past. These factors, as mentioned above, include socioeconomic factors such as the unemployment rate, income and population attributes as well as vehicle and driver-related factors. These latter factors include, among others, alcohol consumption, speed limit laws, vehicle miles travelled, interstate highway mileage, the ratio of rural to interstate highway mileage, the blood alcohol threshold indicative of driving under the influence of alcohol and a time trend.[9] Recently, the question of the potential effect of cell phones on motor vehicle fatalities has become a significant policy issue such that three states (New Jersey, Connecticut and New York) as well as Washington DC ban the use of hand-held cell phones while driving.

The traditional econometric-based literature has examined many of the potential factors effecting motor vehicle accidents and injuries, starting with Peltzman (1975). Obviously, early studies do not consider cell phones, since they were not in use at the time of the studies. In these studies, economic factors such as measures of income and the unemployment rate have been examined.[10] Some have argued that higher incomes are associated with more accidents while others have argued that they are associated with fewer accidents. Since the demand for safety and driving intensity are both related to income and may counteract one another, the net effect needs to be determined empirically.[11]

[2] See, for example, Violanti (1998).
[3] See, for example, Consiglio *et al.* (2003) and McEvoy *et al.* (2005).
[4] See Chapman and Schofield (1998).
[5] See Cellular Telecommunications and Internet Association (2005). The growth in cell phone subscriptions is shown in Fig. 2.
[6] See Glassbrenner (2005).
[7] Cell phones have also been suggested as a potential contributor to disease. This question is not addressed in the present article. See, for example, Maier *et al.* (2000) on this matter.
[8] See Fig. 1.
[9] See Loeb *et al.* (1994) on this.
[10] A time trend has also been used in some studies as a proxy for permanent income, changes in technology or other omitted factors. See Peltzman (1975) and Loeb (1993, 2001). Concern arises in using both a time trend and measures of income in models due to high correlation between such variables. Loeb and Clarke (2007) found a correlation between real GDP and a time trend to be 0.988 and 0.997 when the variables are measured in natural log form for the time period 1970–2001.
[11] Prior studies have found a positive relationship between accidents and income using time-series models and a negative relationship with cross-sectional models. See Loeb *et al.* (1994).

Unemployment rates have been used in many studies as a control for economic activity and have been found to be inversely related to motor vehicle accidents.[12] Miles driven is expected to be positively related to motor vehicle accidents as is alcohol consumption by drivers and the public in general.[13] Further, interstate highway mileage and the relationship between rural and urban highway mileage have also been investigated as to their effects on accidents.[14] In addition, studies have suggested that empirical models should be normalized by population or characteristics of the population, such as the proportion of the population aged 65 or older, or the proportion of the population characterized as youthful.[15] The effect of speed and speed variance has been an issue debated at length in the transportation literature.[16] The effect of speed limits have also been investigated as potential contributors to motor vehicle accidents and have been found in some studies to have some effect on fatalities.[17]

Unlike the above-mentioned variables, cell phones have only recently been investigated regarding their influence on motor-vehicle-related accidents, and then rarely in a traditional regression format. Perhaps the most well-known study to date is that of Redelmeier and Tibshirani (1997). Using cross-over analysis, they analyse 699 drivers involved in property-damage-only accidents in the Toronto (Canada) area during the period 1 July 1994 to 31 August 1995. They find, among other things, that the risk of being involved in such an accident is four times higher when a cell phone is being used. In addition, they find that hands-free devices offer no additional safety as compared to the hand-held devices. However, they find that 39% of drivers involved in these accidents used cell phones to call for assistance after a crash which suggests that cell phones may be advantageous after a crash. Similarly, McEvoy *et al.* (2005) using cross-over analysis and Australian data evaluated 456 drivers aged 17 or older who owned cell phones and were involved in crashes which resulted in hospital visits. Interestingly, they found that the use of mobile phones up to 10 min before a crash was associated with a four-fold increased probability of a crash. Hands-free devices again were found no safer than hand-held devices. Laberge-Nadeau *et al.* (2003), using Canadian survey data (36 078 responses) and logistic-normal regression models found the relative risk of accidents is higher for users of cell phones as compared to nonusers by approximately 38%. However, the risk diminishes when the models are more extensive. Another survey-based study using cross-over analysis was conducted by Sullman and Baas (2004). Their survey resulted in approximately a 50% response rate and investigated all crashes, regardless of severity. Once demographic and other variables were accounted for, they did not find a significant correlation between cell phone use and crash involvement. Examining traffic fatalities, Violanti (1998) using regression analysis finds that cell phones are associated with approximately a, 'nine-fold risk for a fatality over those not using a phone.'[18] This life-taking effect is countered by Chapman and Schofield (1998) who claim that cell phones in Australia should be credited with saving lives. They found that, 'Over one in eight current mobile phone users have used their phones to report a road accident.'[19] Referring to the 'golden hour' (which is critical to trauma victims) and with reference to medical and other emergencies over the last decade they claim that, 'it seems highly plausible that many Australians may have had their lives saved because help was summoned on a mobile phone.'[20] An alternative technique to examine the effect of cell phones on motor vehicle accidents involves the use of measuring response rates, or reaction time, in a simulated laboratory situation. Consiglio *et al.* (2003) found that both hand-held and hand-free devices resulted in a reduction in reaction time in a braking situation. They also found that conversation both in-person or via a cell phone caused reaction time to slow while listening to music did not. As such, there is evidence suggesting that cell phones may have both life-saving as well as life-taking attributes.

[12] See, for example, Evans and Graham (1988), Loeb (1995) and Fowles and Loeb (1995).
[13] See Loeb *et al.* (1994), Fowles and Loeb (1995) and Loeb and Clarke (2007).
[14] See Loeb *et al.* (1994).
[15] See, for example, Loeb (1988), Fowles and Loeb (1992), Keeler (1994) and Loeb and Clarke (2007). It should be noted further that, as in the case concerning real GDP and a time trend, there is also a strong correlation between real GDP and both population and vehicle miles driven. For the sample period 1975–2003, the correlation between real GDP and a time trend is 0.99 while the correlation between real GDP and population and vehicle miles driven is 0.995 in both cases. As such, most models developed do not include more than one of these variables so as to avoid multicollinearity.
[16] See Lave (1985), Fowles and Loeb (1989, 1995), Levy and Asch (1989) and Loeb *et al.* (1994).
[17] See Loeb (1993) and Fowles and Loeb (1995).
[18] Violanti (1998, p. 522).
[19] Chapman and Schofield (1998, p. 5).
[20] Chapman and Schofield (1998).

The current article evaluates the effect of cell phones on motor vehicle fatalities using econometric methods and a time-series dataset covering the period 1975 to 2003. As such, we are able to diminish statistical problems associated with survey data and provide an analysis while controlling for traditional factors in such models. To reduce the likelihood that the models suffer from omission of variables, misspecification of the structural form, or simultaneous equation bias (which may result in biased estimates) along with nonnormality of the error structure and serial correlation, a set of specification error tests are applied to the models.[21] Only models which are not rejected by any of these tests are used in the analysis to follow.

## III. The Model and Data

### *The general model*

A model of the form

$$\text{FATTOT} = \beta_0 + \beta_1\mathbf{X} + \beta_2\text{CELLS} + \mu \qquad (1)$$

is suggested where FATTOT is total motor vehicle fatalities and **X** is a matrix of socioeconomic and motor-vehicle-related variables thought to be determinants of the dependent variable. CELLS is a measure of cell phone availability/usage whose influence on the dependent variable is to be examined. $\mu$ is a random error term assumed to comply with the full ideal conditions underlying the classical linear regression model which would result in Best Linear Unbiased Estimates of the coefficients when the model is estimated by Ordinary Least Squares (OLS). Cell phone usage by drivers is not measured directly but is proxied by cell phone subscribers.[22] Glassbrenner (2005) has estimated that approximately 10% of all drivers at any daylight moment are making use of a cell phone device. Therefore, the number of cell phone subscribers should serve as a reasonable proxy for the potential distracting influence on drivers which may result in an accident and fatality.[23] In the models suggested, CELLS is entered so that the model appears as a polynomial of degree 3. This conforms to similar models in the Industrial Organization literature examining the determinants of Research and Development.[24]

The variables considered for possible inclusion in **X** are

- UNEMP: the civilian unemployment rate.
- ETHOTOTAL: apparent total per capital ethanol consumption (in gallons) based on population aged 14 and over.
- VEHMI: vehicle miles driven (billions).
- TOTALMI: total highway mileage (in thousands).
- INTERMI: interstate highway mileage (in thousands).
- URBANMI: urban highway mileage (in thousands).
- RURALMI: rural highway mileage (in thousands).
- POP: total population (in thousands).[25]
- BAC: a dummy variable indicating the blood alcohol threshold associated with driving under the influence of alcohol. State laws vary over time. A BAC of ‘1’ indicates either a 0.1 or a 0.08 BAC threshold is in effect while a BAC of ‘0’ indicates no such legal threshold exists.[26]
- SPEED95: a dummy variable indicating the repeal of the maximum speed limit by the National Highway System Designation Act of 1995 in December 1995 which allowed states to set their own limits

[21] These include a Regression Specification Error Test, a Jarque–Bera test and a Durbin–Watson test.

[22] In addition, it may capture the effect of cell phone availability to those not involved in an accident on the outcome of an accident.

[23] Again, as the number of cell phones among the general public increases, there may be a reduction in fatalities given an accident due to the increased speed in which medical assistance may be acquired.

[24] See Scherer (1965a, b) and Loeb and Lin (1977). The polynomial function allows for the examination of both the possible life-saving and life-taking effects of cell phones as the number of cell phones increases.

[25] Additional population variables were examined as well where the entire population was decomposed into those aged 16–19, 20–24, 25–44, 45–64, 65 and older. This allowed for examining whether certain groups of the population contributed to accidents more than others. Results using POP were superior to other variations of population. The alternative results are available from the authors.

[26] The BAC data are by state and over time. An annualized value is obtained by weighting each state’s BAC threshold for a given year by its relative share of the population for the year. We are grateful to Michael Grossman for the data and weighting mechanism used to generate this variable.

for the first time since 1974.[27] SPEED95 is set equal to 0.083333 in 1995, set equal to 1 from 1996 to 2003 and set to zero for all other time periods.

CELLS estimated number of cell phone subscribers (in millions).

We anticipate a negative effect on the dependent variable by UNEMPL and BAC. We expect a positive effect by ETHOTOTAL, the ratio of rural mileage to urban mileage (RURALMI/URBANMI) and CELLS. We do not have strong *a priori* expectations regarding the effects of INTERMI and POP.[28]

### The data

Data generally cover the period 1975 to 2003, but may vary depending on the model and variables included. The dependent variable (FATTOT) is measured as total motor vehicle fatalities and is reported in NHTSA (2005). Vehicle miles driven, measured in billions of miles (VEHMI), are reported in NHTSA (2005) as well. The unemployment rate (UNEMP) and population data (POP) are reported in the Economic Report of the President (2005). Total apparent per capita ethanol consumption (ETHOTOTAL) is reported by the National Institute on Alcohol Abuse and Alcoholism and is found at: http://www.niaa.-nih.gov/Resources/DatabaseResources/QuickFacts. Data on highway mileage, i.e. total mileage (TOTALMI), interstate mileage (INTERMI), rural mileage (RURALMI) and urban mileage (URBANMI) are reported in the US Bureau of the Census (various years). The speed limit variable (SPEED95) was generated as a dummy variable taking on the value of '1' for the years in which the National Highway System Designation Act of 1995 was in effect and '0' otherwise. In the year 1995, the variable was set equal to 0.083333 to reflect the proportion of that year the act was in effect. Data associated with the BAC laws are provided by MADD (http://www.madd.org/laws/) and the US Bureau of the Census (http://www.allcountries.org/uscensus/1046_state_legislation_alcohol_and_road_safety.html). Data for the number of cell phone subscribers (CELLS) are in millions and are reported by CTIA (2005) for the years 1985–2004. CTIA does not report the number of cell phone subscribers prior to 1985 and one could infer that none existed. However, AT&T put into place a trial system involving 2000 customers in 1977. As such, rather than assume there were no cell customers prior to 1985, we extrapolate potential subscribers for the period 1977 to 1984. Relatively speaking, these do not amount to significant numbers, but do take account of the fact that cell phones were in very limited use prior to 1985.[29]

## IV. Model Selection and Empirical Results

### Model selection

Equation 1 can be respecified to introduce a polynomial effect of CELLS on the dependent variable as

$$\text{FATTOT} = \beta_0 + \beta_1\mathbf{X} + \beta_2\text{CELLS} + \beta_3\text{CELLS}^2 + \beta_4\text{CELLS}^3 + \mu \quad (2)$$

where $\mathbf{X}$ includes various combinations of the other regressors discussed above.[30] Variations of Equation 2 are estimated by Ordinary Least Squares (OLS). Under the full ideal conditions, OLS results in Best Linear Unbiased Estimates (BLUE). Concern arises due to the possibility of not only serial correlation, given the use of time-series data, but also the possibility of biased estimates due to the potential omission of variables, simultaneous equation problems and misspecification of the structural form of the model. As such, the various specifications estimated were subjected to a set of specification error tests. These tests are used to detect violations of the full ideal conditions. They include the Regression Specification Error Test (RESET) developed by Ramsey (1974), the Jarque–Bera test (J–B) for normality and the Durbin–Watson test (D–W) for serial correlation. RESET examines the residuals of a given regression for the possibility of omission of variable(s), simultaneous equation bias

[27] An alternative dummy variable to account for the speed limit was also evaluated. SPEED87 indicated the years Congress allowed states to increase speed limits to 65 mph on rural interstates. These results are available from the authors.

[28] As mentioned previously, population and vehicle miles drive were found to be highly correlated with other variables, e.g. the time trend and other measures of miles driven. As such, most models estimated restricted the number of such variables included so as to minimize the risk of multicollinearity. A correlation matrix is available from the authors.

[29] Even in 1985, there were only slightly more than 340 000 cell phone subscribers. See CITA (2005). It should be further noted that model (1) was expanded to include additional variables to account for the influence of hospital availability, income, technology and other factors. However, these variables are not included in what follows since their inclusion either did not add substantially to the results reported or they introduced potential specification errors such as multicollinearity or errors resulting in biased estimates or nonnormal errors.

[30] These would include the ratio of RURALMI to URBANMI and Vehicle Miles per Capita (VEHMI/POP), among others.

and misspecification of the structural form of the regressors, any of which may result in biased estimates.[31] Any given specification estimated is rejected if one or more of the above-mentioned tests rejects the hypothesis of the presence of the full ideal conditions. This is a rather severe requirement imposed on the model selection process as compared to relying on student *t*-statistics or $R^2$'s.[32] Those specifications which are not rejected provide reasonable specifications to evaluate at least from a single equation perspective.

### *Empirical results*

Models suggested by Equation 2 were estimated by OLS and examined for specification errors. Table 1 provides summary statistics for variables used in the equations not rejected for specification errors mentioned above or for multicollinearity.[33] Table 2 provides a set of models for FATTOT which were not rejected for specification errors.

**Table 1. Summary statistics of selected variables**

| Variable name | Mean | SD |
|---|---|---|
| FATTOT | 44 356.64 | 3300.725 |
| UNEMP | 6.425 | 1.466 |
| ETHOTOTAL | 2.445 | 0.24 |
| VEHMI | 2049.464 | 478.932 |
| TOTALMI | 3892.643 | 33.260 |
| INTERMI | 44.050 | 3.43 |
| URBANMI | 746.464 | 83.49 |
| RURALMI | 3147.250 | 57.12 |
| POP | 24 9334.5 | 22 114.98 |
| SPEED95 | 0.253 | 0.439 |
| CELLS | 26.401 | 42.235 |
| RURALMI/URBANMI | 4.275 | 0.551 |
| VEHMI/POP | 0.008 | 0.001 |
| BAC | 0.725 | 0.31 |

The estimated coefficients tend to be stable (nonfragile) and consistent across the various specifications. Those reported are not rejected by the various specification error tests and all have adjusted $R^2$'s above 0.91. The coefficient associated with the unemployment rate is consistently negative and statistically significant at better than the 0.005 significance level across all the specifications estimated. The coefficient associated with alcohol consumption is, as expected, always positive and statistically significant at better than the 0.005 significance level. The ratio of rural to urban highway mileage has a positive influence on the dependent variable as seen across all specifications, as expected, with the associated coefficients varying in significance with most near the 0.1 one-tail level. The BAC coefficients were negative and significant at approximately the 5% or better one-tail level. The interstate mileage driven and population variables did not have coefficients which were statistically significant.

The variables of particular interest in this study are variants of CELLS indicating the potential effect of cell phone usage on motor–vehicle-related fatalities. The coefficients associated with the variables which account for cell phone usage are always nonfragile across specifications and are statistically significant at the two-tail significance level of 0.05 or better (with the vast majority of these coefficients significant at the 0.01 level or better). They suggest that the effect of cell phones on fatalities is positive. In addition, cell phone results suggest that their influence on fatalities is nonlinear. The effect on fatalities increases at a decreasing rate as noted by the coefficients associated with CELLS and $\text{CELLS}^2$, but the effect on fatalities is significantly impacted by $\text{CELLS}^3$. At some point, the effect of cell phones may actually decrease the number of fatalities. Using specification (1) from Table 2, we can see that the marginal effect of CELLS on fatalities depends on the level of CELLS. Evaluated at the mean of CELLS indicates a value of 41.575, all else equal. However, examining specification (1) for the volume of cells associated with a maximum or minimum number of fatalities requires that we examine the partial derivative of FATTOT with respect to CELLS. Setting $\partial\text{FATTOT}/\partial\text{CELLS} = 0$ gives rise to a quadratic with the two roots being 34.49 and 97.76. Evaluating the second derivatives results in $\text{CELLS} > 66.13$ is associated with a minimum and $\text{CELLS} < 66.13$ is associated with a maximum. More precisely, evaluating the original specification (1) for the effect of CELLS on FATTOT, holding all else equal, reveals an initial maximum at 34.49 CELLS and a minimum at 97.76 CELLS. As such, the effect of CELLS initially exacerbates fatalities and then fatalities decline with additional phone subscribers. However, the analysis must not cease at this point, for the above maximum and minimum values are local maxima and minima. The function then increases without end after

[31] RESET's ability to detect misspecification associated with structural form is of particular interest given the polynomial specification suggested.
[32] See Ramsey and Zarembka (1971) on this.
[33] A correlation matrix is available from the authors.

**Table 2. Regression results for models of FATTOT[a]**

| Independent variable name | Equation # (1) | (2) | (3) | (4) | (5) | (6) | (7) |
|---|---|---|---|---|---|---|---|
| Constant | 4159.003 (0.247) | 69.774 (0.008) | 87.115 (0.014) | 3346.150 (0.210) | 4698.404 (0.269) | 9910.879 (1.099) | 11 020.58 (1.252) |
| UNEMP | −2241.382 (−8.633) | −2254.079 (−9.014) | −2254.109 (−9.246) | −2248.608 (−8.969) | −1966.420 (−9.692) | −1946.920 (−10.611) | −2178.663 (−9.17) |
| ETHOTOTAL | 17 335.02 (3.460) | 17 814.51 (3.852) | 17 811.30 (4.087) | 17 364.19 (3.554) | 22 919.23 (6.112) | 19 541.31 (5.832) | 14 970.70 (3.332) |
| CELLS | 242.780 (3.306) | 244.027 (3.407) | 244.038 (3.497) | 243.911 (3.415) | 252.338 (3.318) | 181.972 (2.338) | 183.362 (2.422) |
| $CELLS^2$ | −4.761 (−3.838) | −4.842 (−4.1) | −4.842 (−4.224) | −4.815 (−4.081) | −4.614 (−3.590) | −3.77 (−3.043) | −3.965 (−3.270) |
| $CELLS^3$ | 0.024 (4.131) | 0.024 (4.426) | 0.024 (4.570) | 0.024 (4.419) | 0.022 (3.759) | 0.019 (3.41) | 0.020 (3.73) |
| INTERMI | 22.947 (0.194) | 0.232 (0.003) | | | 55.188 (0.456) | | |
| POP | −0.014 (−0.292) | | | −0.008 (−0.224) | −0.030 (−.0616) | | |
| RURALMI/ URBANMI | 3158.385 (1.607) | 3277.626 (1.745) | 3277.854 (1.790) | 3223.214 (1.706) | | | 2647.787 (1.478) |
| BAC | | | | | | −2148.064 (−1.998) | −1822.012 (−1.704) |
| Adjusted $R^2$ | 0.918 | 0.922 | 0.925 | 0.922 | 0.911 | 0.928 | 0.932 |
| D–W[b] | 1.771 | 1.804 | 1.804 | 1.780 | 1.86 | 1.839 | 1.736 |
| J–B[c] | 2.775 | 2.719 | 2.717 | 2.705 | 0.844 | 0.411 | 1.664 |
| RESET[d] | 1.335 | 1.291 | 1.361 | 1.389 | 2.353 | 2.356 | 1.3 |

*Notes*: [a]Numbers shown within parentheses are *t*-statistics associated with the coefficients.
[b]Durbin–Watson statistic.
[c]Jarque–Bera test.
[d]Regression specification error test.

reaching the minimum.[34] This may explain some of the different results found by other researchers.

As such, we first note a contributing effect of cell phones on motor-vehicle-related deaths. This may be due to several factors including inexperience among drivers using cell phones (much like not being able to chew gum and do another task at the same time), the distracting effect of cell phones, and an insufficient number of cell phones among the public to afford a faster response time to an accident due to cell phone calls which might counter the negative effects of cell phone use. After a critical amount of subscribers is reached, the life-saving effect of cell phones among the public may, for example, increase the likelihood of survivorship in an accident due to the ability to immediately call for medical assistance. Hence, the life-saving effects of cell phones outweigh the life-taking effect after some point. However, beyond a certain level once again, the life-taking effect overwhelms the life-saving effect again. With the explosive growth in the number of cell phones, drivers have become more accustomed to using cell phones while driving. This may reflect a change in attitudes and habits regarding cell phone usage over time. This change is documented by NHTSA which reports a 50% increase in drivers using cell phones in the daylight hours since 2002.[35] An examination of Figs 1 and 2 add to the analysis. Figure 1 indicates that motor vehicle fatalities tend to trend downward until the early to mid-1990s. By the year 2000, motor vehicle fatalities were close to 42 000 and rising. Meanwhile, cell phone subscribers had surpassed in number the 97.8 million mark. Hence, the visual evidence adds additional support to the conclusion that cell phones and their usage above a critical threshold add to motor vehicle fatalities.[36]

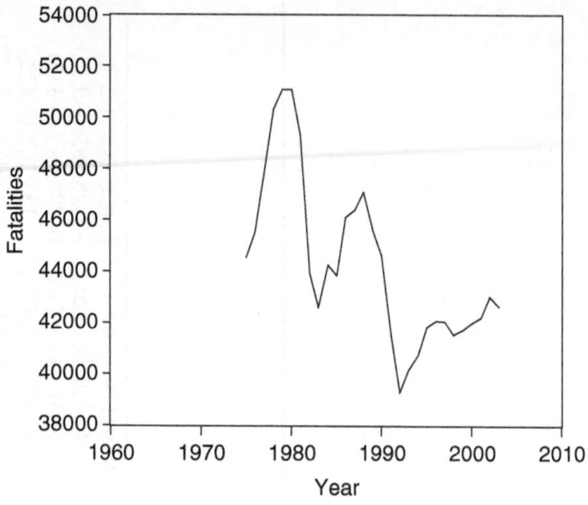


**Fig. 1. Motor vehicle fatalities over time**

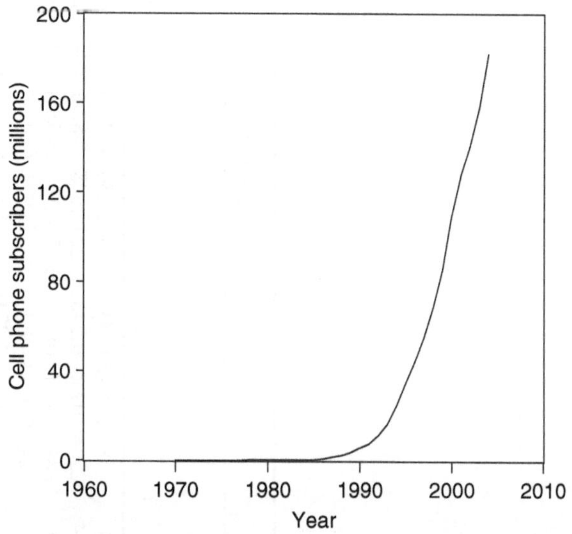


**Fig. 2. Cell phone subscribers over time**

## V. Concluding Comments and Policy Recommendations

This study examines the effect of cell phones on motor-vehicle-related fatalities using econometric models and specification error tests. The models adjust for unemployment rates, alcohol consumption, blood alcohol legislation and other factors as well as cell phones. Data are obtained for the years 1975–2003 and the models are evaluated using OLS. Only models which fail to be rejected for specification errors are considered in the analysis.

As expected, alcohol consumption is shown to have a positive and statistically significant effect on fatalities with coefficients which are stable across specifications. This lends support for public policies

[34] See Fig. 3 for the estimated response rate of fatalities to cell phones.
[35] Reported by the Associated Press in http://www.msnbc.msn.com/id/8545779/. See Glassbrenner (2005) as well on increases of cell phones by drivers.
[36] Models in terms of rates, i.e. fatalities/capita, were estimated as well. The results conform with those presented in Table 2 especially in those models which do not include BAC. These results are available from the authors.

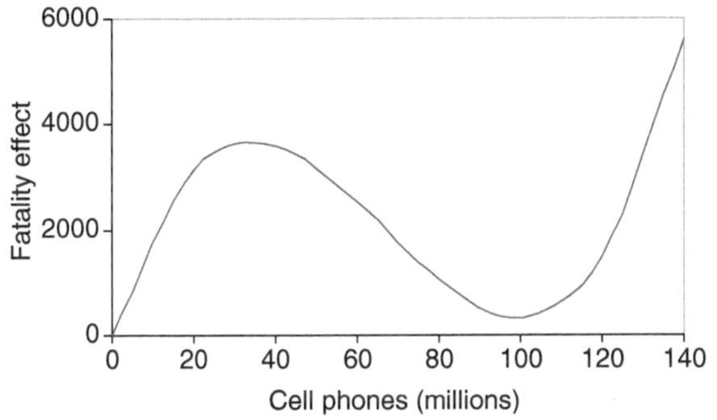


**Fig. 3. Estimated response rate of fatalities to cell phones**

which would result in reduced alcohol consumption. Such policies may include increased taxes on alcohol or possibly raising the minimum legal drinking age.[37] The ratio of rural highway mileage to urban highway mileage also has an impact but at a lower significance level. The unemployment rate, as expected, has a negative and statistically significant effect on fatalities. Similarly, the use of BAC laws to define driving while under the influence of alcohol also reduces fatalities. As such, reducing the blood alcohol limit indicating when driving under the influence may prove to be a valuable policy to reduce motor vehicle fatalities.

Most significantly, cell phones are found to have an adverse effect on fatalities initially as cell phones become more readily available. After a point, some life-saving effects of cell phones overtake the life-taking effects. However, with cell phone subscribers reaching about 100 million or more, the life-taking effect overtakes the potential life-saving effect once again. These results are nonfragile across specifications and are statistically significant. Given that there are over 219 million cell phone subscribers in the United States (as of 2006) leads one to believe that the life-taking effect of cell phones is greater than the life-saving effect. As such, policies which would reduce cell phone use by drivers may be warranted. This might be accomplished through an appropriate fine structure combined with active enforcement.

## Acknowledgements

The authors are indebted to Michael Grossman, Jeffrey Cohen and Jason Barr for valuable suggestions. Loeb gratefully acknowledges the research support of a Rutgers University Research Council Grant.

## References

Cellular Telecommunications and Internet Association (CTIA) (2005). Available at http://www.mindfully.org/Technology/2005/Wireless-Industry-SurveyJan05.htm (accessed 21 January 2009).

Chaloupka, F. J., Saffer, H. and Grossman, M. (1993) Alcohol-control policies and motor vehicle fatalities, *Journal of Legal Studies*, **22**, 161–86.

Chapman, S. and Schofield, W. N. (1998) Lifesavers and samaritans: emergency use of cellular (mobile) phones in Australia, *Accident Analysis and Prevention*, **30**, 815–9.

Consiglio, Wm., Driscoll, P., Witte, M. and Berg, Wm. P. (2003) Effect of cellular telephone conversations and other potential interference on reaction time in a braking responses, *Accident Analysis and Prevention*, **35**, 495–500.

Economic Report of the President (2005) United States Government Printing Office, Washington, DC.

Evans, W. and Graham, J. D. (1988) Traffic safety and business cycles, *Alcohol, Drugs and Driving*, **4**, 31–8.

Fowles, R. and Loeb, P. D. (1989) Speeding, coordination, and the 55-MPH limit: comment, *American Economic Review*, **79**, 916–21.

Fowles, R. and Loeb, P. D. (1992) The interactive effect of alcohol and altitude on traffic fatalities, *Southern Economic Journal*, **59**, 108–11.

Fowles, R. and Loeb, P. D. (1995) Effects of policy-related variables on traffic fatalities: an extreme bounds analysis using time-series data, *Southern Economic Journal*, **62**, 359–66.

Glassbrenner, D. (2005) Driver cell phone use in 2005 – overall results. Traffic safety facts: research note, NHTSA, DOT HS 809967. Available at http://www-nrd.nhtsa.dot.gov/pdf/nrd-30/NCSA/RNotes/2005/809967.pdf (accessed 21 January 2009).

Keeler, T. E. (1994) Highway safety, economic behavior, and driving environment, *American Economic Review*, **84**, 684–93.

Laberge-Nadeau, C., Maag, U., Bellavance, F., Lapiere, S. D., Desjardins, D., Messier, S. and Saidi, A. (2003) Wireless telephones and the risk of road crashes. DOI:10.1016/S0001-4575(02)00043-X.

Lave, C. A. (1985) Speeding, coordination and the 55 mph limit, *American Economic Review*, **79**, 1159–64.

Levy, D. T. and Asch, P. (1989) Speeding, coordination, and the 55 mph limit: comment, *American Economic Review*, **79**, 913–5.

Loeb, P. D. (1988) The determinants of motor vehicle accidents – a specification error analysis, *The Logistics and Transportation Review*, **24**, 33–48.

Loeb, P. D. (1993) The effectiveness of seat-belt legislation in reducing various driver-involved injury rates in California, *Accident Analysis and Prevention*, **25**, 189–97.

Loeb, P. D. (1995) The effectiveness of seat-belt legislation in reducing injury rates in Texas, *American Economic Review – Papers and Proceedings*, **88**, 81–4.

Loeb, P. D. (2001) The effectiveness of seat belt legislation in reducing driver-involved injury rates in Maryland, *Transportation Research: Part E*, **37**, 297–310.

[37] See Chaloupka *et al.* (1993) on the effect of alcohol control policies.

Loeb, P. D. and Clarke, Wm. A. (2007) The determinants of truck accidents, *Transportation Research: Part E*, **43**, 442–52.

Loeb, P. D. and Lin, V. (1977) Research and development in the pharmaceutical industry – a specification error approach, *The Journal of Industrial Economics*, **26**, 45–51.

Loeb, P. D., Talley, W. K. and Zlatoper, T. J. (1994) *Causes and Deterrents of Transportation Accidents: An Analysis by Mode*, Quorum Books, Westport, CT.

Maier, M., Colin, B. and Koivisto, M. (2000) The health hazards of mobile phones, *British Medical Journal*, **320**, 1288–9. Available at http://www.pubmedcentral.nih.gov/articlerender.fcgi?artid = 1127293 (accessed 21 January 2009).

McEvoy, S. P., Stevenson, M. R., McCartt, A. T., Woodward, M., Haworth, C., Palamara, P. and Cercarelli, R. (2005) Role of mobile phones in motor vehicle crashes resulting in hospital attendance: a case-crossover study, *British Medical Journal*. DOI:10.1136/bmj.38537.397512.55.

National Highway Traffic Safety Administration (2005) Traffic *Safety Facts 2003: A Compilation of Motor Vehicle Crash Data from the Fatality Analysis Reporting System and the General Estimates System*, National Center for Statistics and Analysis, US Department of Transportation, Washington, DC. Available at http://www-nrd.nhtsa.dot.gov/pdf/nrd-30/NCSA/TSFAnn/2003HTMLTSF/TSF2003.htm (accessed 21 January 2009).

National Institute on Alcohol Abuse and Alcoholism. Available at http://www.niaaa.nih.gov/Resources/DatabaseResources/QuickFacts/AlcoholSales/default.htm (accessed 21 January 2009).

Peltzman, S. (1975) The effects of automobile regulations, *Journal of Political Economy*, **93**, 677–725.

Ramsey, J. B. (1974) Classical model selection through specification error tests, in *Frontiers in Econometrics* (Ed.) P. Zarembka, Academic Press, New York, pp. 13–47.

Ramsey, J. B. and Zarembka, P. (1971) Specification error tests and the alternative functional form of the aggregate production function, *Journal of the American Statistical Association, Applications Section*, **57**, 471–7.

Redelmeier, D. A. and Tibshirani, R. J. (1997) Association between cellular-telephone calls and motor vehicle collisions, *The New England Journal of Medicine*, **336**, 453–8.

Scherer, F. M. (1965a) Size of firm, oligopoly, and research: a comment, *Canadian Journal of Economics and Political Science*, **31**, 256–66.

Scherer, F. M. (1965b) Firm size, market structure, opportunity, and the output of patented inventions, *American Economic Review*, **55**, 1097–125.

Sullman, M. J. and Baas, P. H. (2004) Mobile phone use amongst New Zealand drivers, *Transportation Research Part F: Traffic Psychology and Behavior*, **7**, 95–105.

US Bureau of the Census (various years) Statistical Abstract of the United States, Washington, DC.

Violanti, J. M. (1998) Cellular phones and fatal traffic collisions, *Accident Analysis and Prevention*, **30**, 519–24.

# Latent class model or mixed logit model? A comparison by transport mode choice data

Junyi Shen

This article applies two recently stated choice survey datasets of Japan to investigate the difference between the Latent Class Model (LCM) and the Mixed Logit Model (MLM) for transport mode choice. A detailed comparison is carried out, focusing on comparing values of time savings, direct choice elasticities, predicted choice probabilities and prediction success indices. Furthermore, a test on nonnested model is also utilized to help determine which model is superior to another one. The results suggest that the LCM performs better than the MLM in both datasets.

## I. Introduction

In the recent 30 years, analysts have made a great endeavour on developing different discrete choice models to relax the assumption of Independence from Irrelevant Alternatives (IIA) in the fundamental Multinomial Logit Model (MNL). Among these models, the MLM is probably the most flexible one (see, for instance, Revelt and Train, 1998; McFadden and Train, 2000; Persson, 2002; Bhat, 2001, 2003; Greene and Hensher, 2003; Bhat and Gossen, 2004; Viton, 2004; Kim *et al.*, 2005, etc.). It generalizes a standard MNL by allowing its parameters associated with the observed variable to vary with a known population distribution across individuals. Alternatively, the Latent Class Model (LCM), which is frequently applied in marketing research, assumes that a discrete number of latent classes are sufficient to account for preference heterogeneity (see, for instance, Boxall and Adamowicz, 2002; Morey *et al.*, 2006, etc.). Comparing with the MLM specification, the LCM has the advantage of being relatively simple, reasonably plausible and statistically testable. However, it is somewhat less flexible than the MLM since the parameters associated with each variable in each class are fixed. In contrast, the main disadvantage of the MLM is that the analysts should specify the assumption about the distribution of parameters. Due to the fact that each model has its virtues and limitations, it is meaningful to compare between these two advanced discrete choice models.

A recent study by Greene and Hensher (2003) compared the LCM with the MLM by using a dataset of road type's choice by car in New Zealand. After a detailed comparison on value of travel time savings, direct share elasticities, choice sensitivities to 50% increase in travel time, and choice probabilities, they concluded that although both the MLM and LCM offer attractive specifications than the MNL, it is inconclusive that which one is 'completely' superior to another despite some stronger statistical evidences support for the LCM in their dataset.[1] Remained as a future study implication, they mentioned that 'we encourage a greater effort to compare and contrast

[1] The inconclusiveness is due to the reason that these two models are nonnested, therefore, normal Likelihood Ratio (LR) test cannot be applied.

such advanced models as one approach to searching for rules on stability in explanation and prediction' (Greene and Hensher, 2003).

Strongly encouraged by their study, we use two stated preference datasets of transport modal choice (monorail, car and bus) in Japan to make a comparison between the MLM and the LCM. Thus, the prime purpose of this article is to seek for whether or not the results of the comparison suggest that the LCM is to some extent superior to the MLM as Greene and Hensher (2003) mentioned in their study.

The rest of the article is organized as follows. Section II provides a brief introduction on the LCM and the MLM. Section III compactly describes our two stated preference datasets in Japan. Section IV presents a comparison between these two models and Section V draws conclusions of the article.

## II. The Latent Class and Mixed Logit Models[2]

### The latent class model

The LCM, unlike the MLM which specifies the random parameters to follow a continuous joint distribution, assumes that a discrete number of classes are sufficient to account for preference heterogeneity across classes. Therefore, the unobserved heterogeneity is captured by these latent classes in the population, each of which is associated with a different parameter vector in the corresponding utility. The LCM has often been used in marketing research instead of ML model, while there are few studies in other fields such as transportation and environmental economics.

The choice probability that an individual $q$ of class $s$ chooses alternative $i$ from a particular set $J$, which comprises $j$ alternatives, is expressed as:

$$P_{iq|s} = \frac{\exp(\beta_s' X_{iq})}{\sum_{j=1}^{J} \exp(\beta_s' X_{jq})} \qquad s = 1, \ldots, S \tag{1}$$

where $\beta_s'$ is the parameter vector associated with the vector of explanatory variables $X_{iq}$. Note that Equation 1 is a simple MNL specification in class $s$.

Additionally, one can construct a classification model as a function of some individual-specific attributes to explain the heterogeneity across classes. The LCM model simultaneously estimates Equation 1 for $S$ classes and predicts the probability $H_{qs}$ as individual $q$ being in class $s$. Then, the unconditional probability of choosing the alternative $i$ is given as:

$$P_{iq} = \sum_{s=1}^{S} P_{iq|s} H_{qs} \tag{2}$$

An issue to be noted is the choice of $S$, the number of classes. Since this is not a parameter, hypotheses on $S$ cannot be tested directly. However, as Louviere *et al.* (2000, Ch. 10) mentioned that a number of methods to decide $S$ have been used based on the Akaike Information Criterion (AIC) and its variants. AIC and Consistent AIC (CAIC), which are given in Equations 3 and 4, are used to guide model selection.

$$\text{AIC} = -2[\text{LL}(\hat{\beta}) - S \cdot K_s - (S-1)K_c] \tag{3}$$

$$\text{CAIC} = -2\text{LL}(\hat{\beta}) - [S \cdot K_s + (S-1)K_c - 1][\ln(2N) + 1] \tag{4}$$

where $\text{LL}(\hat{\beta})$ is the log likelihood at the estimated parameters $\hat{\beta}$, $K_s$ is the number of elements in the utility function of the class-specific choice models, $K_c$ is the total number of parameters in the classification model and $N$ is the number of observations in the sample. The value of $S$ that minimizes each of the measures of AIC and CAIC suggests which model should be preferred (Louviere *et al.*, 2000, Chap. 10).

### The mixed logit model

The MLM allows for a heightened level of flexibility by specifying taste coefficients to be randomly distributed across individuals. Additionally, superior to LCM, MLM can account for potential correlation over repeated choices made by each individual by imposing a first-order autoregressive (AR1) process.[3]

The model is a generalization of the MNL model, summarized as below:

$$P_{iqt} = \frac{\exp(\alpha' + \beta' X_{iqt} + \varphi' F_{iqt})}{\sum_{j=1}^{J} \exp(\alpha' + \beta' X_{jqt} + \varphi' F_{jqt})} \tag{5}$$

where $\alpha'$ is a vector of fixed or random Alternative-Specific Constants (ASCs) associated with $i = 1, \ldots, J$ alternatives and $q = 1, \ldots, Q$ individuals, and one of

[2] Since Greene and Hensher (2003) have provided a detailed description on the LCM and the MLM, therefore, we just give a brief introduction on these two models. For the other literature on the MLM and LCM, see Revelt and Train (1998), Louviere *et al.* (2000), McFadden and Train (2000), Bhat and Gossen (2004), Bishop and Provencher (2004), Greene (2003), Hensher *et al.* (2005), Train (2003), Train and Sandor (2004), Shen (2006), etc.

[3] Greene and Hensher (2003) mentioned that the LCM does not readily extend to autocorrelation, therefore, this aspect is left for future research.

**Table 1. An example of choice set in Saito survey**

| | Monorail | Car | Bus |
|---|---|---|---|
| In-vehicle time including delay time caused by traffic jam (minutes) | 15 | 40 | 50 |
| Access time (minutes) | 15 | Almost 0 | 3 |
| Frequency (minutes) | 10 | At any time | 15 |
| Generalized cost (JP yen) | 360 | 800 | 280 |
| Negative impact on the environment (such as $CO_2$ emission) | Low | 3 times as monorail | 2.5 times as monorail |
| Please choose one most preferable transport mode and ✓ in □ | □ | □ | □ |

these ASCs should be identified as 0. $\beta'$ is a parameter vector that is randomly distributed across individuals. $\varphi'$ is a vector of nonrandom parameters. $X_{iqt}$ is a vector of individual-specific characteristics and alternative-specific attributes at observation $t$, and is estimated with random parameters. $F_{iqt}$ is a vector of individual-specific characteristics and alternative-specific attributes at observation $t$, and is estimated with fixed parameters.

In this specification, a subset or all of $\alpha'$ and the parameters in the $\beta'$ vector can be assumed to be randomly distributed across individuals.[4] These random parameters can then be defined as a function of characteristics of individuals and/or other attributes that are choice invariant. Based on these defined attributes, the mean and standard deviations of specified random parameters and contributions from these choice invariant attributes to random parameters are estimated by using Maximum Simulated Likelihood (MSL) method. The MLM is sufficiently flexible that it provides the modeler a tremendous range to specify individual unobserved heterogeneity. To some extent, this flexibility offsets the specificity of the distributional assumptions (Greene and Hensher, 2003).

## III. Data

We use two survey datasets, which are collected in Osaka of Japan, to compare the LCM with the MLM. The first survey is based on a stated choice experiment carried out in July of 2005 on transport mode choices by the residents in the Saito and Onohara Area of Northern Osaka (hereinafter, called Saito survey). A prime purpose of this experiment is to investigate whether or not individual environmental consciousness is one of the determinants in transport modal choice. The transport modes in the choice set faced by each respondent consist of monorail, car and bus. This dataset is composed of 467 individuals with each answering eight choice sets, therefore, the total observations are 3736. Five attributes are used in the stated choice experiment as follows:

(A) In-vehicle time including delay time caused by traffic jam (in min)
(B) Access time (in min)
(C) Frequency (in min)
(D) Travel cost (in JP yen)
(E) Negative impact on the environment caused by transport modes

For each attribute, we adopted a two-level design except for access time and frequency in car and negative impact on the environment in monorail. Then, 32 choice sets were constructed by a fractional factorial design to reduce the number of choice sets to a manageable level. These 32 choice sets were further blocked into four versions avoiding a dominant selection. Each sampled individual was asked to answer one version. An example of the choice sets is provided in Table 1. Further details on the survey are given in Shen *et al.* (2007).

The second dataset is based on another stated choice survey on transport mode choice of the residents in Eastern Osaka (hereinafter, called Eastern Osaka survey), which was also carried out in July 2005. Different from the first one, this survey focused on both impacts of local natural environment and network accessibility on transport modal choice. Same experimental design strategy as that in Saito survey was used, except that the local natural environment and network accessibility were treated

[4] The distributions of random parameters can be considered, for example, normal distribution, lognormal distribution and triangular distribution, etc.

**Table 2. An example of choice set in Eastern Osaka survey**

| | Monorail | Car | Bus |
|---|---|---|---|
| Average in-vehicle time for one section (minutes) | 3 | 4 | 10 |
| Average delay time due to congestion (minutes) | 0 | 8 | 10 |
| Average cost (JP yen) | 100 | 200 | 60 |
| Frequency (numbers/hour) | 4 | At any time | 10 |
| Local natural environment | Worse than current state | Worse than current state | Worse than current state |
| Network accessibility | Only monorail | Only monorail | Only monorail |
| Please choose one most preferable transport mode and ✓ in ☐ | ☐ | ☐ | ☐ |

as a common condition in each choice set, i.e. they were allowed to vary across choice sets but not across alternatives. A total of 453 valid responses, each with eight choice sets, produce 3624 observations. Table 2 shows an example of the choice sets, and Sakata *et al.* (2006) provides further details on this survey.

## IV. A Comparison Between LCM and MLM

Tables 3 and 4 summarize the estimated results of the two datasets with the specifications of MNL, MLM and LCM.[5] We have specified a number of individual socioeconomic characteristics and added them into the estimated model. However, to conserve space, we omit these results in the tables.

With respect to the MLM, we have defined all time-associated attributes as random parameters and selected a *Normal* distribution for them. Specifying a given parameter to follow a *Normal* distribution is equivalent to making *a priori* assumption that both positive and negative values for this parameter may exist in the population. Concerning the possible positive signs of time-associated parameters, Hess *et al.* (2005) have noted that 'a negative measure for Value of Travel Time Savings (VTTS) for a given individual in effect suggests that this individual would be willing to pay for increases in travel-time. At first sight, this is counter-intuitive. However, several recent articles discuss zero (Richard, 2003) or positive (Redmond and Mokhtarian, 2001) elasticity with respect to travel-time. There are interesting statements like: 'I'd rather have an hour-plus commute than a five-minute commute. In the morning, it gives me a chance to work through what I'm going to do for the day. And it's my decompression time.' (Redmond and Mokhtarian, 2001)'. This citation indicates that if an individual is more satisfied with longer time-associated attributes due to some individual-specific reasons, the positive sign of time-associated attributes could be possible.[6]

AIC and CAIC given in Equations 3 and 4 were used to select the number of classes in the LCM. As a result, both AIC and CAIC were the lowest ones in the three latent classes for both datasets. Therefore, three-class LCMs were estimated for both Saito and Eastern Osaka surveys. From the results in Tables 3 and 4, based on the log-likelihood values, the hypothesis that the MNL model is in favour of either the MLM or the LCM can be safely rejected.

With respect to the comparison between MLM and LCM, we focus on contrasting indicators of willingness to pay, e.g. values of time savings, choice elasticities, predicted choice probabilities of each transport mode and prediction success index, respectively. In addition, a test on nonnested choice models which is based on the AIC proposed by Ben-Akiva and Swait (1986) is applied to help determine which model is relatively more superior in the two datasets applied in this study.

Table 5 summarizes the estimated Values of Time Savings (VOTS). For both datasets, the mean estimates of VOTS by the MLM specification differ substantially with the three latent classes for LCM, although in Saito survey, VOTS of in-vehicle time is similar to that in class 1 and VOTS of access time is similar to that in class 2. Overall, the results from the LCM indicate the fact that for either in-vehicle time, access time and frequency in Saito survey or in-vehicle time, delay time and frequency in Eastern

[5] All the results were estimated by NLOGIT 3.0 (Econometric Software, Inc., 2003).

[6] We have also estimated the MLM with a specification of triangular distribution on time-associated parameters. However, we did not find large differences between normal distribution and triangular distribution specifications on the estimated parameters, value of time savings choice elasticities, etc.

**Table 3. Estimated results for Saito survey (*t*-statistics in parentheses)**

| | | | | | | LCM | | | | | |
|---|---|---|---|---|---|---|---|---|---|---|---|
| Attribute | Alternative | MNL | | MLM | | Class 1 | | Class 2 | | Class 3 | |
| In-vehicle time | All | −0.0758 | (−25.45) | −0.1668 | (−17.12) | −0.0653 | (−4.05) | −0.1160 | (−36.34) | −0.0858 | (−11.47) |
| Access time | All | −0.0265 | (−2.08) | −0.0575 | (−2.59) | −0.0270 | (−3.78) | −0.0642 | (−3.48) | −0.0088 | (−2.94) |
| Frequency | All | −0.0155 | (−3.57) | −0.0247 | (−3.21) | −0.0228 | (−2.04) | −0.0232 | (−4.63) | −0.0097 | (−2.82) |
| Travel cost | All | −0.0027 | (−9.87) | −0.0049 | (−10.13) | −0.0019 | (−3.30) | −0.0056 | (−15.42) | −0.0014 | (−3.50) |
| Negative environmental impact | All | −0.7066 | (−2.78) | −0.5100 | (−3.06) | −3.1898 | (−2.52) | 0.3882 | (1.273) | −3.1662 | (5−5.97) |
| Monorail constant | Monorail | −0.7612 | (−3.19) | −1.7252 | (−3.22) | 19.3000 | (0.02) | −2.0457 | (−7.90) | 0.9842 | (1.71) |
| Car constant | Car | −1.3935 | (−4.41) | −3.4679 | (−4.92) | 0.4838 | (0.00) | −18.5697 | (−0.02) | 4.1862 | (5.48) |
| In-vehicle time standard derivation | All | | | 0.1039 | (11.17) | | | | | | |
| Access time standard derivation | All | | | 0.2109 | (14.79) | | | | | | |
| Frequency standard derivation | All | | | 0.0848 | (12.12) | | | | | | |
| Latent class probability | | | | | | 0.14175 | (7.15) | 0.58520 | (20.30) | 0.27305 | (10.781) |
| Log-likelihood | | −2853.062 | | −2320.686 | | −1954.913 | | | | | |
| Pseudo-$R^2$ | | 0.1844 | | 0.3366 | | 0.4460 | | | | | |

**Table 4. Estimated results for Eastern Osaka survey (*t*-statistics in parentheses)**

| Attribute | Alternative | MNL | | MLM | | LCM Class 1 | | LCM Class 2 | | LCM Class 3 | |
|---|---|---|---|---|---|---|---|---|---|---|---|
| In-vehicle time | All | −0.1251 | (−8.65) | −0.2669 | (−10.23) | −0.1365 | (−5.51) | −0.2825 | (−8.62) | −0.1915 | (−3.55) |
| Delay time | All | −0.0606 | (−8.10) | −0.1338 | (−8.94) | −0.0672 | (−5.10) | −0.1522 | (−10.36) | −0.0501 | (−2.10) |
| Frequency | All | −0.0328 | (−3.18) | −0.1101 | (−8.67) | −0.0710 | (−3.97) | −0.0913 | (−5.94) | −0.0377 | (−2.21) |
| Travel cost | All | −0.0050 | (−13.29) | −0.0083 | (−15.52) | −0.0157 | (−13.19) | −0.0062 | (−10.70) | −0.0022 | (−2.55) |
| Monorail constant | Monorail | 1.3564 | (7.25) | 2.0211 | (7.04) | 1.0647 | (2.42) | 2.1905 | (6.64) | −0.1073 | (−0.18) |
| Bus constant | Bus | 0.3930 | (1.95) | 0.9844 | (3.43) | 0.6429 | (1.43) | 0.3326 | (0.77) | −1.3832 | (−1.54) |
| Local natural environment | Monorail | 0.4150 | (1.85) | 0.4396 | (2.19) | −0.9100 | (−1.55) | 0.9895 | (2.74) | 1.3309 | (2.24) |
| Network accessibility | Monorail | 0.7705 | (3.33) | 0.9924 | (2.60) | 0.7249 | (1.16) | 1.2860 | (3.66) | 1.5493 | (2.44) |
| Local natural environment | Bus | 0.2396 | (0.87) | 0.1647 | (0.42) | −0.9972 | (−1.70) | −0.1079 | (−0.14) | −5.9485 | (−1.61) |
| Network accessibility | Bus | 0.7990 | (2.91) | 1.0638 | (2.60) | 0.8712 | (1.40) | −0.1265 | (−0.16) | 5.8119 | (4.48) |
| In-vehicle time standard derivation | All | | | 0.2799 | (12.16) | | | | | | |
| Delay time standard derivation | All | | | 0.1620 | (9.95) | | | | | | |
| Frequency standard derivation | All | | | 0.1993 | (14.37) | | | | | | |
| Latent class probability | | | | | | 0.35625 | (12.60) | 0.52661 | (18.02) | 0.11714 | (6.43) |
| Log-likelihood | | −2791.523 | | −2390.553 | | −1714.392 | | | | | |
| Pseudo-$R^2$ | | 0.0892 | | 0.2200 | | 0.4406 | | | | | |

**Table 5. Values of time savings for Saito and Eastern Osaka surveys (JP yen per hour)**

| | | | LCM | | |
|---|---|---|---|---|---|
| Time type | MNL | MLM (mean) | Class 1 | Class 2 | Class 3 |
| Saito survey | | | | | |
| In-vehicle time | 1684 | 2042 | 2062 | 1243 | 3677 |
| Access time | 589 | 704 | 853 | 688 | 377 |
| Frequency | 344 | 302 | 720 | 249 | 416 |
| Eastern Osaka survey | | | | | |
| In-vehicle time | 1501 | 1929 | 522 | 2734 | 5223 |
| Delay time | 727 | 967 | 257 | 1473 | 1366 |
| Frequency | 394 | 795 | 271 | 884 | 1028 |

**Table 6. Direct choice elasticities for Saito and Eastern Osaka surveys (probability weighted)**

| Time type | MNL | MLM | LCM |
|---|---|---|---|
| In-vehicle time | | | |
| Monorail | −0.510 (−0.181) | −0.586 (−0.237) | −0.446 (−0.179) |
| Car | −1.304 (−0.276) | −1.367 (−0.398) | −1.361 (−0.306) |
| Bus | −1.418 (−0.676) | −1.343 (−0.666) | −1.374 (−0.776) |
| Travel cost | | | |
| Monorail | −0.397 (−0.243) | −0.400 (−0.263) | −0.423 (−0.313) |
| Car | −0.955 (−0.993) | −1.001 (−0.988) | −1.056 (−0.8699) |
| Bus | −0.375 (−0.331) | −0.398 (−0.419) | −0.455 (−0.785) |

*Note*: Elasticities for Eastern Osaka survey are in the parentheses.

Osaka survey, three segments of low, medium and high VOTS can be found. This evidence supports the claim in Greene and Hensher's (2003) study that the latent influences are to some extent related to an individual's VOTS.

Summaries of the probability-weighted choice elasticities for common attributes (in-vehicle time and travel cost) in two surveys are provided in Table 6. The choice elasticities differ substantially between the MLM and the LCM, especially in Eastern Osaka survey. For response to changes in in-vehicle time, the LCM suggests less sensitivity for monorail and car but more sensitivity for bus than the MLM in both datasets, whilst the magnitude of sensitivity is relatively larger in Saito survey. With respect to changes in travel cost, the MLM predicts less-sensitive response for almost all the modes than the LCM in both datasets with the exception of car in Eastern Osaka survey.

A comparison of predicted choice probability between the LCM and the MLM for two surveys starts from the kernel density estimators of their ratios for each mode that are listed in Figs 1 and 2. From these figures, we may find that for both datasets, the distribution around 1 is skewed to the right for monorail and to the left for car and bus. This evidence indicates that at the individual level, the choice probability of monorail predicted by the LCM is relatively larger than that predicted by the MLM, whilst the choice probabilities of car and bus are relatively smaller than those predicted by the MLM. It is consistent to the result at the aggregate choice probability level for the sampled population. The respective aggregate probabilities for monorail, car and bus are in Saito survey LCM: 0.6784, 0.1881, 0.1335 and MLM: 0.6586, 0.1889, 0.1525, and in Eastern Osaka survey LCM: 0.5759, 0.1216, 0.3025 and MLM: 0.5369, 0.1456, 0.3175.

OLS regressions are further applied to investigate the relationship between the LCM probability and the MLM probability. The results of OLS regressions are provided in Table 7. From the relatively low $R^2$ for OLS regression, we may conclude that the relationship between the predicted choice probabilities under the LCM (for three latent classes) and the MLM (a normal distribution on the random parameters) is relatively weak at the individual level.

The prediction success indices suggested by McFadden (1979) are calculated and summarized in Table 8. From these indices, we found that in both datasets the LCM has more predictive capability than the MLM.

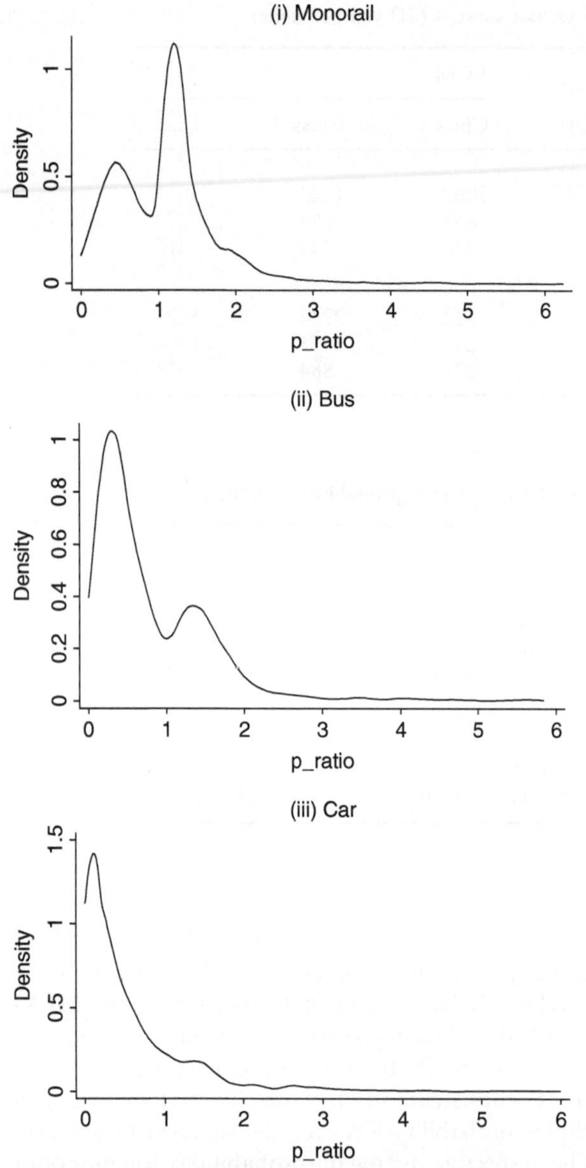


**Fig. 1. Kernel density estimate for probability ratio of LCM to MLM in Saito survey**

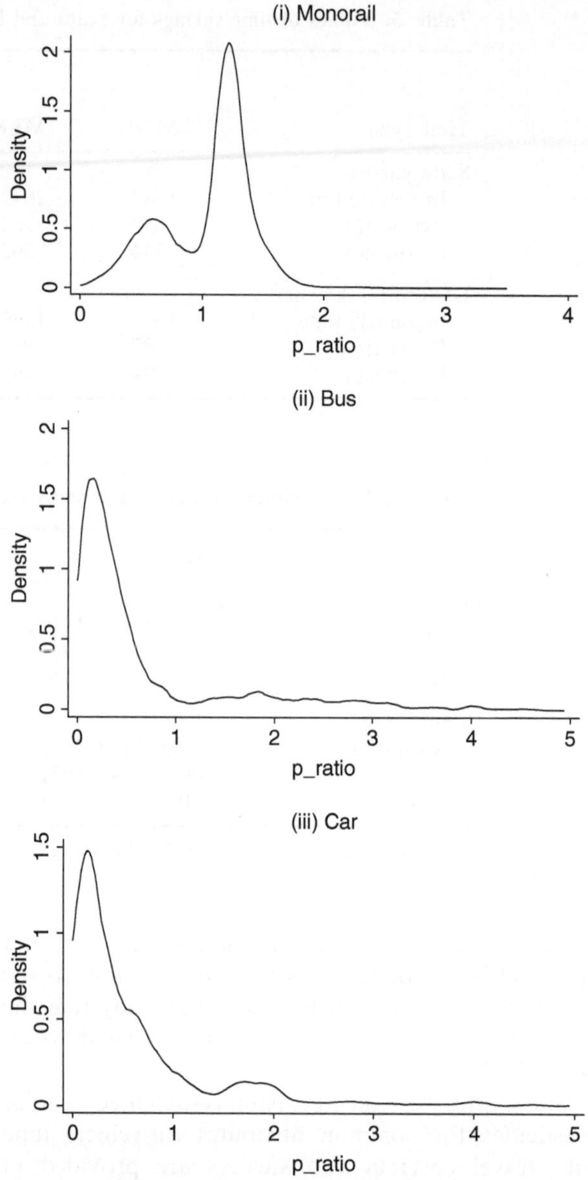


**Fig. 2. Kernel density estimate for probability ratio of LCM to MLM in Eastern Osaka survey**

Finally, we apply a test on nonnested choice models which is based on the AIC proposed by Ben-Akiva and Swait (1986). The test is carried out as follows. Suppose there are two nonnested Models 1 and 2. Model 1 explains choices using $K_1$ variables, while Model 2 explains the same choices using $K_2$ variables. Assume that $K_1 \geq K_2$ and either the two models have different functional forms or the two sets of variables are different by at least one element. Define the fitness measure for model $j, j = 1, 2$:

$$\rho_j^2 = 1 - \frac{L_j - K_j}{L(0)} \tag{6}$$

where $L_j$ is the log-likelihood at convergence for model $j$ and $L(0)$ is the log-likelihood for constants only. Ben-Akiva and Swait (1986) show that under the null hypothesis that Model 2 is the true model, the probability that the fitness measure in Equation 6 for Model 1 will be greater than that of Model 2 is asymptotically bounded by a function given in Equation 7:

$$\Pr\left(|\rho_2^2 - \rho_1^2| \geq Z\right) \leq \Phi\left(-\sqrt{-2ZL(0) + (K_1 - K_2)}\right) \tag{7}$$

where $Z$ is the difference of the fitness measures between Model 1 and Model 2 and assumed larger

**Table 7. OLS regressions of predicted probability estimated by the LCM and MLM**

| | Saito survey | | | Eastern Osaka survey | | |
|---|---|---|---|---|---|---|
| | Monorail | Car | Bus | Monorail | Car | Bus |
| Constant | −0.03118 | −0.01796 | −0.0473 | −0.1205 | −0.03407 | −0.04991 |
| P_MLM | 1.132968 | 1.012928 | 1.07295 | 1.253378 | 1.175096 | 1.046462 |
| $R^2$ | 0.395 | 0.448 | 0.456 | 0.384 | 0.340 | 0.277 |

*Note*: Dependant variable is P_LCM. All the parameters are significant at 99.9% level.

**Table 8. Prediction success indices for Saito and Eastern Osaka surveys**

| | MNL | MLM | LCM |
|---|---|---|---|
| Saito survey | 0.1049 | 0.1440 | 0.3259 |
| Eastern Osaka survey | 0.0435 | 0.0622 | 0.2218 |

than zero, $\Phi$ is the standard normal Cumulative Distribution Function (CDF). Therefore, Equation 7 sets an upper bound for the probability that one incorrectly selects Model 1 as the true model although Model 2 is the true model.

Using the above definition, we calculate that the probabilities in Equation 7 for Saito survey and Eastern Osaka survey are $P \leq \Phi(-27.039) \approx 0$ and $P \leq \Phi(-36.773) \approx 0$, respectively, assuming that the MLM is Model 1 and the LCM is Model 2. Therefore, we may conclude that in both datasets to which we applied the test, the LCM is superior to the MLM.

## V. Conclusions

This article provides a detailed comparison between two advanced specifications of discrete choice model, i.e. an LCM and an MLM. Following the study of Greene and Hensher (2003), the article compares the values of time savings, direct choice elasticities and predicted choice probability derived from these two models. In addition, the prediction success indices and a nonnested model test are further applied to investigate the difference between these two models, while these results indicate that the LCM performs statistically better than the MLM in our two datasets.

Although our results are consistent with those concluded from Greene and Hensher (2003), which claims that the LCM is supported by stronger statistical behaviours than the MLM in their dataset, we caution that it still cannot make this evidence as a conclusive suggestion that the LCM is definitely superior to the MLM in all cases. More and more studies on comparison between these two specifications are appreciated in future, because only after a number of accumulated studies, a systematical meta-analysis could be considered to seek for some rules on concluding which model specification is better or not.

## References

Ben-Akiva, M. E. and Swait, J. D. (1986) The Akaike likelihood ratio index, *Transportation Science*, **20**, 133–6.

Bhat, C. R. (2001) Quasi-random maximum simulated likelihood estimation of the mixed logit model, *Transportation Research Part B*, **35**, 677–93.

Bhat, C. R. (2003) Simulation estimation of mixed discrete choice models using randomized and scrambled Halton sequences, *Transportation Research Part B*, **37**, 837–55.

Bhat, C. R. and Gossen, R. (2004) A mixed multinomial logit model analysis of weekend recreational episode type choice, *Transportation Research Part B*, **38**, 767–87.

Bishop, R. C. and Provencher, B. (2004) Does accounting for preference heterogeneity improve the forecasting of a random utility model? A case study, *Journal of Environmental Economics and Management*, **48**, 793–810.

Boxall, P. C. and Adamowicz, W. L. (2002) Understanding heterogeneous preferences in random utility models: a latent class approach, *Environmental and Resource Economics*, **23**, 421–46.

Greene, W. H. (2003) *Econometric Analysis*, 5th edn, Pearson Education International, New York.

Greene, W. H. and Hensher, D. A. (2003) A latent class model for discrete choice analysis: contrasts with mixed logit, *Transportation Research Part B*, **37**, 681–98.

Hensher, D. A., Rose, J. M. and Greene, W. H. (2005) *Applied Choice Analysis: a Primer*, Cambridge University Press, Cambridge.

Hess, S., Bierlaire, M. and Polak, J. W. (2005) Estimation of value of travel-time saving using mixed logit models, *Transportation Research Part A*, **39**, 221–36.

Kim, Y., Lee, J. D. and Koh, D. (2005) Effects of consumer preferences on the convergence of mobile telecommunications devices, *Applied Economics*, **37**, 817–26.

Louviere, J. J., Hensher, D. A. and Swait, J. D. (2000) *Stated Choice Methods: Analysis and Applications*, Cambridge University Press, Cambridge.

McFadden, D. (1979) Quantitative methods for analyzing travel behavior of individuals: some recent developments, in *Behavioral Travel Modeling* (Eds) D. A. Hensher and P. R. Stopher, Croom Helm, London.

McFadden, D. and Train, K. (2000) Mixed MNL models for discrete response, *Journal of Applied Econometrics*, **15**, 447–70.

Morey, E., Thacher, J. and Breffle, W. (2006) Using Angler characteristics and attitudinal data to identify environmental preference classes: a latent-class model, *Environmental and Resource Economics*, **34**, 91–115.

Persson, T. H. (2002) Welfare calculations in models of the demand for sanitation, *Applied Economics*, **34**, 1509–18.

Redmond, L. S. and Mokhtarian, P. L. (2001) The positive utility of the commute: modeling ideal commute time and relative desired commute amount, *Transportation*, **28**, 179–205.

Revelt, D. and Train, K. (1998) Incentives for appliance efficiency in a competitive energy environment: random parameters logit models of households' choices, *Review of Economics and Statistics*, **80**, 647–57.

Richard, A. J. (2003) Some evidence of travelers with zero value-of-time, *Transportation Research Record*, **1854**, 107–13.

Sakata, Y., Shen, J. and Hashimoto, Y. (2006) The influence of environmental deterioration and network improvement on transport mode choice, Working Paper in Economics and Business No. 06–04, Graduate School of Economics and Osaka School of International Public Policy (OSIPP), Osaka University.

Shen, J. (2006) A review of stated choice method, *International Public Policy Studies*, **10**, 97–121.

Shen, J., Sakata, Y. and Hashimoto, Y. (2007) Is individual environmental consciousness one of the determinants in transport mode choice?, *Applied Economics*, **40**, 1229–39.

Train, K. (2003) *Discrete Choice Methods with Simulation*, Cambridge University Press, New York.

Train, K. and Sandor, Z. (2004) Quasi-random simulation of discrete choice models, *Transportation Research Part B*, **38**, 313–27.

Viton, P. A. (2004) Will mixed logit change urban transport policies?, *Journal of Transport Economics and Policy*, **38**, 403–23.

# Index

Page numbers in *Italics* represent tables.
Page numbers in **Bold** represent figures.